Colonial Legacy in North East India

About the Editors

Shukhdeba Sharma Hanjabam (MSW, Ph.D.) is Head, Department of Social Work, Indira Gandhi National Tribal University, Regional Campus, Manipur. Makhan Kangpokpi District, Manipur. He completed his PhD. from School of Social Work, Tata Institute of Social Sciences, Mumbai and post doctoral from University of Florida, Florida, USA (2014-15) as Fogarty International Centre Fellow. He is also the life member of North East India History Association; Manipur Historical Society; and Indian National Trust for Art and Cultural Heritage (INTACH), New Delhi. He also had successfully completed research projects under the sponsorship from ICSSR, New Delhi and Manipur Commission for Protection of Child Rights, Manipur.

Aheibam Koireng Singh (MA, Ph.D.), is Assistant Professor, Centre for Manipur Studies, Manipur University, Canchipur, Imphal West District, Manipur. He is formerly the General Secretary of Manipur University Research Club. He is also the life member of Indian Tourism Congress, Manipur Historical Society, and North East India History Association. He specializes in India's North East regional studies of election, ethnicity, inter-group and inter-community relations, conflict, peace building, and issues of governance. His authored and edited books, *'Ethnicity and Intercommunity Conflicts: A Case of Kuki-Naga in Manipur'*, *'Miniature India in Motion: Movements in Recent Past and Present Manipur'* are well received for its rich material content and critical insights.

Colonial Legacy in North East India

Edited by

Hanjabam Shukhdeba Sharma
Aheibam Koireng Singh

Jointly Published
for
Intellectual Forum of North East India
Guwahati
by

CONCEPT PUBLISHING COMPANY PVT. LTD.
NEW DELHI-110059

ISBN-13: 978-93-88937-64-1

First Published 2020

Published and Printed by

Concept Publishing Company Pvt. Ltd.
A/15-16, Commercial Block, Mohan Garden,
New Delhi-110059 (INDIA)
T : 91 11 25351460, 91 11 25351794
E : publishing@conceptpub.com; *W* : www.conceptpub.com

Cataloging in Publication Data--Courtesy: D.K. Agencies (P) Ltd. <docinfo@dkagencies.com>

National Symposium on Revisiting Colonial Legacy in North East India (2018 : Imphal, India)

Colonial legacy in North East India / edited by Hanjabam Shukhdeba Sharma, Aheibam Koireng Singh.

pages cm

"Outcome of the National Symposium on Revisiting Colonial Legacy in North East India on 2–3 February, 2018, at the Central Hall of Ghanapriya Womens' College ... jointly organised by Intellectual Forum of North East ..."—Acknowledgements.

Includes bibliographical references and index.
ISBN 9789388937641

1. India, Northeastern—History—Congresses. 2. Anti-imperialist movements—India, Northeastern—Congresses. 3. India, Northeastern—Ethnic relations--Congresses. I. Hanjabam, Shukhdeba Sharma, 1983- editor. II. Singh, Aheibam Koireng, editor. III. Intellectual Forum of North East India (Gauhati, India), organizer, publisher. IV. Ghanapriya Womens' College (Imphal, India), host institution. V. Title.

LCC DS483.7.N38 2018 | DDC 954.1 23

Foreword

I have great pleasure to learn that the book titled, "Colonial Legacy in North East India" will soon see the light of the day which is essentially an outcome of the symposium on the same theme organized jointly by the Intellectual Forum of North East; Dhanamanjuri University, Imphal; Department of Social Work, Indira Gandhi National Tribal University, Regional Campus, Manipur; and Centre for Manipur Studies, Manipur University, Canchipur on 2–3 February, 2019. It is also a matter of great personal delight and fulfilling experience for me as well, as I was actively associated with the said symposium right from the initial stage till its logical end. It was also more or less made successful and fruitful largely because of the contribution by the participating resource persons and delegates, many of them are internationally famed scholars and luminaries from different walks of life. I owe my indebtedness to them for the immense contribution made by them with their sharing of insightful analysis and thorough knowledge on the subject relevant with the themes of the symposium.

As for me, I strongly feel that understanding and appreciating the cultural indignity is a must for self-realization. For that the social, political, economic and cultural practices of the land needs to be re-researched for better understanding of societal developments and better future. I am sure and certain that this will help in analyzing the historical events and know the cultural ethos of the people of the country where the British Colonialism ruled once. The very much presently discussed, "Citizen Amendments Bill" is also a colonial legacy. 'Lamgi Sanna machi sangi', the local usage meaning 'the worth of other culture has primacy over native culture' is still in relevance. Though it is already in the past, their culture evades the local culture in every sphere of life still today. Emphasizing and reinstating the indigenous practices and principles is highly the need of the hour to gain confidence in our own cultural practices. Imitation is the worse habit that deteriorates self-determination.

I am sure this book will gain greater dissemination to people from all walks of life including the young minds to reach out and help them understand the present scenario of the society to enable them realize the beauty of the culture and tradition. I am also hopeful that this book will contribute in appreciating each other's beliefs, faith and culture of different community inhabiting in the North East as well as the country which ultimately will help in bringing peace and harmony.

I also congratulate the editors and give them due credits for documenting and keeping in record the proceedings of the symposium in book form by bringing out this present volume in print at the least possible time which in the posterity to come as well as for the present generation will be a good asset towards understanding the impact of colonial legacy, the damages made it and the need for resurrecting our pristine cultural wealth and practices.

September 2019
Imphal

Shri Th. Radheshyam Singh
Minister
Education, Government of Manipur

Acknowledgements

This book is an outcome of the National Symposium on Revisiting Colonial Legacy in North East India on 2–3 February, 2018, at the Central Hall of Ghanapriya Womens' College, a constituent college of Dhanamanjuri University, Imphal which was jointly organised by Intellectual Forum of North East; Dhanamanjuri University, Imphal; Department of Social Work, Indira Gandhi National Tribal University, Regional Campus, Manipur; and Centre for Manipur Studies, Manipur University, Canchipur. Many individuals and organisations have helped in the successful organisation of the said seminar which ultimately led its proceedings seeing the light of the day in this present book form.

Firstly, we sincerely acknowledge and express sincere appreciation to Thokchom Radheshyam Singh, Hon'ble Minister (Education), Government of Manipur and accredit him the most for the success of the seminar. He, irrespective of his hectic busy schedule, had supported and involved at all stages of organising the symposium right from the start with keen personal interest and enthusiasm which indeed was very encouraging and inspiring to the whole team of the seminar. We also thank Dr. Sapam Ranjan Singh, Hon'ble Member of Manipur Legislative Assembly and Chairman, Manipur Tourism Development Corporation for gracing the valedictory function. We are also grateful to ICSSR (Indian Council of Social Science Research), New Delhi for partially supporting the symposium.

We also like to thank the Vice Chancellor, DM University; Principals of Constituent Colleges, namely Ch. Sheelaramani of DM College of Arts; Dr. Jadu Singh, DM College of Sciences; Dr. Asem Nabachandra of DM College of Commerce; LMS Law College, Dr. R.K. Tamphasana of GP Women's College and Officials of Directorate of University and Higher Education, Government of Manipur particularly Shri Malengngamba Chenglei, Director and Shri T. Ojit Singh, State Nodal Officer, RUSA.

We appreciate the support of Prof T.V. Kattimani, Vice Chancellor; Prof. Alok Shotriya, Dean School of Social Sciences, Indira Gandhi National Tribal University (IGNTU), Amarkantak; Dr. Ng. Ngalengnam, Director; and Faculty Members and Research Scholars of IGNTU, Regional Campus, Manipur.

We also like to thank Shri Jarnail Singh, Administrator, Manipur University; Prof. S. Mangi Singh, former Director, Centre for Manipur Studies; Dr. Vijayalaxmi Brara, Associate Professor and Dr. Amal Sanasam of the Centre.

We appreciate the contribution of Intellectual Forum of North East (IFNE), Guwahati particularly Shri Sumanta Chaliha, President; Shri Rakesh Kalita, General Secretary; and Convenor, Swapnil Shermale; and Vishal Sinha.

We also extend our thanks to the State Government particularly Chief Secretary, Dr. J. Suresh Babu for declaring our Invitee, Justice K.G. Balkrishnan, Former Chief Justice, Supreme Court of India. We would like to thank Shri I. Dinesh Kumar Singh, then the Under Secretary-cum-Assistant Registrar, Manipur Human Rights Commission and presently Sub-Divisional Officer, Moreh, for his service to our invitee.

We thank all the resource persons, who have come from different part of India and shared their valuable inputs towards the theme of the seminar. Further, we thank the paper contributors of the seminar. Some of them have presented papers and some have submitted paper on our request.

We also acknowledge and would like to put on record the logistic support of Seva Bharati, Manipur and service rendered by its volunteers in the successful organisation of the seminar.

We also gratefully extend our hearty thanks to Dr. R.K. Tamphasana, Principal and the whole GP Women's College team consisting of faculties, staffs and students for hosting the seminar and also for showing great hospitality.

Last but not the least, we owe our indebtedness to each one and all who helped in one way or the other in organising the symposium and ensuring that this publication sees the light of the day.

Message

I am glad that the proceedings of the symposium on "Revisiting Colonial Legacy in North East India", which was held at Imphal from February 2 to 3, 2019, are being published in the form of a book. The event was jointly organised by the Intellectual Forum of North East; Dhanamanjuri University, Imphal; the Department of Social Work, Indira Gandhi National Tribal University, Regional Campus, Manipur; and the Centre for Manipur Studies, Manipur University, Canchipur.

'Bharat' is well-known for its socio-cultural, historical and geopolitical continuum beyond the regional boundaries. As a result of the colonial influence on Indian minds, over the years, we have lost the sense of unity. The centre of national discourse had been shifted from unity to diversity, peddling fake narratives to create a schism in our society.

'Let noble thoughts come to us from all sides': It is our civilisational ethos. As a civilisation, we are not averse to any stream of knowledge only because it is originated outside Bharat. At the same time, we do not welcome anything which is slapped against us or invasive in nature. It will eventually delink us from our cultural roots. So the decolonisation of Indian minds should be our top priority.

I hope, with the publication of this book, the idea of Bharat and sense of unity that we put forward, will reach to a larger audience all-over the country, particularly in the North-East region of Bharat. I wish you all success with this book.

Shri Nandakumar
National Convenor, Pragya Pravah

Contents

SECTION II

Anti-Colonial Movement

SECTION III

Colonial Legacy

SECTION IV

Colonial Legacy and Inter-Community Relationship

SECTION V

National Integration

Abbreviations

A.D.	-	Anno Domini
BL	-	British Library
CP	-	Central Provinces
DIG	-	Director in General
DONER	-	Development of North Eastern Region
GoI	-	Government of India
INA	-	Indian National Army
J&K	-	Jammu and Kashmir
Lieut. Col.	-	Lieutenant Colonel
MNF	-	Mizo National Front
NEC	-	North Eastern Council
NEFA	-	North Eastern Frontier Agency
NNC	-	Naga National Council
PA	-	Personal Assistant
RAF	-	Royal Air Force
RSS	-	Rashtriya Swayamsevak Sangh
TRC	-	Tinkao Ragwang Chapriak

List of Contributors

Swapnil Shermale is Convenor, Intellectual Forum of North East (IFNE), Guwahati.

Dr. B.B. Kumar (Braj Bihari Kumar) is Chairman, Indian Council of Social Science Research (ICSSR), New Delhi.

Dr. K. Gyanendra Singh, Associate Professor (Economics), Department of Humanities and Social Sciences, National Institute of Technology, Mizoram.

Dr. Budha Kamei is Assistant Professor, Department of Tribal Studies, Manipur University of Culture, Imphal.

Dr. Th. Nishikanta Singh is Assistant Professor, Department of History, Maharaja Bodhchandra College (Government of Manipur), Imphal.

Dr. K. Ruhinikumar Sharma, is Assistant Professor, Department of History, Ideal Girls' College (Government of Manipur), Imphal.

Shri Som Kamei is an Indian Postal Service Cadre and presently posted as Postmaster General (Assam Circle).

Dr. Jangkhomang Guite is Assistant Professor, Centre for Historical Studies, Jawaharlal Nehru University, New Delhi.

L. Nishikanta Singh, VSM & BAR is Chairperson, Manipur Public Service Commission. He retired as Lt. General, Indian Army.

Dr. Bhabananda Singh T. is Associate Professor, Department of History, C.I. College (Government of Manipur), Imphal.

Dr. K. Himalay Singh, PVSM, UYSM, AVSM, YSM retired as Lt. General, Indian Army and former Chairperson, Manipur Public Service Commission.

Prof N. Lokendra Singh is Professor, Department of History, Manipur University, & President (Elect), North East India History Association.

Dr. Pureshwore Nameirakpam is teaching at National Sports Academy, Government of Manipur, Imphal.

Shri N. Munish Singh is Regional Director, Indian Council of Cultural Research, Ministry of External Affairs, Government of India.

Prof. M. Amarjeet Singh is Professor at Centre for North East Studies and Policy Research, Jamia Millia Islamia (A Central University), New Delhi.

Dr. Atul Debbarma is Hon'ble Member, Tripura Legislative Assembly and medical Doctor by training.

Rami Niranjan Desai is Research Adviser, Centre for Soft Power, India Foundation, New Delhi.

Dr. Laitonjam Muhindro is Assistant Professor, Department of Political Science, S.K. Women's College (Government of Manipur).

Prof. W. Nabakumar is Guest Professor, Department of Anthropology, Manipur University, Imphal.

Prof Kuldip Chand Agnihotri is Vice Chancellor, Central University of Himachal Pradesh.

Shri J. Nandakumar, is National Convenor, Prajna Pravah.

Prof Rakesh Sinha is Hon'ble Member, Rajya Sabha and Member, Indian Council of Social Science Research (ICSSR), New Delhi.

Dr. Th Bimola Devi, Assistant Professor, Department of Culture, Manipur University of Culture, Imphal.

SECTION I
Civilization Perspectives

1
Prologue to Colonial Legacy in North East India

Swapnil Shermale

The seed of British colonialism in the region of present day North East India was sown with the treaty of Yandaboo signed between the King of Ava and the British on 24 February, 1826 started the British rule in Assam. In 1830, Cachar came under British jurisdiction. Subsequently, in 1854 the hill areas of Cachar were annexed followed by Lakhimpur in 1835 and Sylhet in 1858. Manipur had retained its status as an independent region (princely state), as well as the Khasi Hills, but Jaintia Hills came under the British in 1835. The Naga Hills was finally annexed as a district in 1866, followed by the Garo Hills in 1869. The "Chin-Lushai Expedition" of 1889-1890 by the British Government finally led to the colonial permanent occupation of Lushai Hills. Manipur also eventually came under British rule following the defeat in Anglo Manipuri War of 1891. In the early 18th Century, the British Empire sought to establish trade routes with Tibet leading Sikkim to fall under British suzerainty. So, the whole of the region of present day North East India (NEI) formed originally by seven states of Assam, Meghalaya, Mizoram, Nagaland, Arunachal Pradesh, Tripura, Manipur, and Sikkim had been under British colonialism starting from varied times in the first quarter of the nineteenth century till Independence in 1947.

Colonialism or colonial rule was a historical phenomenon: conquest, emigration and subjugation happened in history. Colonialism is the establishment and maintenance for an extended term of rule over an alien people that is separate from and subordinate to the ruling power. Colonialism means domination of an alien minority, administrators, businessmen and soldiers asserting their racial and cultural superiority over the subjugated people.

The time-honoured consciousness in the region undergoes colossal transformation with the colonisation of the region. The existing ways of life have been severely disrupted leading to the near extinction of many of its cultural and ideological aspects after coming into contact and interacted with the emergent ways of life brought about by the colonisers. The colonial administrators exploited the local subjects and resources in order to fulfil their own interests. Ethnicity and various divisive measures were also introduced as administrative policy with far reaching consequences. The colonial administration utilized the services of the Christian missionaries to legitimize their rule over the conquered people. In the process, the colonisers outrightly rejected the native cultural practices including the belief system as 'heathen', 'barbaric', and 'uncivilised'. This transformation compelled the native population to struggle to get used to the new order that benefits the colonial masters.

In the light of what is being mentioned, a symposium was organised jointly by the Intellectual Forum of North East; Dhanamanjuri University, Imphal; Department of Social Work, Indira Gandhi National Tribal University, Regional Campus, Manipur; and Centre for Manipur Studies, Manipur University, Canchipur 2–3 February, 2019 to address the impact of colonial legacy on various sub-themes.

In the inaugural function dignitaries also share their thoughts and insights on the topic of the seminar. Dr. R.K. Tamphasana, Principal, Ghana Priya Women's College, a constituent college of Dhanamanjuri University stated that colonial rule in North East India began with the signing of Treaty of Yandaboo on 24 February, 1826 between the King of Awa and the British rule in authority which marks the beginning of colonial rule in Assam, and the subsequent eventual conquest following that including the Naga Hills in 1866, Garo Hills in 1869, Lushai Hills in 1890 and Manipur in 1891. During the hundred years of British rule in provision, the earlier socio-economic political system was completely transformed and a new cultural system based on European system on the concept of property system, governance, religious and cultural life have emerged thereby impacting colossal transformation of religion.

Justice K. Balkrishnan, Former Chief Justice of Supreme Court and also Former Chairperson of National Human Rights Commission (NHRC) who graced the inaugural function as the Guest of Honour says: "We are thinking of the British legacy and British legacy is about the whole wealth. It is not used as bad, good, positive or negative. Now it is our country, our culture. We can move ahead, we can change whatever system which is possible on the rest of the country. Geographically, North East is a difficult terrain, some of the state is very difficult for the communication facilities. But the people are very normal and literally wise. Literacy rate is very high. Only when there is a peaceful atmosphere in the country, we can move ahead for a better progress and development. When there is all sorts of bickering between any group, whether political groups, cultural groups, if they continue to fight each other then there is no place for governance, no place for progress, no place for development, there will only be violence. North East states suffer a lot because of this violence. It is time for us to stop factional infighting. It is time for us to take in one line and move ahead. Students should not indulge in disruptive activities. They are the assets of the nation and future of the nation is in their hands. They can best contribute by studying sincerely in their academic pursuit. Science is fast developing in medicine, agriculture, and many other, we are to make use of these technologies. Today, that is possible and makes it available to the world, make it available to this country, and make it available to this region of this country. Progress, progress and progress, that's the way we can have a major life."

Prof. Rakesh Sinha, Hon'ble Member, Rajya Sabha and Member, Indian Council for Social Science Research (ICSSR), New Delhi, Special Invitee who later in the academic session also presented paper says, "In Manipur, if I were to speak on colonial legacy, entire North East is a land of the people which has enough capacity to protect its cultural personality. Colonial rule has made severe impacts all-over the country but it could not change the originality of North East people. That is the beauty and resilience of North East people. The North East people have struggled to free the lands from the British rule and most important, Rani

Gaidinlu was one of the leaders who led the movement in Manipur. Rani Gaidinlu in 13 years of age, she led the struggle. When she was called Rani, she was not a queen by birth. When Pandit Nehru paid a visit in the prison, she found the dynamic leader, and he called her Rani. Tileshwari Barua of Assam also martyred for the cause of the nation at the very young age of eleven. This example is to be found in North Eastern states. There are umpteen examples when men and women of North East struggled, sacrificed not only to protect the land, but also frontier, culture, legacies etc." While highlighting the need to protect the cultural identity, he further said that the entire North East region continued to remain marginalised and exploited. India should learn true nationalism, cultural unity and women empowerment from the North East. There is no need of mainstreaming the North East.

Prof. Kuldip Chand Agnihotri, Vice Chancellor, Central University of Himachal Pradesh said Indian history will be a complete one only when the contributions of North East, North West and South Indian were included, otherwise it will remain as North Indian history, said Kuldeep, while adding that the Western society and Indian society are two different entities—the last unit of a society in the Western world is individual while it is the family in the Indian society. So, western always talk about individual rights while the Indians fight for the family rights. He also applauded Late Prof. Gangmumei Kamei as the first scholar who made concerted effort to decolonize the colonial history of North East. He also put forward strongly that history of North East India should deservingly become the part of mainstream of India.

Shri Th. Radheshyam, Hon'ble Minister Education, Government of Manipur, Chief Guest of the inaugural function said that understanding and appreciating the cultural indignity is a must for self-realization. He expressed that the socio-political, economic and culture practices of the land needs to be re-research for better understanding of societal developments and better future. He said that the symposium will help in analyzing the historical events and know the cultural ethos of the people of the country where the British Colonialism ruled once. He also stated that the present very much discussed Citizen Amendments Bill is also a colonial legacy. 'Lamgi Sanna machi sangi', the local usages meaning the worth of other culture has primacy over local culture is still in relevance. Though it is already in the past, their culture evades the local culture in every sphere of life still today, he added. Emphasizing that reinstating the indigenous practices and principles is highly the need of the hour to gain confidence in our own cultural practices. He added that imitation is the worse habit that deteriorates self-determination. He urged the gathering of the professors and scholars present in the seminar to reach out to the young minds and help them understand the present scenario of the society to enable them realize the beauty of the culture and tradition. The Minister also said that appreciation of each other's beliefs, faith and culture of different community inhabiting in the State as well as the country can help in bringing peace and harmony.

Shri Nandakumar, National Convenor, Pragya Pravah, President of the inaugural function stated that discussion has to be done in the right direction. The speciality of 'Bharat' is the socio-cultural, historical and geo-political continuum irrespective of the region. There are lots of such things we have to bestow. Now-a-day, what is happening because of our myopic view due to colonial influence and legacy, he said, "we are more concentrating on the differences, we are not concentrating on the duality, searching for the unity." Let all noble thoughts come from any part of the world. We accepted the ethos. We have also benefited from the colonial masters, there is no doubt about that. Regarding the core of 'Bharat' is concerned, but those thoughts which are against the unity of India, integrity, peace of mind, peace of the society. Mahatma Gandhi used to say, "let all great thoughts come to my own, I won't close my windows and doors against them, but will shut doors and windows to those who would damage and mess up the room." Further, he said that colonialism did impact the native art forms, and what has been happening in the country is the 'blur view of the colonial era', and are not concentrating on 'our potentials to unite the country'.

In the valedictory function, Prof. Nani Gopal Mahanta, Department of Political Science, Gauhati University, Guest of Honour said that legislators in the country need to understand the impact of colonialism and the issue of dying languages. The political, judicial and administrative system of India is largely impacted by the remnants of colonialism and its continuing legacy. The issue of boundary in India and isolation of tribal and non-tribal in North Eastern part of the country is due to the coloniser's prejudiced notion of 'White Man's burden' as they branded the natives as barbaric and uncivilised and legitimised their Colonial rule and the missionary activities as a civilising mission. He also stated that, Gauhati University had recently introduced a paper called, 'Stalwarts of Assam', and make it a compulsory, so that young generations are aware of the contributions made by the forefathers and the rich heritage and traditions handed down to them by their preceding generations. This needs to be replicated in the state of Manipur also.

Prof. Kuldip Chand Agnihotri, Vice Chancellor of Central University of Himachal Pradesh, said in his guest of honour speech that European fails to understand India, but, unfortunately they tell what India is and we follow their story. As a legacy of colonialism, we have disowned our language, forefather and history. In the process, blindly following the epistemology and processes of knowledge production brought about by wrongly informed homogenising notions of Westerners to the amount of undermining the diversity have destroyed the age old civilsational heritage of engaging critically in dialogue and discourses and have consequently numbed the consciousness of the Indians irrespective of the region they belong. He emphasised that in order to develop and advance further, Colonial ethnography should be outrightly rejected and be replaced by auto-ethnography pursuing the sources and fieldwork giving primacy to the knowledge arising out of engaging in their respective native language and source. Stating that the basic idea of science and development comes from mother tongue, the Vice Chancellor urged the people of North East to speak, think, express and conduct research in their native languages.

Prof. N. Lokendra Singh, Dean, School of Social Science, Manipur University stressed on the importance of critically questioning the outcome of Colonial historiography as they measure the worth of other cultures from their own yardstick which is very prejudiced and bias. He also emphasised on engaging in research which is scientific and empirically verifiable so as to stop relying on colonial ethnography.

This present volume is more or less an outcome of the symposium so mentioned and also enriched with some solicited ones. The structure of the book comprises prologue which is the introductory furnishing the symposium's inaugural and valedictory proceedings of the discourse on the topic by eminent persons who are competent to give informed opinion with rich material contents and insightful analysis, and a glimpse of subsequent chapters which are organized under five sections, namely Civilization Perspectives; Anti-Colonial Movement; Colonial Legacy; and Inter-Community Relationship and National Integration.

Chapter 2, "India's Trade-Route Links with its Eastern-Neighbours: A Historical Perspective" by B.B. Kumar which was first published in *Dialogue*, July-September 2007, Volume 9, No. 1, describes that India, since the remotest past, was linked to its eastern neighbourhood through land and sea routes. The land routes passed through North-East India. The Silk Route linkages of Central Asia, China and Tibet passed through Western India and Kashmir. Tibet was linked to the North India also through Himalayan passes. The sea route links were through east coast ports—Tamralipti and others—in Bay of Bengal. The sea lanes from the western coast on Arabian Sea passed through Indian Ocean encircling Ceylon. India had not only the hectic trade, but cultural, historic and religious links also. In fact, India, East and South East Asia formed part of the same Cultural Continuum.

Chapter 3, "Economic History of Manipur: Some Explorations" by K. Gyanendra Singh is an improved version of the paper which was first published in *African and Asian Studies*, 15 (3016) pp. 393-407 in 2016. Manipur, an erstwhile princely state of North Eastern India, suffered in the hands of Burmese during 1819-1825 and again in the hands of British in 1891. Since 1891, the state had been under the control of the British Government of India. With the change in hands of the seat of administration, the economy of the state underwent drastic changes. The chapter analyses the salient features of the economy of Manipur during the feudal and colonial era following pure economic history approach. It observes that the otherwise self-sufficient food economy of the feudal era was distorted during the colonial period. The colonial policy not only robbed the rice economy but also shunned the paths of industrialisation, thus preventing the natural transition of an economy. The policy of monetisation and commercialisation of agriculture led to export-led-retardation of the people and de-industrialisation of the economy with feeble trends towards tertiarization of the economy.

Chapter 4, "Trade Relations of Manipur with Her Neighbours

in the Pre-British Period: An Overview" by Kamei Budha Kabui attempts to examine the trade relation of Manipur with the neighbouring countries before 1891. It mainly deals with the internal and external trade, trade route, exchange systems, market, and introduction of coins etc. In primitive economy, trade was mainly characterized by barter system, there was no regular market. The price of goods was determined generally by through bargaining between buyers and sellers against their respective goods. Markets came up at the roadside during the reign of Khagemba. With the increase of market places, buying and selling of goods with native coin (Sel) became popular, but it was limited in circulation. The king was the sole authority to mint the coin. Internal trade was conducted exclusively by the women. The hill tribes also exchanged their products among themselves or with that of the valley dwellers. Besides the internal trade, Manipur had trade relation with Burma, China and other Indian states. The main items of import and export were raw silk, paper tea, ponies, ivories, cotton etc. Before 1891, the people of Manipur did not depend much on external trade for their basic need because almost all the necessities were produced within the state. External trade meant to sell the native goods to other states and buy limited items which were not of basic needs. It was confirmed from the evidence that when Manipur was cut-off from other states at the time of war, the economy was not affected. The route of external trade was on land routes. The data are based on available primary and secondary sources.

Chapter 5, "Coinage in Manipur: Technique, Structure, Metallurgy and Process of Minting" by Th. Nishikanta Singh while emphasising that coins are the most important of all antiquities that seem to be imperishable, arrives at a conclusion on the basis of the material evidences and few available works by noted scholars that it was the sixth century A.D. which witnessed a new era in the history of numismatics in Manipur.

Chapter 6, "Pre-Colonial Economy of Manipur: An Overview" by K. Ruhinikumar Sharma attempts at reconstructing the pre-colonial economic history of an ancient kingdom situated in an area sandwiched between India and a region called Southeast Asia. The term 'pre-colonial' refers to the period prior to the British conquest of Manipur in 1891. Historians and economists considered economy as the primary determinant of any social formation. Though sketchy, archaeological and literary sources supported by chronicles established beyond doubt the existence of a hunting-gathering economy in early Manipur and subsequent transition to a settled agrarian economy in Manipur valley. The study also examines the organisation of labour and production and the states' control over the resources and in production process. From the sources examined, it may be concluded that Manipur had experienced primary state formation process and was able to emerge to the stage of a full-fledged feudal state. But her gradual development in its own was interrupted by the Anglo-Manipur War of 1891 resulting in the establishment of colonial rule and colonisation of the economy.

Chapter 7, "Beyond Her Role as an Anti-Colonial Freedom Fighter: The Cultural and Religious Legacy of Rani Gaidinliu" by Som Kamei by going beyond her role as an anti-colonial freedom fighter, highlights her impact on the highly misunderstood and misinterpreted cultural and religious aspect of Rani Gaindinliu's contribution in the strengthening of indigenous religion in NE India, more specifically on her Zeliangrong community which occupy a geographically contiguous area spread over the three states of Assam, Manipur and Nagaland.

Chapter 8, "Anglo-Kuki War 1917-1919: The Forgotten Great War Theatre" by Jangkhomang Guite highlights that the Kukis of North East India and Burma joined hands in fighting with the British forces for more than two years but was brutally suppressed. The military operations surrounding the Manipur Valley and extending over to the Somra Tract and the Thaungdut State in Burma costs huge exchequer to the imperial British government. The Operations unleashed an enormous amount of organized state violence, ranging from shoot at sight to indiscriminate burning of villages, wholesale destruction of property and livestock, prevention of cultivation and rebuilding of villages, forced mass displacement in jungles or in 'concentration camps', and collective punishment. The leaders were deported after the war. It registered an important landmark in the history of freedom movement in the whole North East India and inform us the crucial moment in the military history of colonial India which perhaps marked the last episode of colonial violence being perpetrated freely under the military doctrine of 'moral effect' before it was finally exposed at Jallianwala Bagh Massacre on 13 April, 1919.

Chapter 9, "Analysing the Anglo-Manipur and Anglo-Assam Wars : Understanding British Colonial Military Strategy in the North East India" by L. Nishikanta Singh highlights that in Anglo-Assam War, 360 fighting soldiers under a Captain were involved in Assam whereas in the case of Anglo-Manipur War, nearly 6500 soldiers, under a Major General, were required to tackle Manipur. The Anglo-Manipur War could be divided into three phases. In the first two phases, the British force of nearly 680 soldiers had to retreat. In fact, a total seven British officers died. The British rescue effort resulted in the battle of Thoubal lasting 10 days. The Manipuris compelled the British force to withdraw. The Manipuris were superior in strength. The only Victoria Cross, highest British gallantry award of this war was awarded in the battle of Thoubal indicating the ferocity of the fighting. In the third phase, three brigade group task forces on three different axes (roads) were used. This was basically to prevent concentration of force of the Manipuri forces and ensuring their dispersal. The British on the other hand wanted a concentrated application of their forces on the centre of gravity of Manipur, i.e. Imphal by converging all three task forces on the same date, i.e. 27 April at Imphal. This force of nearly 5500 soldiers including a reserve battalion was led by a Major General. For the battle of Khongjom, the British initially used a total of nearly 350 soldiers and four guns (cannons), but the overall strength of task force was 1800 soldiers. The Manipuris had constructed an oval shaped defence which was basically trenches, ditches, sanger (parapet) along a stream full of water. The British commenced their attack by using the guns (cannons) to shell the Manipuris position. This was followed by concentrated aimed small arms fire. Even after some parts of their defences were captured by the British, the Manipuris did not give up instead continued to put up a very stiff resistance. In fact, the contest became a hand-to-hand fight. There was no worthwhile resistance after Khongjom.

Chapter 10, "Women's Movements in Colonial and Post-Colonial Manipur" by Dr. Bhabananda Singh deals with the women's movement in Manipur, the annals of which are of bravery, courage and self-sacrifice with determined focus, characteristic spontaneity, prowess, effectiveness and a long history behind. This chapter intends to take a closer look of these movements, the cause, nature, outcome and the continuum. It attempts to reveal the problems of the society and how women have responded in their own way searching for an effective solution, the dynamicity of the movement in responding to the changing socio-economic and political situation of the times. It highlights that women of Manipur had played a very significant role in the society, from myths and legends to contemporary times. In the colonial times, the women's movements were mostly focused on struggle against economic and political exploitations of the colonized people. Two important movements were the first and second Nupi Lals. In the post-colonial times, the movements ranged from fight against the evils of alcoholism, movement for higher political status and defending human rights. However, all throughout the absence of feminist trends has been prominently noticed in the Women's movement in Manipur.

Chapter 11, "Impact of British Colonial Commercial Policies in North East India" by K. Himalay Singh highlights that North East India has been and continues to be one of the least developed regions of the country. The coming of the British in the region brought the growth of modern sector, which, however, did not bring about a high standard of living to the people of the region due to their limited participation in the economic activities. By the end of nineteenth century, the economy of Assam had developed all the characteristics of a dual economy. The modern sector served alien interests, employed capital and labours from outside the region, and catered to an external market. As a result, the traditional sector and the hill areas of the region that had hitherto been underdeveloped remained in enclave and untouched by the process of development. The British after pushing up their administration to North East India did not help the region in bringing about economic development for the benefit of the area. Whatever industries they had set up were done only to further their own interests. Hence, during the colonial period limited economic development took place, and that too was confined to the tea and oil producing areas of Assam plains and in some mineral producing areas in the Khasi Hills of Meghalaya. In the rest of the hill areas barring a few pockets, the traditional tribal economy of the primitive type of agricultural jhumming and pastoral economy, among others, persisted. This variation in the respective economies of the hills and plains is the functions of different physical features, different social relations, and the neglect and isolation of the region by the colonial masters. This in turn produced a multi-structural economy in the region and this position continued till India's Independence.

Chapter 12, "Second World War and North East India" by N. Lokendra Singh addresses and explores a significant historical theme, which is crucial for understanding the post-Second World War Naga society and polity, its nature as well as the extent of socio-economic and political changes, which took place during the war period which not only paved the way for the emergence of new social forces but also prepared the necessary pre-conditions for a strong popular movement for bringing about broad economic and political changes in Naga Hills during the immediate post-Second World War period. The chapter concludes that in the midst of such profound socio-economic changes that in June 1946 Zapu Phizo, an Angami leader returned to the Naga Hills after his long war time sojourn in Burma to preach his gospel of Naga independence. Although the NNC (Naga National Council) which he had founded initially demanded local autonomy of Naga Hills within the state of Assam, after India's independence, they began to demand the cessation of the place from India.

Chapter 13, "British Coloniolism and Agrarian Change in Manipur: 1891-1947" by Pureshwor Nameirakpam attempts to bring out the agrarian structure and institutions in the pre-colonial period and how these institutions underwent change, evolution or outright abolition during the British colonialism with Manipur becoming one of the British colonies after 23rd April, 1891 in South East Asia and how the significant changes which took place as a result of colonisation impacted upon the economy and its productive base especially agriculture.

Chapter 14, "Colonialism and its Effect on the Culture of North East India" by Ningthoujam Munish Singh at the very outset traces the advent of British Colonialism in North East India by the treaty of Yandaboo in 1826 by virtue of which most hill parts were gone under their suzerainty. As a consequence, the missionaries with active colonial patronage interfered in the social and cultural practices of the tribes of North East India thereby eroding their pristine socio-cultural and religious practices eventually destroying their solidarity enjoying communitarian activities. The chapter concludes that detribalizing the various tribes of North East India was at its peak during the colonial period.

Chapter 15, "Social Implications of Colonial Intervention" by

M. Amarjeet Singh brings into focus that the rapid transformation which took place in Assam in the nineteenth century led to large scale migration into Assam. Also, in order to serve the colonial interests, the administrative boundaries were redrawn. Moreover, the Bengali became the language of Courts of Justice and of the government schools during 1837-1874. It was an act of disregarding the indigenous inhabitants of Assam. Likewise, the assumption that the advent of Hinduism in Manipur affected the social relationships between the plain dwellers (the Meiteis) and the hill dwellers (the Nagas and Kukis) is debatable. It is rather due to the colonial policy of setting up of separate administrative boundaries. Thus, in the name of administrative convenience, several policies having far-reaching implications were introduced during the colonial rule in North East India. Such interventions had brought ethnic identity as an inevitable emotional resource for political mobilisation by different communities today.

Chapter 16, "Colonial Policy and Inter-Community Relationship" by Atul Debbarma concludes that the colonial policies had affected every aspect of human life of north-eastern people in particular and all over India in general. It is easy to destroy but difficult to construct. The colonial policies framed centuries ago did not end after the departure of British government from Indian soil. The soul of colonialism is still alive and actively haunting in different *avatar* as Breaking India force to smash Indian nation into pieces. In the age of app revolution, there is no need of physical presence at all to engineer the destruction of India, a virtual person is equal to a million real people and is enough to disturb inter-community relationship.

Chapter 17, "Colonial Legacy of Identity and Insurgency in North East India" by Rami Niranjan Desai articulates that the role of the British administration, their policies of exclusion and isolation and the crucial role of Christianity in building neo-colonial identities was successful to an extent. But, the eventual failure of the Crown Colony plan gave the region an opportunity to integrate, just as over six hundred other tribes did in India. However, the legacy of colonialism in the North-East will be defined in history by their denial of equality and opportunity to the people of North East India.

Chapter 18, "Colonial Implication and South Nagalim Movement: Socio-Political Unrest and Trust Deficit in Manipur" by Laitonjam Muhindro highlights that the South Nagalim movement has predictably served to catalyse and consolidate oppositional democratic politics along ethnic lines and furthering hill-valley divide in Manipur. This trend has exacerbated in the last two decades as NSCN-IM seems to seek a negotiating leverage from the deepening hill-valley divide. It creates more trust deficit amongst different ethnic communities living in this tiny state with the coming of Framework Agreement in between NSCN-IM and GoI.

Chapter 19, "State Policies Towards the Tribal: A Rethinking on the Indian Experience" by W. Nabakumar and Th. Bimola focuses on 'directed change' in the form of the developmental programmes taken up by the State for the socio-economic upliftment of the tribal people which have been acting as the exogenous force of bringing about institutional and structural change in tribal societies as it frequently leads to the unforeseen, unpredicted goal, sometimes socially disastrous, rather than the targeted goal. This is what is actually happening in the contemporary tribal societies of India in general and of Manipur, the home state of thirty seven recognized Scheduled Tribes, in particular. It concludes that the previously homogenous ranking tribal societies are found to be transforming into the economically heterogeneous, class societies owing to current strategies of development. Finally, the structure of many tribal societies is now cracking under several strains.

Chapter 20, "Defending Integrity by Strengthening National Voices" by Kuldeep Chand Agnihotri deals with three movements which find special mention in the contemporary history of Jammu and Kashmir (J&K). First is the movement launched by the Muslim Conference in 1931 in which Hindus were killed for the first time after the defeat inflicted on foreign Afghan state by Maharaja Ranjit Singh. Kashmir was liberated from the foreign rule of Afghans by Ranjit Singh in 1818. This movement claimed the lives of 21 people on whose graves obeisance is still paid by some people even today. The second was the movement started by the Sheikh Abdullah led National Conference with the primary demand of this movement was for and annulment of the treaty of 1946 which strategy was deeply detrimental to the whole of India to the extent that it has the potential of the whole of J&K becoming a part of Pakistan if succeeded. Third, is the historic movement conducted by Praja

Parishad from 1949 to 1952 in which 15 people were martyred in an uprising in protest against the mounting apprehension that due to wrong policies pursued by the duo of Nehru and Sheikh, people living in Jammu and Ladakh, Hindu Sikhs of Kashmir Valley, Gujjars and Shias might be compelled to embrace Pakistan.

Chapter 21, "Dismantle Colonial Relics" by J. Nandakumar argues and emphasizes that the cancerous tentacles of colonialism have eaten into the vitals of *Bharatiya* culture. There is an urgent need to reverse the process and undo the damage it has done on our minds. It sums up that all the evil effects of colonisation can be summarised into six 'Is', such as Inferiority, Ignorance, Inertia, Incompetency, Ill-will and Irreverence. Anything Hindu is being ridiculed as communal, obscurantist, and retrograde which is essentially propaganda of the colonisation agenda of the West.

Chapter 22, "Role of Rashtriya Swayamsevak Sangh in Freedom Movement" by Rakesh Sinha is a reproduction of the article "Not a Negative Role" which was first published in *Hindustan Times* on 5 September, 1997. This chapter articulates that the history of the RSS, spanning more than two decades before India's Independence, is one of active participation in the anti-colonial struggle and unconditional cooperation not only with the Congress but also with any other group committed to the liberation of the motherland.

2
India's Trade-Route Links with Its Eastern-Neighbours

A Historical Perspective

B.B. Kumar

Land Routes and Trade Through the North-East

The North-East India had trade links with Tibet and Burma through land routes. There was an ancient land route from Peshawar to Parvatipur (now in Bangladesh) passing through Vazirabad, Lahore, Jalandhar, Saharanpur, Lucknow, Tirhut and Katihar. It extended further to Assam[1] from Parvatipur.[2] It mostly passed keeping Ganges to the south. A southern route from Lahore to Bhagalpur, through Raivind, Firozepur, Bhatinda, Delhi, Allahabad, Varanasi, and Patna, branched off to Ganga Sagar (Calcutta) from Patna. The route extended from Bhagalpur to Kajangal in Rajmahal and then to Calcutta.[3]

In fact, Gangasagar/Calcutta route went to the Bay of Bengal port of Tamralipti, which has numerous mention in our Classical literature. Another route branched off from this southern route to Kamarupa and Chinese traveller, Yuan Chuang met the emperor, Harsha Vardhana at Kajangal[4], and they must have used the same route for travelling to that place from the Kamarupa. The two monarchs marched towards Kannauj with their armies from that place. Harsha Vardhana proceeded along the southern route and Bhaskara Varman followed the northern one.[5] The route to Kamarupa extended up to the Yunnan province of China.[6] Kamarupa formed an important part of this trade route. An alternative trade route from India to China passed through Chumbi valley in Sikkim and Tibet. The ancient Silk Route passed through the north and the north-west. A proposal was made in the early part of the last century to open up Patkai trade route.[7] That, however, could not materialize due to various reasons. That was, perhaps, to follow the ancient route linking Brahamputra valley to the South-East Asia and Yunnan province of China. One of the reasons of not restoring the ancient trade routes through Brahmaputra valley towards the east was the higher cost of road construction. The interests of the British owned Steam-Navigation Companies operating in the rivers of Burma were supposed to be adversely affected by such land routes and their opposition certainly played crucial role in the decision.

An attempt was made during Second World War to link India to Burma (now Myanmar) and China through Brahamputra valley by constructing famous Stillwell Road. In fact, there is a fresh proposal to rebuild the road. The road from Arunachal Pradesh border in India to Myitkyina in Myanmar needs—about 180 kms—rebuilding. The road may be rebuilt and slightly extended to connect the country through North-East region to Kunming, the provincial capital Yunnan of China, through Myitkyina and Lashie in Myanmar. Myitkyni Kunming Road is highly developed. The latter is linked to Hongkong by an express highway. Connectivity of Lashio with South and Central Myanmar provinces bordering Laos, Thailand and Malaysia is highly developed. The Governments of India and Myanmar have agreed to open Moreh (India)—Tamu (Myanmar), Champhai (Mizoram, India)-Hri (Myanmar) routes and border at Lungwa (in Nagaland, India) for border trade, under former's 'Look East Policy'. This will eventually lead to better road connectivity between India and East and South East Asia. Asian Railway project is also expected to be implemented soon bringing the countries nearer.

The Brahmputra valley was linked up with Burma (Myanmar) through Manipur also. But, one or two routes linking the valley with Manipur were most difficult.[8] This route was not an important one for border trade between Assam and Burma due to difficult terrain. The human movement between India and Burma through Surma valley and Manipur started in the remote past. According to Sir A. Phayre, "The route by which Kahatriya princes arrived (in Burma) is indicated in the traditions as being through

Manipur..."[9] According to Capt. Dun, "There can be no reasonable doubt that a great Aryan wave of very pure blood passed through Manipur into Burma in pre-historic times."[10] Johnstone has mentioned: "In the days when the Indian branch of the Aryan race was still in its progressive and colonising stage, this district (Manipur) was repeatedly passed over by one wave after another of invaders intent on penetrating into the remotest part of Burma."[11]

It may be mentioned that there were regular routes between Burma and India which were used by the traders, colonisers and the Buddhist Missionaries. D.G.E. Hall mentions about one such road linking Lower Burma and India *via* the bank of the Irrawady, the bank of the Chindwin and the Manipur.[12] K.M. Panikkar has mentioned about another route through these hills to China.[13] It is obvious that the existence of such land routes facilitated the trade between North-East India with Tibet and Burma on one hand and Bangladesh on the other. The land routes through Manipur continued to operate up to the present day. There were at least three routes connecting Surma valley with the Manipur valley and two connecting the latter with the Kabaw valley in the Chindwin river valley in the present day Burma.[14] There were many minor routes connecting Brahmaputra valley with Tibet which were used for the trade.

North-East India produced many items which were marketed outside the region. *Mahabharata*[15], *Harshacharit*[16] etc., mention about the products of Kamarupa. Silk clothes, ivory products etc. from Kamarupa continued to be appreciated outside the region. Many items were imported from China, Tibet and Burma through this region and exported outside India from this country. One of the routes of the import of Chinese clothes was through Yunnan and Assam[17], and the same was sent to the Bay of Bengal through Brahmaputra. It may be mentioned here that Brahmaputra was navigable from Gwalando in Bangladesh (the confluence of the Ganges and Brahmaputra) to Dibrugarh, and up to Sadiya during the floods.[18] Cinnamon was exported from China, Tibet and Burma. The route of its import and of many other products was through Assam.

There were many minor trade-routes linking the region with the foreign countries through which considerable trade was carried. Considerable trade was also carried between the villagers of both sides of the international border. Such trade, though illegal and called smuggling still continues. "The tribes inhabiting Indo-Tibet and Indo-Burma border had trade links with their neighbours across the border. Some of the tribes of Arunachal Pradesh used to be expert traders. The Monpas, the Sherdukpens, the Boris, the Ramos, the Bokars, the Pailibos continued to have trade links with the Tibetans. The Boris used to visit Nayi Lube market in Tibet and barter their raw hides, and chillies for rock salt, woolen clothes, raw wool, Tibetan swords, Tibetan vessels, ear-rings and brass bangles. They used to barter salt, iron and utensils brought from Tibet with the other groups of the Adis."[19] The Bokars exchanged their surplus chillies, butter, hides, tamen (a creeper used for dyeing) for the cattle, sheep and goats, swords and woollen goods in the Tibetan markets.[20] The Shimongs and Ashings used to carry their clothes to the Tibetan markets and exchanged them for salt, beads etc.[21]

It may be pointed out that two principal trade routes, out of the several important ones in the Siang district, pass through the Bori and the Bokar countries to the Tibetan plateau.[22] The Tibetans used to come down through the Kepung La Pass to the Ashing area of Arunachal Pradesh and further down up to Pasighat for exchanging the rock-salt, iron, hand-woven clothes, swords, musk, imitation turquoise necklaces, blue porcelain beads, yarn of different colours, snuff, China silver and wooden bowls and metal pots for mithuns, raw hides, deer horns, and white and red rice.[23] These trading activities reportedly continued in large scale up to the sixth decade of this country, as reported by Sachin Roy.

Gait has reported about the hectic trade between the Assam and Bengal[24] and also between Assam and Tibet.[25] According to Gait, Rudra Singh "is said to have received the submission of all the hill tribes, and to have established an extensive trade with Tibet."[26] This clearly indicates that the border trade also depended on the law and order situation of the country concerned. The quantum of trade might have varied from time to time, but it continued uninterrupted on our northern border in the past. Mackenzie has also reported about the border trade with Tibet. He quotes from Hamilton's description of the trade between Assam and Tibet based on the Pemberton's Report. "Tibetan caravans conducted by 20 persons used to come down annually to a mart of Chouna on the Assam border after two months journey from Lassa and conveyed silver bullion to the amount of about one lakh of rupees, and a considerable quantity of rock salt for sale to the Assam merchants at Geegunshur four miles away. The large quantities of rice brought by the merchants at the latter place were purchased and imported into Tibet from Assam by the Tibetan Merchants. Tussa silk cloth, iron and lac found in Assam, skins, buffalo horns, pearls, and corals, first imported from Bengal were traded by the Assamese merchants. The Tibetan merchants brought woollens, gold dust, salt, musk, horses, Chinese silk, etc. The annual fair was temporarily stopped due to Burmese occupation. Attempt was made to revive it in 1833. The fair was started at Udalguri later on."[27]

Marts are regularly held (daily, biweekly, weekly or annual) at the foot-hills of the Himalayas throughout the country and also at the foot-hills bordering Bangladesh, Burma and Tibet. The border trade of Assam, Meghalaya, Mizoram and Tripura was mostly carried through such marts. R.M. Nath has written about the trade of the Garos with Bangladesh: "The Garos living in the areas bordering Goalpara, Mymensing and Rangpur districts as also the Garos of the interior came down to the plains to sell their cotton and chillies and purchase paddy, salt, cloth and other necessities; and rulers of the states exacted taxes from them. To deal with the Garos, each ruler used to appoint a Laskar at every pass of duar. Often times the fraudulent tactics of the merchants and the officers of the states, were retaliated by the Garos by chopping off their head which were sold at high premium in the hills the price varying according to the wealth and position of the merchant or the officer."[28]

The Khasis and the Jaintiyas used to visit the marts of Bangladesh in the south and that of the Assam in the north. The Khasis used to visit the marts up to the central part of the Nowgong. Iron was manufactured in the hills and exported in the shape of hoes to the Assam valley and in lumps of pig iron to the Surma valley, where it was used for clamps by the boat-builders. An estimated 20,000 maunds of iron were exported from the hills in 1853.[29] The ancient trade routes and the marts played important roles in the internal and border trade in the North East region. The discussion about them provides insights in the historical perspective. The importance of the trade routes and the marts for the people may be understood from the fact that the British authorities used to close down the trade routes and prevent the marauding tribes from attending the marts to force them to behave. Mackenzie has described such closures and the impacts of the same. He wrote:

> "In April 1861, the dwars were closed to Naga traders by order of the Commissioner of Assam, in consequence of the murder of one Tonoo Cachari in the Geleki Dwar, used by the Namsang and the neighbouring clans. In the February following, the Nangota Abor Nagas, who were not known to us to be the guilty tribe, surrendered five of their number as those who had committed the murder. The surrender, it appeared, they made under pressure brought to bear on them by the Boree Nagas of Tabloong, Jaktoong, Kamsang, and Namsang, who being such distressed by the closure of the Dwars threatened to attack the Nangotas if they did not give up the offenders."[30]

Mackenzie further observed:

> "In November 1867, the Geleki guard-houses was again attacked at night .... The Dwars were at any rate closed to trade; the out-posts strengthened; and neglected stockades hastily repaired. The stoppage of trade again proved a successful policy. The Tabloong, Namsang, and other Nagas who were carrying on a most profitable traffic with the tea gardens, which they could not afford to loss, speedily combined, and in a few months' time they succeeded in tracing out the raiders, and arresting by force or strategy two of their leaders, who were delivered over to the British authorities for punishment. These men proved to belong to the Yungia Abor Nagas, a remote clan in the upper hills, who actuated by a love of plunder and a craving for skulls had led a stealthy war party through the trackless jungle to the plains below; and had, as they said attacked the police-station under the notion that it was a settlement of ryots - a mistake not very creditable to the discipline of the post."[31]

The remarks made above underline the importance of trade including the border trade, for the people of this region. Some points emerging from the above-mentioned facts, which need to be kept in mind, are:

(i) The North-East India was not the closed corner of the country; it had wider trade links. The region was linked up across the border through major and minor trade routes.
(ii) The region continued to have flourishing trade with the neighbouring countries.
(iii) The trade flourished whenever the law and order situation was sound and suffered at the time of anarchy.
(iv) The quantum of illegal border trade now is almost the same as that of the legal trade with its neighbours; the border trade potential is really very high.

The partition of India created unnatural border and the age-old trade ties with the part of Bengal called East Pakistan (now Bangladesh) were snapped. The trade with Tibet received severe jolt after the occupation of Tibet by China, and specially after the Indo-Chinese Border Conflict in 1962. Situation on both sides of the Indo-Myanmar border remained fluid. The border trade highly decreased after independence of India, and specially after the sixth decade of the nineteenth century. The situation further aggravated due to the lack of roads and the speedier modes of communication. The costs of bringing in the locally needed items, and that of exporting the local produce became prohibitively high. The production of many agricultural and horticultural items, such as, potato, orange, pineapple, ginger, and other perishable products in the southern border areas of Meghalaya, became non-economic. The people suffered. In this background, the steps envisaged by the Central Government to facilitate trade with Bangladesh and Bhutan generate optimism. The border trade with Tibet and Myanmar should also be encouraged.

The economy of the border areas is always of supplementary and complementary nature and this aspect of economy should always be kept in mind while promoting the border trade. Only such border trade shall make the economy healthy. Appropriate steps should, however, be taken to prevent the flow of narcotics and the arms between the neighbours. The trade of the items produced in the third country, such as, the Korea and Japan, should also be discouraged in this case.

Sea Linkages and the Status of Indian Shipping

Indian cultural, religious, historical and trade links with its neighbours since remotest past through sea-routes is a well-known phenomenon. Navigation, and the related words, such as 'navigate', 'navigator', 'naval', "nautical' are related to Sanskrit, '*nava*', f. RigVedic, '*nau-*', and similar words in a large number of Indian languages for boat.[32] '*Navika-*' (Sanskrit, m.; Pali, '*navika-*' m.; *Prakrita*, '*navia-*', m.; Hindi, *Navika*) is sailor, helmsman.[33] Scrt naus, GK. naus, Lat nav-(em), navos, and old Norse nor for ship are also related words.[34] *Navya* (Rigveda, f.) is navigable stream, stream; in *Pali*, nava, f., is canal.[35] *Navy*, abbreviated from navigator, sailor, was the name formerly given to workmen engaged in making canals or 'navigation', i.e. of passages that could be navigated.[36] According to eminent historian, Dr. Radha Kumud Mookerjee, "that art of navigation was born in river Sindh 6000 years ago. The very word navigation is derived from Sanskrit word Non (Nav-ship) Gaith.[37] The ship-building in India was in the advanced state. Sir John Malcolm wrote: "Indian vessels—so admirably adapted to the purpose for which they are required that, notwithstanding their superior science, Europeans were unable during an intercourse with India for two centuries to suggest or to bring into successful practice one improvement."[38]

Dr. Robert Heine Geldern and Dr. Gordon F. Ekholm, in the Civilisations of Ancient America (1951) have stated: "Ships of size that carried Fahien from India to China (through stormy China water) were certainly capable of proceeding all the way to Mexico and Peru by crossing the Pacific. One thousand years before the birth of Columbus Indian ships were far superior to any made in Europe up to the eighteenth century."[39]

He further writes:

> "There appears to be little doubt but that ship building and navigation were sufficiently advanced in southern and eastern Asia at the period in question to have made trans-Pacific voyages possible.... In the third century, horses were exported from India to the Malay Peninsula and Indo-China, an indication that there must have been ships of considerable size.... When the Chinese Buddhist scholar Fahien returned from India around A.D. 400, he embarked

> on a ship which carried more than two hundred sailors and merchants and which, therefore, must have been larger than the ships of Columbus and early Spanish explorers. This ship sailed directly across the ocean from Ceylon to Java."[40]

Many European travellers have written about Indian shipping. They include Marco Polo (1254-1324 A.D.), Niccolo dei Conti (1395-1469 A.D.), and Lodovico de Varthema (1470-1510). The latter two were Italians. Niclo dei Conti records that India built some ships 'larger than ours'. The ships used to have five sails and five masts each capable of containing 2,000 butts. The capacity of some of the ships were about 60,000 cubic feet. The bottom was constructed with three layers of planks to enable them to resist the onslaughts of cyclonic weather, and some ships had compartments built in such manner that the voyage was possible even after a part was shattered.[41] Lodovico de Varthema has described Calicut as a flourishing ship-building centre.[42] There were large number of ship-building centres in Bengal.[43]

There are numerous references of the ships and the voyages in the Vedic texts, epics, and other texts. There is description of a strongly constructed vessel, called *plava* in *Rig Veda*. It is said to withstand the battering of storms and having wings.[44] The wings, according to Sridharan, were perhaps some sort of archaic stabilizers.[45] There is mention in a passage that merchants journeyed across the ocean to distant countries in pursuit of wealth.[46] In a prayer for prosperity in the lands across the seas to god Agni in the *Rig Veda*, it is said: "O Lord, take us in a ship across the oceans for our well-being."[47] God Varuna is credited with the knowledge of the sea-routes followed.[48] According to another reference, Varuna and Vasishtha sailed to mid-ocean in a well-rigged ship.[49] A naval expedition was sent out by the Rishi-King Turga under the command of his son Bhujyu; the ship wrecked in a storm, and King Tugra and some of his followers were rescued by the Ashvini Kumaras in their hundred oared (shataritra) galleys.[50] *Rig Veda* also mentions about the *Rishis* of the two seas.[51] Nau-manda, referred in *Satapatha Brahmana*, denotes two rudders of a ship.[52]

Ramayana mentions about five hundred well-built ships with *swastika* signs, flags, displaying full sails and fitted with large gongs.[53] Sugriva instructs his monkeys to go to the islands of the sea[54] and in the land of the Koshakaras[55] in search of Sita. Koshakaras' land is interpreted to be China.[56] A boat fitted with some mechanical device (*yantra-yuktam*} and flags; and strong enough to stand storms and waves (*sarva-vata-saham*) is mentioned in the *Mahabharata*.[57] Maritime navigation is also refered in the *Baudhayana Dharmasutra*[58]. *Deegha Nikaya* mentions the use of birds by mariners to ascertain direction of land during sea-voyage.[59] *Mahabharata* also mentions about Sahadeva going to many islands to bring the subjects from there.[60] There is a reference with admiration in the *Varaha-Purana*[61] of the merchants who sailed fast far into the shoreless, deep and fearful waters of ocean in search of valuable pearls. Panini, in. *Ashtadhyayi*, refers to both coastal island cargoes (*dvaipya*)[62] and mid-ocean island cargoes (*dvaipa, dvaipaka*).[63] The ship building activities and looking after ocean navigation and inland river transport was entrusted to the superintendent of ships Navadhyaksha during Maurya period."[64]

Yuktikalpataru was written by King Bhoja of Dhar in Malwa. It offers an elaborate and analytical treatise of ship-building in ancient India.[65] It gives an account of four kinds of wood according to *Vriksha Ayurveda* (Botany). Those are light and soft, light and hard, soft and heavy, and hard and heavy. The properties of two different kinds are blended in *Dvijati* class. The ships made of the second class of wood bring wealth and happiness; it may be safely used for crossing the sea and bring happiness. It cautions against the use of different classes of wood or the use of iron for ship-building. It recommends painting four masted ship white, three masted red, two masted yellow and single masted blue.[66] Two categories of ships are grouped as *Samanya* (ordinary; used for inland river traffic) and *Vishesha* (special; used for ocean-going). The dimensions and the capacities of the ships vary. The length, breadth and height of each kind of ship is given in cubits.[67] Each cubit equals 1.5 feet. Radhakumud Mukerjee has given the dimensions of different kinds of ships in feet.

Ten varieties of the *samanya* category of ships are: *kshudra* (24'×6'×6'); *madhyama* (36'×18'×12'), *bhima* (60'×30'×3), *capala* (72'×36'×36'), *patala* (96'×48'×48'), *bhaya* (108'×54'×54'), *dirgha* (132'×66'×66'), *patraputa* (144'×72'×72'), *garbhara* (168'×84'×84'), and *manthara* (180'×90'×9). *Vishesha* category of ocean-going ships are classified into *dirgha* and *unnaia*.

Dirgha class of the ships have ten types: *dirghika* (48′×6′×4.8′), *tarani* (72′×9′×7.2′), *lola* (96′×12′×9.6′), *gatvara* (120′×15′×12′), *gamin* (144′×18′×14.1′), *tari* (168′×21′×16.8′), *janghala* (192′×24′×19.2′), *plavini* (216′×27′×21.6′), *dharini* (240′×30′×24′), and *vegini* (264′×33′×26.4′). Five varieties of *unnata* type of ships are *urdhva* (48′×24′×24;), *anurdhva* (72′×36′×36′), *svarnamukhi* (96′×48′×48′), *garbhini* (120′×60′×60′) and *manthara* (144′×72′×72′).[68] *Bhima, bhaya* and *garbhara* ships of *samanya* category are unsafe for navigation because their dimensions do not allow them to keep steady and well balanced on water. *Dirghika* and *tarani* of *dirgha* category, likewise, bring good-luck and the others bring ill luck. Likewise, *anurdhva, garbhini* and *manthara* ships of the last category bring misfortune.[69] The deck-housed ships were classified into *sarvamandira, madhyamandira* and *agramandira* depending on the construction of cabins.[70] The ships of enormous sizes were used in the past, as we find from the literary sources. The ship of prince Vijayasimha carried 700 men. Eight hundred persons of the party of his bride travelled in a ship, as mentioned in the Pali chronicle, *Mahavamsa*.[71] As mentioned in the *Samudda-vanija-jataka*, one thousand carpenters of a village, failing to deliver goods for which they were paid in advanced, built a ship secretly and set sail for an island overseas.[72] *Janaka Jataka* mentions about a ship-wreck of seven hundred passengers.[73] In *Sankha Jataka*, there is mention of a huge ship.[74]

Decoration of the Indian vessels with sheets of gold, silver, copper and their alloys was done.[75] However, the use of iron was avoided to avoid danger due to magnetic attraction. Jinadatta Suri in his *Kalasvarupakulakama* mentions the legend of magnetic rock and says that a ship riveted with iron is attracted by loadstone, breaks, sinks and cannot cross the sea. On the contrary, a ship without iron crosses deep sea in strong wind; bring profit and prosperity.[76] A ship used in successful sea voyage is described being "without iron" (*nilloham*) in *Bhavisyattakaha*.[77] As iron, though known in India, was not used, planks of the hull were joined by stitching. The tennon and groove system of joining planks horizontally can be seen in the vessels painted at Ajanta.[78] Stitching with palm-fibre or with cord of jute or coir dipped in cashew-nut pitch was also done.[79] In the fish-joinery technique, wedge-shaped pieces of wood were inserted in the joints of the planks. It can be seen in the sculptural representation of a boat carrying three ascetics on the eastern gateway of Sanchi Stupa No. I.[80] Here, it needs mention that the ships are depicted in the paintings elsewhere also, as is found in the Ajanta caves[81], Borobudur[82], Harappan sites[83], Moahnjo-daro[84], Bharhut sculptures[85] and Andhra coins.[86]

The stitched hulls, according to some Arab writers, are pliant and resilient, and are less easily broken than nailed ships in case of their striking any reef.[87] But, the danger of sinking was there due to entry of water through leakage[88], and proper arrangements were made to prevent the same. The chief sailor examined all the joinings and caulked even small holes before starting the journey.[89] *Acarangsutra* mentions about the emergency blocking of the holes.[90] More regular practice of caulking is mentioned in *Tilakamanjari.*[91] Sailors were appointed with specific duty to pour out water[92] and to plug holes.[93] The mariner's compass was known to the Indians.[94] Foreigners also reported the fact.[95] The sailers used their knowledge of the areas visited[96] and that of the astronomical knowledge.[97] Indians had the knowledge of the trade winds. Avashyakacurni[98] informs about sixteen types of winds, including the twelve types of the same mentioned in Abu Hanifa Dainuri's book on nautical science.[99]

It was necessary for a pilot to learn *Niryamakasutra* for handling ships at Sopara, acording to *Jatakamala.*[100] Practical training was given to the sailors, according to *Tilakamanjari.*[101] *Tilakamanjari* has the story of Taraka, who was made chief of the sailors by Chandraketu. Perhaps he received practical training under the latter. Taraka, very soon, learnt the complete art of shipping (*naupracaravidya*); knew the duties of helmsman. He repeatedly sailed in deep waters, visited *dvipantara,* saw even small waterways, carefully observed rough and smooth places, and thus properly practised the works of sailing the ship.[102] For becoming successful sailors, the sons of chief navigators received education of nautical sciences.[103]

The sailors also learnt medicine/chemistry.[104] The information about sea voyages is scattered in Indian literature. The manuscript of the work *Navashastrama* (called Kappala in one case) is found in the library of the old college of Fort St. George (Madras).[105] The copy of the *Niryamaka sutra,* however, is not available presently.[106] Excavations at Lothal in Gujarat have unearthed the dock, measuring 710′ length, 120′ width and 23-foot opening in one side, capable of handling sea and river navigation. It was situated near Arabian Sea once. According to S.R. Rao, the skill and technical knowledge displayed in the construction of the dock presupposes a sound knowledge of hydrography and maritime engineering.[107] It is reported that Indian coasts were studded with harbours from which merchant vessels sailed to Persia, Arabia, Africa and Red Sea ports.[108] Indian navigational links with South-East Asia are well-known. The author of the *Periplus of the Erythrean Sea* mentions two kinds of ships; *sangara*, the coastal vessels, and the *colaindia*, bulky and strong sea-going vassel, used for trade with Malcca, and perhaps also with China.[109] Megasthenes and Pliny have written about the ship-building in Maurya period.[110] Andhra- Satavahana, Chola-Pandya and Gupta kings also encouraged oversea trade[111]; through numerous Indian ports.[112] A naval department was maintained during Akbar's time.[113] Measures were taken by Shaista Khan, Aurangzeb's Governor in Bengal to strengthen naval force to quell Arakanese and Portuguese piracy.[114] There were about 500 ships in Shivaji's fleet.[115]

Indian literature is full of the references of the sea voyages and oversea-trade. Apart from the books refered above, the information about shipping/navigation and the references of the traders and sailors is scattered in the *jatakas* (such as *Bayeru Jataka, Mahajanaka, Sankha Jataka* etc), Avadanas, Jain texts, *Katha Saritasagara*, Tamil texts, *Paddinappalai* and *Manimekhalai Simhalavadana, Rajavalliya, Brihatkathashlokasangraha, Samaraiccakaha, Mihndapanho; Upamitibhavaprapancakatha, Brihatkathakosha, Kathakosha, Bhavishyattakaha, Navadhammakaha* etc. '*Bhavisyattakaha*'[116] and '*Tilakamanjari*'[117] provide very detailed and graphic description of the sea-voyage. *Avadanakalpalata* of Kshemendra describes the unlimited zeal of the sailors.[118] Varahamihira describes sea and its riches in glowing terms.[119]

The worship and special ceremonies and rites related to sea voyage are described in many books.[120] Among lexicons, *Deshinamamala, Ahhdhanaratnamala* and *Vaijayanti* provide important information. We find *Deshi* terms for the ship in the first one. The second book provides terms related to sea, shore, waves, tide, and acquatic animals.[121] *Vaijayanti* provides terms for different categories of ships, its parts, classes of passengers and sailors.[122] Terms for varieties of ship and its parts are given in

Varnaratnakara.[123] Books are also available which provide terms related to shipping/ships in other languages.[124] Texts like *Tilakamanjari, Nayadhammakaha* and *Jatakas* list the essentials carried during voyages. In case of shipwreck, survivers used to take as much *ghee* and sugar as was possible to digest and used to cover their bodies and garments with oil for protection. They used to place a flag on the tree-top and burn fire so that to attract attention of the passing ships and get rescued.

It is evident from the above-mentioned write-up that the status of Indian shipping was very high. Scholars like Dr. Robert Heine Geldern, Dr. Ekholm and Chaman Lai firmly believed in Indo-American links centuries before Collumbus.[125] But there was marked decline during medieval period in this field. The reasons are not difficult to find. Al-Beruni has described the ruinous effects of Mahmood's raids on India. He looted immense wealth and ruined our heritage. The Indians "became like atoms of dust and their sciences retired far away from the conquered areas to distant Kashmir, Benares and other places." The second holocaust two centuries later initiated the worst process of intellectual, social and economic pauperization. Bakhtiyar Khilji, not only plundered the country and captured political power, but also destroyed our great institutions of learning. Universities like Nalanda, Vikramshila, were attacked and destroyed; our libraries were burnt. India became knowledge-starved and inward-looking. The sea trade became less protected and the piracy increased tremendously. This happened due to increased internal wars and instability. This resulted into tabooing of the sea voyage, and journey in the certain regions. Manu prohibits inviting Brahmins undertaking sea voyages to religious feasts being not fit to carry out religious functions.[126] Sea voyage is treated as one of the five reprehensible practices according to *Baudhayana Dharmasutra.*[127] It is a prohibition only during Kali-age (*Kalivarjya*), according to Hemadri.[128]

This suggests the prohibition to be of later origin. The taboo was against the Brahmins according to Kane[129] and that against *dvija* according to 'Vyavaharamayukha'[130], 'Apastamba'[131] and 'Vasishtha'[132] advise avoiding contact with the barbarians.

Notes

1. Dr. Motichandra, *Sarthavaha*, p. 12; Patna, 1953.
2. *Ibid.*
3. *Ibid.*
4. Vasu, N.N., *Social History of Kamarupa*, vol. I, p. 151.
5. *Ibid.*
6. Motichandra, *op. cit.*, p. 127.
7. Mackenzie, A., *The North-East Frontier of India*, Reprint, Delhi, 1981, p. 64.
8. Singh, R.K. Jhaljit, *A Short History of Manipur, Imphal*, 1965; p. 3.
9. Phayre, A., *Histroy of Burma*, p. 3.
10. Dun, *Gazetteer of Manipur*, p. 6, foot-note.
11. Johnstone, James, *My Experience in Manipur and Naga Hills*, p. 280.
12. Hall, D.G.E., *History of South-East Asia*, p. 121.
13. Panikkar, K.M., *India and China*, p. 17.
14. Singh, R.K. Jhaljit, *op. cit.*, p. 3.
15. Maha.
16. Agarwal, Dr. Vasudevasharn, *Harsh Charit: Ek Samskritik Adhyayan*, pp. 170-72.
17. Motichandra, *op. cit.*, p. 127.
18. *Ibid.*, p. 12.
19. *Ibid.*, p. 127.
20. Roy, Sachin, *Aspects of Padam Minyong Culture*, p. 32.
21. *Ibid.*, pp. 32-33.
22. *Ibid.*, p. 32.
23. *Ibid.*, p. 33.
24. Gait, Edward, *A History of Assam*, Reprint, Guwahati, 1994, p. 285.
25. *Ibid.*, p. 171.
26. *Ibid.*
27. Mackenzie, *op. cit.*, p. 15.
28. Nath, R.M., *The Background of Assamese Culture*, p. 111.
29. Gurdon, P.R.T., *The Khasis*, Reprint, Delhi, 1990, p. 58.
30. Mackenzie, *op. cit.*, p. 97.
31. *Ibid.*, pp. 97-98.
32. Turner, R.L., *A Comparative Dictionary of the Indo-Aryan Languages*, London, O.U.P., 1973; entry no. 7081 on p. 406.
33. *Ibid.*, entry no. 7082, p. 406.
34. Wyld, Henry Cecil, *Universal English Dictionary*, p. 765.
35. Turner, *op. cit.*, p. 406.
36. Wyld, *op. cit.*, p. 765.
37. Chaman Lai, *India Mother of Us All*, p. 48.
38. Chaman Lai, *op. cit.*, p. 48; quoted from *Journal of Royal Asiatic Society*, Vol. I.

39. *Ibid.*, p. 49.
40. *Ibid.*
41. Mamta Chaudhury, *Ship Building in Ancient and Medieval India in The Cultural Heritage of India*, Calcutta, The Ramakrishna Mission, 1991, p. 203; quoted from R.H. Major: *India in the Fifteenth Century*, II (Hakluyt Society, London), pp. 10, 21 and 27.
42. *Ibid.*, quoted from *Travels of Varthema*, ed. G.P. Badger (Hekluyt Society, London), pp. 152ff.
43. *The Cultural Heritage of India*, p. 203.
44. *Rig Veda*, 1.24, 35-36.
45. Sridharan, K., *A Maritime History of India*, Government of India, Publication Division, Delhi, 1965; p. 10.
46. *Rig Veda*, 1.48.3.
47. *Ibid.*, 1.97.8.
48. *Ibid.*, 1.25.7
49. *Ibid.*, VII.88.3-4.
50. *Ibid.*, 1.116.3.
51. *Ibid.*, x. 136.5.
52. *Satapatha Brahmana*, II.3.3.15.
53. *Valmiki's Ramayana*, 11.89; 11.16.
54. *Ibid.*, IV.40.25.
55. *Ibid.*, IV.40.23.
56. Mukerjee, Radha Kumud, *Indian Shipping*, Longman's Green & Co. Bombay, 1919; p. 55-56; quoted in *Cultural Heritage of India*, p. 198.
57. *Mahabharata*, 1.143.5-7,
58. *Baudhayana Dharmasutra*, 1.2.4; II.2.2.
59. *Deegha Nikaya*, 1.222.
60. *Mahabharata*, II.28.44, 46.
61. Lallanji Gopal, *Indian Shipping in Early Medieval Period*, quoted in *India's Contribution to World Thought and Culture*, Dr. Lokesh Chandra and others (ed.); p. 115.
62. *Ashtadhyayi*, 4.3.1063.
63. *Ibid.*, VI 3.58.
64. Kautilya's *Artha Shastra*, II.28.
65. The manuscript was available in Calcutta Sanskrit College Library.
66. *Yuktikalpataru*, Pandit Ishvara Chandra Sastri (ed.), Calcutta, 1917; quoted in Cultural Heritage of India on p. 201.
67. *Ibid.*
68. Radhakumud Mukerjee, *op. cit.*, pp. 22-24.
69. *Ibid.*
70. Chaman Lal, *op. cit.*, p. 52.
71. *Cultural Heritage of India*, p. 200.
72. *Ibid.*
73. Chaman Lal, *op. cit.*, p. 53.
74. *Ibid.*

75. Mamata Chaudhury, *op. cit.*, p. 201.
76. Lallanji Gopal, *op. cit.*, p. 109.
77. *Ibid.*,
78. S.R. Rao, "Shipping in Ancient India", in *India's Contribution to World Thought and Culture*, p. 97.
79. *Ibid.*, pp. 97-98.
80. *Ibid.*, p. 98.
81. Three masted ships are seen in Ajanta murals.
82. In Borobudur sculptures multi-masted ships are seen.
83. Ship engraved on a postsherd was found at Dhulia.
84. Seal engravings and terracotta amulet from Mohenjodaro have ships with cabins.
85. Steering oars of the ships depicted in Bharhut sculptures might have served as rudders.
86. Andhra coins are found to have depiction of steering oars of the ships.
87. G.P. Hourani, *Arab Seafaring in the Indian Ocean in the Ancient and Early Medieval times*; p. 90.
88. *Dohakosh*, XIV. 87.
89. Lallanji Gopal, *op. cit.*, p. 109.
90. II. 3.1.10.20.
91. Lallanji Gopal, *op. cit.*, p. 109.
92. *Ibid.*
93. *Ibid.*
94. Moti Chandra, Sarthavaha, Patna, 1953, pp. 147, 209; R.K. Mookerjee, *op. cit*, pp. 47-48.
95. Vide Jacques de Vitry, *History of the Kingdom of Jerusalem*, quoted by Lallanji Gopal, *op. cit.*, p. 112.
96. Lallanji Gopal, *op. cit.*, p. 112.
97. *Ibid.* p. 116.
98. *Ibid.*, p. 111.
99. *Ibid.*
100. The manuscript of the book is not available.
101. *Tilakamanjari*, pp. 129-30.
102. *Ibid.*, p. 144.
103. Lallanji Gopal, *op. cit.*, p. 116.
104. *Bhavisyatakaha*, VII. 1.84-85.
105. *Vide* 'A Catelogue Raisonee of Oriental MSS' in the Library of the Late College of Fort St. George, Madras.
106. India lost a vast treasure of books during post-Bakhtiyar Muslim invasion.
107. S.R. Rao, *Further Escavations in Lothal, Lalit Kala*, No. II, Lalit Kala Akademi, New Delhi, April 1962, p. 17.
108. *Periplus of the Erithrean Sea*; Wilfred H. Schoff, Calcutta, 1912; p. 46.

109. *Ibid.*, p. 243.
110. Mookerjee, R.K., *op. cit.*, pp. 102-3.
111. S.R. Rao, "Shipping in Ancient India", in *India's Contribution to World Thought and Culture.*
112. *Ibid.*, pp. 92-97.
113. *Ain-i-Akbari.*
114. Mamata Chaudhury, *op. cit.*, p. 203.
115. *Ibid.*, p. 204.
116. Quoted by Lallanji Gopal, *op. cit.*, p. 115.
117. *Ibid.*
118. *Avadanakalpalata*, IV. 2.
119. *Varahamihira, Brihatsamhita*, Agastyacara, XII. 2-6.
120. *Tilakamanjari* describes the worship of God Ratnakara (ocean) before undertaking the voyage. *Bhavisyattakaha* informs about the rites performed while floating a ship. The merchants, before boarding the ship used to offer homage to the ocean, bow down to the gods and elders and give alms to the poor, as mentioned in *Samaraiccakaha*. *Brihatkathakosha* and *Upamitibhavaprapancapatha* inform about auspicious rites performed and preparations made before sailing. The start of the journey, after *puja*, blessings of the family members and the relatives, and the blessings of the sooth-sayer, used to be the most joyous occasion for all including the crew and the passengers, according to *Nayadhammakaha*.
121. *Adhidhanaratnamala*, III. 625-660.
122. *Vaijayanti*, II. 29-39.
123. Lallanji Gopal, *op. cit.*, p. 115.
124. Terms used in early Bengali literature are given in T. Dasgupta's *Aspects of Bengali Society*, p. 17.
125. Chaman Lal, *op. cit.*, pp. 75-92.
126. *Manu Smriti*, III. 158.
127. *Baudhayana Dharmasutra*, II. 1.51.
128. Quoted by Lallanji Gopal, *op. cit.*, p. 114.
129. *Ibid.*
130. Quoted by Kane; *History of Dharma Shastra*, III, p. 936.
131. *Apastamba*, I. 32
132. *Vasishtha Smriti*, VI. 41.

3
Economic History of Manipur

Some Explorations

K. Gyanendra Singh

I

Manipur, a north-eastern state of India, with a total geographical area of 22,327 sq. km., is a charming place with a small and oval valley at the centre and surrounded by hills. The state naturally splits up into two tracts, *viz.* the hills and the dales. The valley area occupies about 10 per cent (2,238 sq. km.) of the total geographical area and the rest 90 per cent (20,089 sq. km.) is the hills. The state has 352 km. long international border with Myanmar to the south-east and 502 km. long border with the adjacent states of Nagaland on the north, Cachar district of Assam on the west and Mizoram on the south and south-west.

II

Manipur has a history of state formation right from 33 A.D. According to the Royal Chronicle '*Cheitharon Kumpapa*', the first maker of Manipur is Nongda Lairen Pakhangba. It is widely believed that like the other Mongoloid groups in the north-eastern states of India, Meeties, who is the dominant inhabitant of the state and settled in the valley area, also migrated from south-west China (S.N.A. Parratt, 2005: 2-22). The kingdom of Manipur suffered in the hands of the Burmese (present day Myanmar) for seven years during 1819-25.[1] After regaining her freedom from the Burmese, she fell again in the hands of the British in 1891. With the departure of the Raj in 1947, the kingdom regained her sovereignty but was merged with the Indian Union on October 15, 1949 and graduated a full-fledged state of India on January 27, 1972.

III

The Feudal Economy

The feudal economy was basically agrarian in nature. Agriculture was the mainstay of the economy. The kingdom was known for its rice economy. The inhabitants of the valley had specialised in the art of wet rice cultivation while the hill people widely practised *jhum* cultivation. As transplantation of paddy and use of plough drawn by bullock and buffalo was introduced in Manipur only after the arrival of the Muslim war captives in the beginning of the 17th century, it appears that the technique of shifting cultivation was used even for wet rice cultivation in the valley.

The valley, being blessed with fertile land, rivers, streams, lakes, had a stable food economy. Though the size of the cultivated land is not known for certainty, it is widely believed that about one-fourth of the valley area was cultivated (R. Brown, 2001: 85). Prior to the first Census in 1881, a rough estimate showed that area of Manipur was 17,920 sq. km. and the valley area was 1664 sq. km., which forms about 9 per cent of the total geographical area (W. McCulloch, 1980:1). According to the first Census of Manipur 1881, the population was 2,21,070 persons (B.C. Allen, 2002: 45).

A rough estimate of the yield rate showed that on worst land the paddy yield was 100 baskets[2] or 2700 kg. per *pari*.[3] On best lands the yield rate was 4320 kg. to 5400 kg. per hectare.

So, the average yield rate was 4050 kg. per hectare (R. Brown, 2001: 86).

The structure of the feudal agrarian economy is also well defined by the land holding pattern of the prevailing period. Although no historical account is available on the nature of land relations at this time, oblique evidences like the introduction of the system of *pana* (division) by Loiyumba[4], suggest that land was under the control of the kings (G. Kabui, 1991: 111). The cultivable land was distributed by the king according to the system of *lallup*.[5] In other words, every male who served as *lallup* was given one hectare of land for cultivation. Besides, land was given to officials and nobles. An official named *Phunan Selungba* (Land Settlement Officer) looked after all the matters related to land (R. Brown, 2001: 85). All the land under cultivation was taxed according to the category of land[6] and taxes were paid in kind. These taxes ranged between 1 per cent to 6 per cent of the total produce on the best land and 2 per cent to 12 per cent of the total produce on the worst land. So, the land relationship was non-exploitative if rent is the criterion (Ch. Priyoranjan Singh, 2005: 151).

Since people in the valley practised wet rice cultivation, they had developed some crude form of irrigation. They used to dredge the course of river and make channels near the foot of the hills to carry the hill streams to the fields. However, a good harvest was still dependant on timely monsoon and the role of irrigation was minimal. A severe flood or drought often led to the failure of crops. But food scarcity was a rare phenomenon during this period of time. The kings of Manipur had developed a centralised system of storing paddy in common granaries known as *keis* in each village. At times of crop failure, kings used to distribute paddy from these granaries to the people (G. Kabui, 1991: 218-219).

Besides rice production, other agro-based products of the valley were potatoes, sweet potatoes, brinjals, cucumber, pumpkins, onions, pepper, tobacco and different varieties of *dhal*. In the hills, rice, cotton, oil seeds, pepper, tobacco, vegetables of various kinds, potatoes, sweet potatoes, ginger and yam were produced (R. Brown, 2001: 84). However, except rice and cotton, other products were raised mainly for household consumption and hardly had any importance from commercial point of view.

Though Manipur excelled in agriculture, its manufacturing base was extremely weak. Its manufactures were few and subsistence in nature. It comprised, of coarse, clothes, leather, cooking pots, pottery, jewellery, iron and steel, carpentry etc. (R. Brown, 2001: 89). Weaving was the most important industry of the state. Raw cotton was ginned and spun into thread by women. Cotton in large quantity was raised by the hillsmen and so the supply of raw cotton came mostly from the hills. The clothes produced were of excellent quality and extraordinarily cheap (B.C. Allen, 2002: 87). Another very important manufacture was salt. The state was blessed with a large number of salt springs. There were four principal salt-wells, *viz. Ningail, Chandrakhong, Sikhong* and *Waikhong*. The salt obtained was quite pure and free from smell. Its wholesale price was about Rs. 6 a *maund* (R. Brown, 2001: 9-10). Salt was an important item of trade as well as a source of revenue. Hill people mainly took salt in return for raw cotton and firewood. The bazaars in the Cachar valley, adjacent to the hills were also supplied.

Besides manufacturing coarse cloths and salt, other manufactures of the state included leather manufactures. The skins of deer and calf were used and the products included saddles, shoes, belts, pouches etc. Brass, copper and bell metal were used for making cooking pots. But clay was used for ordinary pots and water jars. Jewellery was another important craft and the products included rings, bracelets, necklets, armlets etc. These items were chiefly made of brass and bell metal (R. Brown, 2001: 89). Gold imported from Calcutta were also used (B.C. Allen, 2002: 90). In iron and steel works, the manufactures included *daos*, spears and arrow heads. Iron was available in valley and a small quantity was also found in the hills. Another important activity of the people was carpentry. The valley people were much praised for their artistic carpentry works and could exactly imitate English works (R. Brown, 2001: 90).

The state was not very open to trade. Major trade of the state was carried on with Cachar. Major items of export included cloths, yarns, buffaloes and ponies. In return, Manipur imported betel nut and *pan*, cloth, yarn, brass and other metals and *hukkas*. The state enjoyed a positive trade balance with Cachar. In 1868-69, the total exports from Manipur to Cachar was Rs. 3533 and total imports from Cachar was Rs. 1975 (R. Brown, 2001: 88), leading to a positive balance of Rs. 1558.

The state, being a closed agrarian economy, had a very limited source of revenue. Moreover, the economy was not fully monetised. Although a native currency called *Sel* was in circulation, most of the taxes were paid in kind. The only important source of revenue was the Kabaw valley compensation of Rs. 6000 per annum received from the Imperial government by the kings of Manipur. The other sources of revenue were taxes on fishing, exports and imports, transit duties and tributes from the outcast communities (W. McCulloch, 1980: 36). A rough estimate showed that the revenue of the valley was in between Rs. 12,000 to Rs. 15,000 per annum (R. Brown, 2001: 89).

The feudal economy of Manipur may, thus, be characterised as self-sufficient and self-contained system largely insulated within the valley without much interaction with outside world. The ruling aristocracy, no doubt, used to enjoy higher social status but without much economic inequality. The agrarian base of the economy and egalitarian approach towards resource mobilisation, particularly in relation to collection of taxes, had made the feudal state economically weak. The feudal authority hardly had resources to strengthen its armoury even while the neighbouring powers were gaining strength. With the rise of Burma in the east and imperial British in the west, the balance of power tilted against Manipur. Instead of gaining strength in order to face the new challenges and order, the surrounding political environment, the feudal state of Manipur had to come to terms with these powers at the cost of her own interest. This had ultimately led Manipur to slide into the grips of British colonial power.

IV

The Colonial Period

With the defeat of Manipur in the hands of the British in the Anglo-Manipur War of 1891, the kingdom had lost its sovereignty. Though the British did not completely annex Manipur into her empire, it exercised full control over the administration of the kingdom and the king existed in name only.[7]

The defeat of the state in the hands of the British had led to the transformation of the traditional socio-economic and political structure. The land holding system underwent a major change. The British introduced the *Rayatwari*[8] system which bestowed private land ownership and deprived the kings of the traditional rights over land. Accordingly, a new *patta*[9] system was introduced, according to which, anyone having a claim over land after 1892 was to obtain a *patta* from the government. These *patta* holders were given inheritable and transferable rights on their land. A uniform tax of Rs. 5 per hectare was realised. With the monetisation of the economy and introduction of private land ownership, the feudal economy began to give way to commercialisation of agriculture.

Under the new land system, the nobles and influential people began to apply for land on a mass scale. The colonial government issued *pattas* for as many as 35,000 acres during 1892-93 only and in the next year for 62,218 acres (N. Lokendro Singh, 1998: 51), registering an annual increase of almost 78 per cent *patta*. In 1901, the area under paddy was 1,05,708 acres. It further increased to 1,78,290 acres and 1,88,425 acres in 1931 and 1941 respectively (Ch. Priyoranjan Singh, 2005: 158). Thus, in 40 years time the area under cultivation increased by 78 per cent in the valley area only. Indeed, the introduction of *Rayatwari* system had revolutionised the agricultural sector of Manipur. The sense of ownership had encouraged people to invest in agriculture as well as provided recognition of their *bona fide*.

Alongside the increase in demand for land, population also started growing. The 1891 Census reports were lost in the Anglo-Manipur War and so no data is available for the said year. Table 3.1 shows the growth of population since 1901.

In 40 years time, the population of Manipur increased by 80 per cent. Though the absolute population figure increased over the years, the decadal growth rate was in fact low and insignificant. The decadal growth rate declined from 21.70 per cent in 1911 to 10.92 per cent in 1921. It slightly increased to 16.04 per cent in 1931 but again declined to 14.92 per cent in 1941.

We may safely conclude that Manipur was in the first stage of demographic transition, i.e., a stage of high growth potential but of low actual growth, during the colonial period.

Table 3.1: Growth of Population in Manipur (1901-1941)

Year	*Population (persons)*	*Growth Rate (percentage)*
1901	284465	–
1911	346222	21.70
1921	384016	10.92
1931	445606	16.04
1941	512069	14.92

Source: Government of Manipur, 2005.

As is expected of being in the first phase of economic transition, the vast populace was engaged in agriculture. Table 3.2 shows the occupational distribution of Manipur in 1901.

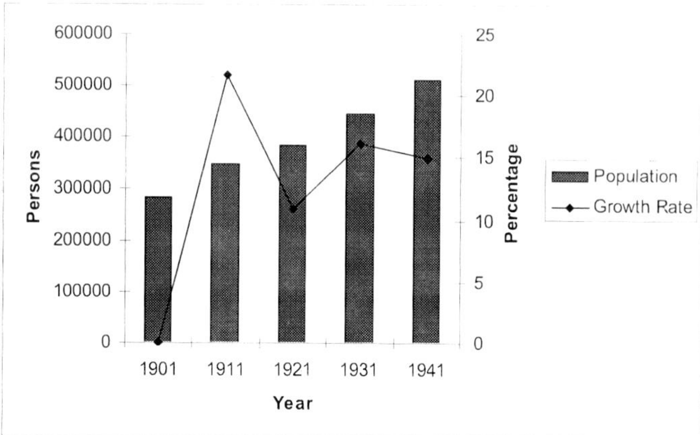

Fig. 3.1: Growth of Population in Manipur (1901-1941)
Source: Table 3.1.

Table 3.2: Occupational Distribution of Manipur in 1901

Occupational classification	*No. of Persons*	*Percentage Share*
Pasture and agriculture	207265	73
Preparation and supply of materials	62988	22
Services*	14212	5
Total Population	284465	100

Source: B.C. Allen, 2002: 66.
* Services include government service, personal service, commerce, transport, storage, professions, unskilled labour not agricultural, means of subsistence independent of occupation.

In 1901, the colonial government conducted a census in Manipur along with British India. It appears that the format of the census used in Manipur had not been tailored made to suit the conditions of the state. In spite of the limitations of the one-size-fit-all approach of the colonial government, one can have some rough idea about the occupational structure of the people of Manipur at the beginning of the twentieth century. It may be noted that 73 per cent of the population was engaged in pasture and agriculture. Another 22 per cent of the population were engaged in 'preparation and supply of substances'. These activities include weaving and other subsidiary activities which people, especially women, used to take up during and after harvest off-season. Although 'preparation and supply of substances' invariably indicate non-farm activities, but in most cases, these were either subsidiary or complementary activities. In fact, manufacturing and processing activities in every traditional society initially grew out either as subsidiary or complementary activities before graduating into a whole time profession. Thus, manufacturing and processing activities began as an embodiment of an agrarian society. A labelling of the 'preparation and supply of substances' as secondary activities may lead to an erroneous conclusion. Looked from this perspective, the percentage of people engaged in agriculture in Manipur in 1901 would be much higher than what Allen made us to believe (73%). As is expected, a 5 per cent of the population was engaged in services.

The closed agrarian economy of Manipur was opened to free trade during the colonial period. There was not only change in export basket but this period also witnessed the emergence of a new dominant business class, the *Marwaris,* who entered into Manipur as comprador to colonial authority. In no time, *Marwaris,* armed with huge market network, established their hegemony over both the external as well as the internal trade. The opening of cart route to Dimapur, Nagaland *via* Mao Thana, Manipur in 1896 further added impulse to the ongoing trade (B.C. Allen, 2002: 112).

Table 3.3: Exports from Manipur to the Surma and Assam Valley

(Value in Rs.)

Name of Articles	*Average value of Exports during three years 1902-1904, via*			
	Jirighat (1)	*Mao Thana* (2)	*Total* (1) + (2)	*Percentage*
Cattle	27022	2610	29632	11.02
Timber	85577	-	85577	31.83
Rice husked	731	93998	94729	35.23
Others*	41617	17341	58958	21.92
Total Export	**154947**	**113949**	**268896**	**100**

Source: B.C. Allen, 2002: 111.

* Others include canes, *rattans,* cotton twist, yarn, piece goods, *ghee,* dry fish, spices other than betel nuts, bamboos and other articles.

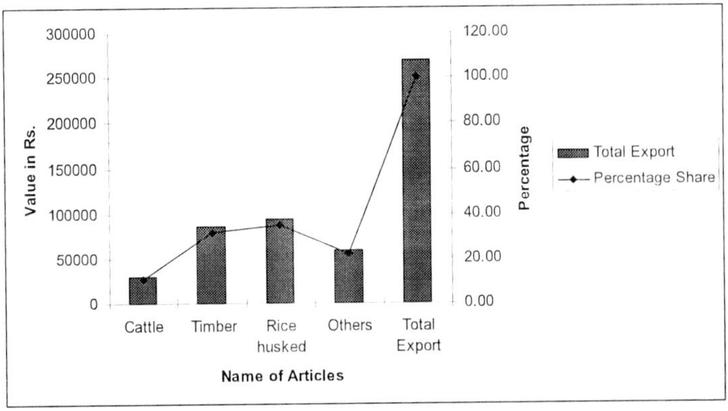

Fig. 3.2: Exports from Manipur to the Surma and Assam Valley
Source: Table 3.3.

Table 3.3 shows the average value of exports from Manipur to the Surma and Assam valley in Assam during the three years 1902-04, *via* the two trade routes, *viz.* Jirighat and Mao Thana of Manipur. While Jirighat route connects Manipur valley with Surma valley (present day Cachar district of Assam), Mao Thana route connects her with Assam valley *via* Nagaland. As it is seen, Manipur was a source of rice, cattle and timber. Rice was the main item of exports, its value averaging at Rs. 94,729 in three years, i.e. 35.23 per cent of the total exports. Timber and cattle were the other two main items, with their values averaging at Rs. 85,577 (31.83%) and Rs. 29,632 (11.02%) respectively in three years. Thus, rice, timber and cattle were the principal export items of Manipur (Table 3.4 and Fig. 3.3).

While the state was a source for rice and forest products like timber, it served as a market for the manufactured goods produced outside. Among the main items of imports, cotton twist, yarn and piece goods contributed the highest share, its value averaging at Rs. 63,848 for three years, i.e. 26.31 per cent of the total imports. Betel nuts and salt are the two other major items of import with their value averaging at Rs. 60,382 (24.89%) and Rs. 20,771 (8.56%) respectively.

The colonial trade policy had a backwash effect for the emerging manufacturing activities in Manipur. The worst affected were the traditional weaving and salt industries. The handmade products of Manipur could not compete with the cheap machine

Table 3.4: Imports to Manipur from the Surma and Assam Valley

(Value in Rs.)

Name of Articles	*Average value of Imports during the three years 1902-1904, via*			
	Jirighat	*Mao Thana*	*Total*	*Percentage*
	(1)	(2)	(1) + (2)	
Cotton twist, yarn and piece goods	9687	54161	63848	26.31
Dry fish	19636	211	19847	8.18
Salt	1418	19353	20771	8.56
Betel nuts	57532	2850	60382	24.89
Others*	15628	62162	77790	32.06
Total Import	**103901**	**138737**	**242638**	**100**

Source: B.C. Allen, 2002: 112.

* Others include horses, ponies, mules, wheat, grams, pulses, liquors, brass, copper, mineral oils, ghee, sugar refines and other articles.

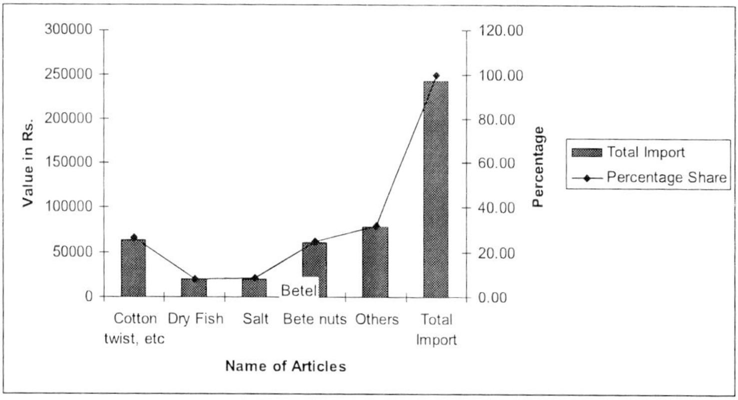

Fig. 3.3: Imports to Manipur from the Surma and Assam Valley

Source: Table 3.4.

made products of Britain. As a result the traditional weaving faced gradual extinction. Besides price competition, cultural competition between tradition and modernity had also caused a shift of the preference of the people towards British made cloths. The traditional salt making was also gradually heading towards extinction due to import of cheap foreign salt. The local salt which was priced at four *annas* a *seer* could not compete with the imported salt which was priced at seven *Pisa* a *seer* (B.C. Allen, 2002: 94). This had led to gradual disappearance of the local salt from the market. The traditional metal industry was another victim which declined due to increasing import of aluminium and enamel products.

Thus, colonial commercial policy stood on the way of emerging manufacturing activities in Manipur. The natural transition of Manipur from agrarian to industrial society had not only been shunned but the natural process of social transition had also been put to reverse gear by way of setting a de-industrialisation process that even routed the traditional manufacturing and processing activities.

With the coming of the British and subsequent monetisation of the economy, the revenue of the state had also increased. The traditional system of *lallup* was abolished and substituted by a house tax of Rs. 2 per annum in the valley and Rs. 3 in the hills. The house tax in the valley was, however, replaced by a uniform homestead tax of Rs. 5 in 1900 due to irregularities and tax evasion. A uniform land tax of Rs. 5 per hectare was also realized in lieu of kind tax. This was raised to Rs. 5.15 per hectare in 1913 following the abolition of *pothang*[10] (N. Lokendro Singh, 1998: 54). With the introduction of foreigner tax, the revenue of the state had further increased.

One can observe from Table 3.5 that land revenue formed the major source of revenue of the state. The share of land revenue to total revenue was more than 65 per cent during these years. Increasing land revenue and increasing number of *patta* holders while read along with increasing export of rice lead us to conjecture that the commercialisation of agriculture was taking place at a faster rate.

Table 3.5: Revenue Receipts of Manipur (% Share)

Categories	*1901*	*1902*	*1903*	*1904*
Land revenue	65.51	65.15	65.21	71.08
Foreigner's tax	1.16	1.08	1.26	1.47
Hill house tax	13.78	16.32	15.13	11.76
Fisheries	7.31	7.46	8.28	6.11
Salt revenue	1.83	2.19	1.93	1.50
Forests	8.50	6.54	5.93	6.69
Others	1.91	1.26	2.26	1.39
Total Revenue	**100**	**100**	**100**	**100**

Source: Calculated from B.C. Allen, 2002: 139.

Hill house tax was another main source of revenue contributing about 15 per cent. The revenue from forests and fisheries also increased during this period of time contributing about 7 per cent and 8 per cent respectively. However, the revenue from salt was very minimal to the extent of less than 2 per cent. The increasing share of revenue from land and forests and decreasing share of revenue from salt indicates the essence of colonial economic policy-promotion of the primary resources and destruction of the traditional industry.

With the introduction of money tax, there was a sudden need for surplus cash. But cash was very hard to obtain during this period of time owing to very low price of rice. The average price of rice during the 1930s was around 30 *seers* per rupee, the major source of money income of the people. Coupled with this factor was the non-availability of any gainful job in other sectors during the post-harvest off-season. The manufacturing sector was dying and trade was largely controlled by the *Marwaris*. According to Ch. Priyoranjan Singh[11] (2005: 153), after paying the land tax of Rs. 5, which was increased to Rs. 5.15 in 1913, a farmer was left with Rs. 8 and 15.65 *annas* as surplus cash. Out of this he had to pay the house tax of Rs. 2 per annum which was increased to Rs. 5 since 1990. Under such conditions, not only the position of the farmers began to deteriorate but they also began to borrow money from rich moneylenders, mainly the *Marwaris*, at a high interest rate which subsequently led to the surrender of their lands.

V

Thus, the British colonial power had established a kind of diarchy in Manipur. While the administration of the state and the maintenance of the law and order was the responsibility of the king, collection of revenue was under the control of the British officials. Although Manipur was not annexed to British India, the economy of the state was integrated with the colonial market. The trade potentials in rice, timber and cattle had been fully exploited. The benefit from enhanced agriculture went to the *Marwaris* as they used to control the rice trade. The outbreak of *Nupi Lan* (Womens' War) in 1939 against the unprecedented export of rice by the *Marwaris* is well documented in the history of Manipur (K. Manimohan Singh, 2006). The benefits from enhanced revenue went to the colonial masters. However, the benefits arising out of the transition from feudal agrarian relations to colonial agrarian relations had, to some extent, gone to the ordinary people in that that they had been bestowed the ownership of land. Of course, this benefit had been accrued to people only at a high cost as the colonial master had raised land taxes considerably. To be precise, while the people of Manipur were better-off socially with the abolition of obligatory feudal services like *lallup* and *pothang*, they were not benefitted economically as far as rise in real income is concerned. The higher tax rate and larger tax base had robbed the surplus generated by the peasantry. Production in agriculture increased due to fresh private initiative following the introduction of *Rayatwari* system. Of course, colonial government refrained from modernising agriculture which would have called for state investment in agro-inputs particularly irrigation. Colonial commercial policy although revolutionised agriculture by way of synchronising land ownership, marketing of rice and rice export, it routed the emerging manufacturing activities in Manipur by way of substituting local manufactures by cheap imported ones. While the people were experiencing export-led-retardation, the economy was experiencing some sort of de-industrialisation with a feeble trend towards tertiarisation due to the little expansion in trade and commerce.

Notes

1. Many were taken to Burma and many fled to nearby Cachar including the King. Seven years rule led to depopulation. Burmese took away thousands of native farmers, artisans, arambai experts, weavers etc. Population of the valley was estimated at 10,000 (R.K. Jhalajit Singh, 1992: 248). R. Brown (2001: 64) estimated the male population in the valley at 3,000 with a scanty proportion of women and children. The valley was overgrown with dense grass jungle, clumps of bamboo and young trees. Highways, roads and lanes were obliterated and rice fields were turned to shallow swamps.
2. One basket contains about 60 pounds. 1 pound = 0.45 kg. So, one basket contains about 27 kg.
3. One *pari* = 2.5 acre or 1 hectare.
4. During the reign of Loiyumba (1074-1121 A.D.), a royal edict known as 'Loiyamba Shinyen' was introduced. It is regarded as the first

written constitution of the Manipur kingdom. He divided the land into six administrative divisions/*panas*, *viz*. Aangoupa Lup, Nongmai Lup, Aakong Lup, Khurai Lup, Chingcha Lup and Khaicha Lup. Every family was assigned a particular duty which the king himself distributed and accordingly served in the *pana* (G. Kabui, 1988: 307-311).

5. According to *lallup*, every male aged between 17 and 60 were required to work 10 days in 40 days for the state without remuneration. Women were exempted from this service. Among men, the blacksmith, goldsmith, carpenters etc. pursued their different crafts in the Raja's workshop for the stated time, while the bulk of the population, the field workers, served as soldiers and made roads or dug canals (J. Johnstone, 2002: 110).
6. The cultivated land was categorised into nine types *viz*., Tauna Lou, Sarkari Lou, Pham Lou, Sepoy Lou, Mana Lou, Brahmin Lou, Temple Lou, Royal Family Lou and Pangal Lou (N. Lokendro Singh, 1998:14-20).
7. The Anglo-Manipur War of 1891 subjected the office of the king and succession to the throne conditional to the recognition by the British. It was made obligatory for the king to obey the 'orders' of the British government (C.U. Aitchison, 1931: 198 and N. Sanajaoba, 1993: 309). The affairs of the state would be managed in accordance with 'Rules for the Management of the Manipur State' sanctioned by the British Government of India. In the management, the king would be assisted by a Durbar, whose President will be the king and the Vice President would be held by a gazetted officer of Eastern Bengal and Assam government (K. Manimohan Singh, 1989: 1-9). Thus, we may say that Manipur had effectively lost her independence after the Anglo-Manipur War of 1891.
8. Every registered holder of land is recognized as its proprietor and pays taxes direct to the government. Under this system, land revenues were imposed directly on the individual cultivators who are registered as proprietors and who actually worked on the land.
9. A legal document issued by the government in the name of the actual owner of a particular plot of land.
10. According to *pothang*, the villagers had to carry luggage of the officials while they were on tour and pool their labour to maintain the village roads and common properties like schools, granaries etc.
11. Ch. Priyoranjan Singh, assumed that one hectare of land gave 37.9 *maunds* of paddy and after deducting his subsistence requirements for five persons he would be left with 10.65 *maunds* which would give him Rs. 13 and 15.65 *annas*, p. 153.

References

Aitchison, C.U. (1931). *A Collection of Treaties, Engagements and Sanads Relating to India and Neighbouring Countries,* Vol. XII. Calcutta: Central Publication Branch, Government of India, 1931.

Allen, B.C. (2002). *Gazetteer of Naga Hills and Manipur*. New Delhi: Mittal Publications.

Brown, R. (2001). *Statistical Account of Manipur*. New Delhi: Mittal Publications.

Government of Manipur (2005). *Statistical Abstract Manipur*. Imphal: Directorate of Economics and Statistics.

Johnstone, J. (2002). *Manipur and the Naga Hills*. New Delhi: Gyan Publishing House.

Kabui, G. (1988). "A Note on Loiyamba Shinyen (1110 A.D.) (The First Written Constitution of Manipur)", In *Manipur Past and Present,* edited by N. Sanajaoba, 307-311. New Delhi: Mittal Publications.

— (1991). *History of Manipur,* Vol. 1. New Delhi: National Publishing House.

McCulloch, W. (1980). *Valley of Manipur*. New Delhi: Gyan Publications.

Parratt, S.N.A. (2005). *The Court Chronicle of the Kings of Manipur: The Cheitharon Kumpapa*. London: Routledge.

Sanajaoba, N. (1993). *Manipur Treaties and Documents (1110—1971), Vol. 1*. New Delhi: Mittal Publications.

Singh, Ch. Priyoranjan (2005). "Manipur's Economy: Historical Roots and Structural Evolution", *Eastern Quarterly,* III: 149-159.

Singh, K. Manimohan (1989). *Hijam Irabot Singh and Political Movements in Manipur*. New Delhi: B.R. Publishing Corporation.

— (2006). *Nupi Lan*. Imphal: K. Premlata Devi.

Singh, N. Lokendro (1998). *The Unquiet Valley*. New Delhi: Mittal Publications.

Singh, R.K. Jhalajit (1992). *A Short History of Manipur*. Imphal: R.K. Jhalajit Singh.

4
Trade Relations of Manipur with Her Neighbours in the Pre-British Period

An Overview

Kamei Budha Kabui

Introduction

Manipur is one of the states located at the extreme north-eastern corner of India. With an area of 22,327 sq. kms, Manipur of today is bounded in the north by Nagaland, in the east and south by Myanmar (Burma), in the south-west by Mizoram and in the west by Assam. A very charming hilly state, which had once separated from Assam and Myanmar before the creation of present Nagaland, Arunachal Pradesh, Meghalaya and Mizoram out of Assam; Manipur had enjoyed the fortune and glory in the past and experienced sorrow and vicissitudes of her long history. It had been witnessed the transformation from a primitive tribal state to an independent kingdom and later on from native state of British India to a state of the Indian Union. The chapter is a humble attempt to look into the trade relations of Manipur with her neighbours like Burma, Indian states etc. during the pre-colonial time on the basis of available primary and secondary sources.

Method and Materials

The approach of the study on which this chapter is based is purely historical; the required data have been extracted from the available primary and secondary sources. The Royal Chronicle, tour diaries of colonial officers, annual administrative reports, gazetteers, and other published works are the important sources of the study.

Traditional Economy of Manipur

The Kingdom of Manipur came into existence under *Pakhangba* in 33AD after the amalgamation of the different principalities into *Ningthouja*'s principality. Barter system was the main feature of traditional economy of Manipur. The barter system was gradually replaced by the bell-metal coin (Kabui 1991: 262). However, the coin did not help much either in the internal or external trade of Manipur. Barter system carried on as an important means of business transaction till the introduction of British currency in Manipur. There was no regular market and the common practice was to get the goods exchanged at the houses of producers and consumers and sometimes, at a place depending on the mutual conveniences of these people. Both men and women actively took part in the trade activities. It is an interesting feature of pre-colonial economy of Manipur.

With the aim to solve the problem of barter system, the succeeding kings of *Pakhangba* introduced bell metal coin (*Sel*) as a medium of exchange of the state. Maharaja *Ura Konthouba* (568-658) issued bell metal coins. But this can be regarded as the starting of monetization of the barter system in Manipur (Mutua, 1985: 2). *Khagemba* also issued coins and introduced the practice of payment tax in cash. It was during the reign of *Garibniwaz* (1709-1748), fees for land recording was started to be paid in the term of *Sel* (Kabui, 1991:262). It is also mentioned that *Chourajit Singh* (1803-1813), *Marjit Singh* (1813-1819) and *Gambir Singh* (1826-1834) issued gold and silver coins, but also in a very limited quantity (Gunindro, 1985:75-84). But, the introduction of coins could not completely replace the barter system. The activities of trade in Manipur had to be carried on with the barter system in one thing or the other alongside the circulation of coins.

Minting of Coins

The king imported the bell metal from Burma. The minting process is very simple. The metal is first cast in little pellets and these are then softened by fire and place on the anvil; one blow of the hammer flattens the pellet into an irregularly round figure; a punch, with the word *Sri* cut on it, is then driven on it by another blow which finishes the process. The coin so produced is small in size weighing only about 16 grains (Brown, 2011:89).

The king was the final authority for minting the coin. Lack of any financial institution, there was no strict rule in matter of issuing coins. The face value of the coin appeared to be equal to its intrinsic value. Therefore, bell metal coin could not be converted into the *Sel* by taking its weight. It was only circulated within the administrative territory of the Maharaja. Because of this, the external trade was to be conducted through barter system.

Internal Trade

The internal trade was carried on within the state. There was trading interaction between the hill tribes and the Meiteis. In the valley, trading activity was conducted exclusively by the women. Besides their household duties, women went up to the villages where there were salt wells to collect salt in exchange for fish, rice etc. according to the demand of the salt manufacturers. Similarly, some traders again took rice, salt and other goods to the villages nearby the lakes and bartered them for fish, water nut etc. (Mrs. Grimwood 1975: 55). The hill tribes also traded among themselves, and at times came down to the valley for exchange of goods from the Meitei traders. They traded in the item of goods such as plantain leaves, cotton, cane, bamboo products, spear, clothes etc. (Political Agents' tour dairy: No. 45 of 10th November, 1908 and No. 43 of 23rd October 1901). The Kuki tribes used musket fire arms. They obtained the crude gun powder from the Meitei traders. The Meitei in turn got it from the Chinese merchants who visited the state during the reign of *Khagemba* in 1630. It is revealed that internal trade was the pricing of the goods so exchanged. The value of goods was determined generally through bargaining between buyers and sellers against their respective goods (Political Agent's Tour dairy, No. 10, February, 1896). But, so far as the internal market was concerned, the inhabitants of both the valley and the hills could freely exchange various goods according to their mutual agreement based on the needs and products without any restriction. This social contact strengthened the relationship between the hills and valley people.

Market System

Keithel means market in local dialect. The word *Keithel* is derived from *Kei* means storing place where food grains are stored and *Thel* means displaying the purchasable items. Since the beginning of seventeenth century, some markets came to be established; Maharaja *Khagemba* opened formally eleven markets in different parts of Manipur with *Sana Keithel* at the heart of the Imphal valley as the biggest market in 1614 (Khelchandra, 1987:5). According to T.C. Hodson, the *Khwairamband* market was started by the end of the year 1580. It is also mentioned that King *Mongyamba* was the founder of the same market (1995:23). Later on, the number of market places increased with the royal patronage. During the period of Seven years devastation (1819-1826), the whole activity of the market place was totally stopped.

The market activities in Manipur were the business transaction of the women. There were different types of market; some outside the Imphal areas started its activities in the early morning and came to an end before afternoon and in some markets the activities started in the afternoon. They were known as morning and evening markets. There were some markets which opened only in a week. It was known as *Hapta Keithei*. It would be difficult to find more industrious women in India than the Manipuri women (Dun, 1981:23).

R. Brown describes the market operation system in the valley. There was no proper marketing shed. It was conducted in the open air by women, but the principal meeting place for women trading there was on a vacant plot of ground near the brick bridge in the Imphal capital. In the early part of the day, the women congregate with their wares, for sale. In the afternoon this market place is deserted and all women migrate to the side of the road leading to the gate, and very short distance from the bridge. The authority of the state did not make any attempt to construct the market shed. Women exposed to rain or sun as the case might be. Principal items of goods marketed were such as dry fish, rice, vegetables, clothes, ornaments and sweetmeats. About 3000 women used to assemble in the afternoon bazaar, men with the exception foreigners were not allowed to enter the market place; all the buying and selling was conducted by women (1975:89).

Trade Routes

Since ancient time, Manipur is linked by trade routes with South Asia, South East Asia and Central Asia; through these routes she had commercial and cultural contact with the neighbouring countries. There were hill routes travelled by immigrants, traders, invaders etc. Manipur had a poor road and communication system during the pre-colonial period. People of Manipur were lucky to have in the valley some rivers such as the Imphal, the *Nambul*, the *Iril*, the *Thoubal* etc. all of which pass through the valley. They served as the water ways for connecting Imphal and the villages in the eastern, south-eastern part of the valley. Though unsuitable for navigational purposes, they were used for transporting agricultural products about 15 to 20 mounds by boat. In the hills, the *Barak* river was used for transporting some agricultural products to *Syhlet* (Bhattacharjee, 1977: 87).

The land route was a link connecting between different villages within the state of Manipur. It was during the reign of *Khagemba*, routes were constructed and maintained. He constructed *Makak* road and provided riverine network of transportation by boats. During the reign of King *Paikhomba* (1668-98), a road from *Chinga* to *Mongsagei* was improved in 1672 and succeeding rulers must have built several other routes by utilizing *Lallup* service (Kabui 1991: 220). E.W. Dun (1981:9) wrote, the traditional routes in the valley that roads here were also like that of the roads found in rice growing countries like Assam and Burma etc. The roads were wide enough for one cart, but not sufficiently broad enough for two carts passing one another, when rain comes, the roads become slippery and traffic becomes difficult, no trees were planted on either side of the road, and bridges over rivers were built with wood and bamboo. In the hills, roads were paths connecting villages. But, it may be pointed out that all the routes leading to Indian states and Burma are all passing through the hilly tracts inhabited by the hill tribes.

External land route was a connecting line between Manipur and other neigbhouring countries. Some of the immediate neighbours which are connected by the ancient land routes are Cachar, Assam, Sylhet, Burma, China etc. The main routes are Western routes (Acquee Route, Kala Naga Route, Khongjai Route), Southern routes (Heirok Route and Imole Route) and Northern routes (Pemberton, 1979: 51). The above routes were used by the people of Manipur and other kingdoms since ancient time. Pilgrims, immigrants, and traders travelled these routes. Laden animals and ponies were the main means of transportation.

External Trade

The Manipuris have a history of two millennia old political organization, a stable cultural network supported by a well developed literary language and several hundreds of scriptures, gold, and silver currency which provides a living testimony to its economic organizations inside and trade and commerce with the South-East Asian countries outside (Sanajaoba, 1988:23). Manipur had trade links with other states since ancient time. It happens to be the trade routes between South Asia, South East Asia and Central Asia (Kabui, 1988: 11). The Neolithic culture of Eastern India has revealed that Manipur had close relations with Burma, China and other Indian states. The discovery of blue porcelain bowls, bell metal coins and guns etc. in the excavation of the *Kameng* village and the palace of Maharaja Jai Singh also gave evidence of having relations between Manipur and other Indian provinces on various periods (Annual Administrative Report of Manipur 1940-41). As native coin was circulated within the state only, external trade was done through barter system.

Trade with China

Trade between China and Manipur was conducted by the merchants of *Yunnan* province of China. They reached Manipur through Burma and brought the goods, *viz.* raw silk, paper tea, and various kinds of fruits. They took away wax, ivories, clothes, cotton and ponies (Gazetteer of Burma 1983: 453). The royal chronicle records that in 1630, the Chinese merchants of *Yunnan* province visited the kingdom and from them learnt the art of manufacturing gun powder. The trade continued as late as 1813 (Kabui, 1991: 13-14). However, the trade between the two states could not be developed due to certain factors: trade with China depends on the attitude of Burma, because Manipur traders had to pass through Burma and secondly China had shifted her interest of trade towards the Western countries since the beginning of nineteenth century (Ali, 1988:174). The development of trade with Dutch, Portuguese and English by sea was reduced the volume of China export to Manipur through the hilly routes (Ahmed, 1981: 178-181). It is fact that China's trade with Manipur had brought about certain economic innovations like the introduction of silk and silk worm and gun powder. This is the influence of Chinese commercial contact with Manipur.

Trade with Burma

Burma is one of the countries, which Manipur had commercial contact since ancient time. Though there had been a number of military aggressions on each other from either side, off and on trade link continued to be maintained between the two countries. Trade was done mainly through three land routes (Pemberton, 1979:51). During the reign of *Maharaja Labanyachandra* (1798-1801), there was brick trade and commerce between the two states. It was during the reign of *Marjit Singh* (who ruled for 6 years peacefully) that commercial ties were brought closer and developed further. This friendly relationship with Burma felicitated external trade. During this period, silk was exported to Burma (Dun 1981: 61). This relationship could not last due to misunderstanding developed between the two kings. *Marjit Singh* permitted his people to cut teak timber in *Kabaw* valley which naturally offended the friend. *Bagyidaw* invited *Marjit Singh* to attend at the ceremony of his accession to the throne of Burma, but *Marjit Singh* did not attend on some excuse. King *Bagyidaw* ordered an expedition to Manipur with one hundred thousand armies under the command of *Maha Bandula* (Kamei, 2015: 5-6) and the trade was suspended between the two states.

Manipur imported the bell metal from Burma. Other goods imported from Burma, but again exported to other Indian states included bullocks, ponies, tea seeds etc. (Annual Administrative Report of Manipur, 1875). The *Thadou* Kukis used to take salt, iron, ornaments, cotton etc. from Burma in exchange with cane and bamboo products at *Yazagyo*, an important market in the Chin Hills of Burma (Roy, 1973: 59-60). The important item of export of Manipur was raw silk. Moreover, finished clothes, the leaves which cover the cob of maize which was used in making cigarette were also exported to Burma.

Trade with Assam, Bengal, Naga Hills and Tripura

Manipur was self-reliant in her traditional economy, but she had commercial contact with the other Indian states. The neigbhouring Indian states with which Manipur exchanged goods are Assam, Cachar, the Naga Hills, the Lushai Hills, Tripura and Bengal. However, the traders of Manipur had closer contact with Cachar because the Manipuris used to exchange goods for the products of other states mostly through Cachar. The important goods exported by Manipur were like cotton, chillies, tea seed, elephant, buffalo, silk, clothes, wax etc. While, the main import goods were betel nuts, coconuts, iron, brass goods, bell metal etc. (Annual Administrative Report of Manipur 1873 to 1877-78; Hunter 1975: 175 and 428). The villagers inhabiting in the western border of Manipur took the advantage of exchanging their products for salt with Cacharis. The trade with Lushai Hills was mostly carried on by the Kuki tribes of Manipur. They took iron from the valley and bartered it for guns and clothes with the people of Lushai Hills (Hunter, 1975: 428). The villagers of the state near the Naga Hills used to exchange salt for brass vessel with the Nagas. In the cold season, Maharaja Gambhir Singh (1832-33) conquered different Naga villages of the Naga Hills including Kohima; this gave opportunity to the Manipuri traders to visit Naga Hills safely (Roy, 1973: 73). There was trade with Tripura and Manipur. During the reign of *Khagemba*, there was trade with the people of Tripura whose influence was extended over Cachar and northern Mizoram (Kabui, 1991:215).

Since the external trade was conducted through the hilly routes, the volume of trade was found to be limited. Another problem was that when Manipur was at war with some other countries, the external trade of Manipur disturbed during the period. But, since the product of Manipur itself served almost all the necessities of Manipur, the people suffered scanty even when Manipur stopped its external trade.

Conclusion

After observing the above facts, we can conclude that Manipur had extensive trade and commercial activities before the British occupation of Manipur. Barter system was the main characteristic of their economy and trade, but the price or value of the goods is determined by bargaining between buyers and sellers against their respective products. With the establishment of market places, buying and selling of goods with native coin (*Sel*) became popular, but circulation of coin was limited. Internal trade was conducted exclusively by the women. The hill people also exchanged their products with the valley dwellers. Besides, the internal trade, Manipur had trade relations with Burma, China and other Indian states. Before 1891, the people of Manipur did not depend much on external trade for their basic needs, because almost all the necessities were produced within the state. Thus, Manipur had self-sufficient economy in the pre-colonial period.

References

Annual Administrative Report of Manipur 1873 to 1877-78.

Annual Administrative Report of Manipur 1875.

Annual Administrative Report of Manipur 1940-41.

Ashraf Ali (1988). *Economic History of Manipur*. Unpublished Ph.D. Thesis, M.U.

Ibungohal and Khelchandra, *Cheitharol Kumbaba*, Imphal, 1987.

Dhires Bhattacharya (1963). *Understanding India's Economy* (Part one). Calcutta: Progressive Publishers.

E.W. Dun (1981). *Gazetteer of Manipur*. Delhi: Vivek Publishing House.

Ethel St. Clair Grimwood (1975). *My Three Years in Manipur*. Delhi: Vivek Publishing House.

Gangmumei Kabui (1991). *History of Manipur: Pre-Colonial Period*. Vol. 1, New Delhi: National Publishing House (1988).

Gangmumei Kamei (2015). *A History of Modern Manipur* 1826-2000 (A Study of Feudalism, Colonialism and Democracy). Vol. 1, New Delhi: Akansha Publishing House.

Gazetteer of Burma, Vol. 1, (1983). Delhi: Cultural Publishing House.

Glimpses into Land and People of Ancient Manipur in Manipur: Past and Present, Vol. 1, Naorem Sanajaoba (Ed.), New Delhi: Mittal Publications.

J.B. Bhattacharjee (1977). *Cachar under the British Rule in North East India*. Delhi: Radiant Publishers.

J. Roy. (1973). *History of Manipur*. Calcutta: East Light Book House.

L.L. Ahmed (1981). *A Comparative History of the Far East*. New Delhi: S. Chand and Company Ltd.

N. Basanta Singh (1998). *Socio-Economic Change in Manipur* 1891-1947. Imphal.

N. Khelchandra Singh (1987). *Phamlon*. Imphal: Manipuri Sahitya Parishad.

P. Gunindro Singh (1985). *Manipur Numismatics*. Imphal: Mutua Musuem.

Political Agents' Tour dairy, No. 10, February, 1896.

Political Agents' tour dairy: No. 45 of 10th November, 1908 and No. 43 of 23rd Oct. 1901 R.B. Pemberton. 1979, *Eastern Frontier of India*. New Delhi: Mittal Publications.

R. Brown (1975). *Statistical Account of Manipur*. Delhi: Sankran Prakashak.

T.C. Hodson (1995). *The Naga Tribes of Manipur*. Delhi: R.B. Publishing House.

—, (1908). *The Meithes*, New Delhi: R. B. Publishing House.

W.W. Hunter (1975). *A Statistical Account of Assam*. Vol. 2, Delhi: B.R. Publishing Corporation.

5
Coinage in Manipur

Technique, Structure, Metallurgy and Process of Minting

Th. Nishikanta Singh

Of all antiquities that seem to be imperishable, coins are the most important, since they bring to our own age the culture and customs of the forgotten generations when they were in current usage. The antiquity of coinage in Manipur is still obscure. There have been a few works on the antiquity of coinage history of Manipur. No serious attempt has so far been made to study the various interesting aspects of these coins. Different scholars have different opinions about the date of introduction of coinage in Manipur. Wahengbam Yumjao Singh, a distinguished archaeologist states that the earliest coins of Manipur had depicted the legend in Nagari script.[1] On the testimony of W. Yumjao Singh's discovery, it has been assumed that Pakhangba (33-154 A.D.), the first king of Manipur introduced a coinage of the bell-metal pieces known as *Sel*.[2] In support of the contention, Mutua Jhulon Singh advocates that Nongda Lairen Pakhangba, the king of Manipur who ruled from 33 A.D. to 154 A.D., had issued coins.[3] T.C. Hodson seems to be in perfect agreement with Yumjao Singh, because he was shown a big bell-metal coin by some Manipuris. He believed it to have been stuck by Pakhangba. The coins according to him, is shield shaped disk of bell-metal, very thin, but of large size, measuring rather more than three-half inches in diameter, it has no mark on it of any kind.[4] Suniti Kumar Chatterji has given his assent to this view.[5]

The above view of Yumjao may be examined on two grounds. Firstly, no evidence in the text is available to prove that shield-shaped disk like things had been used on or before the reign of Pakhangba as the royal insignia of Manipur. Secondly, the identification of any coin depicting no particular legends as the coins of Pakhangba is not free from ambiguity. Yumjao Singh takes 164 *Samvat* (*Saka Samvat*) as the date of issue of Manipuri coins. Here, two varieties of coins may be studied comparatively from different angles. One variety of coin explored by Yumjao Singh have the legend as "Cheitra Sudhi Tarasha Vada 2 Samvada" as four lines in Nagari script.[6] And the second variety of coin is identified as one of the coins issued by King Garibaniwaj (1709-48 A.D.) in 1646 Samvada. This coin has the legend as "Cheitra Sudhi Tarashavada 2 Samvada 1646" in four lines in Nagari script. Except the last numeral figure '6' both of them have similarity in shape, size and number of lines of the legend. From the study in the palaeographical point of view also the Nagari script depicted on the coins explored by Yumjao Singh have a close conformity with that of Garibaniwaj's coin. On the other hand, the Nagari script depicted on the coins would not be the script of the second century A.D. During the second century A.D. Archaic Manipuri script was used in Manipur. Actually Devanagari script began to be inscribed on the coins of Manipur (after the introduction of Hinduism in Manipur) not earlier than the seventeenth century A.D.[7] The tradition of minting coins had not become popular during the second century A.D. And after a thorough examination of all the available coins in Manipur, we have drawn the conclusion that the antiquity of the said coin is quite dubious. It could not be precluded that before the discovery of coin by Yumjao Singh the last digit no. (6) might have been effaced from unknown reasons. This explains that in the absence of '6' (the last digit no. 6), he deciphered it as the coins belonging to 164 *Samvat*.[8] This coin must be ascribed to Garibaniwaj, because in the *Saka* era 1646 (+78 A.D.), he was the king of Manipur. Moreover, large number of coins of his period including the coin dated 1646 have been discovered. Thus, we may assure that 164 *Samvada* (*Saka Samvat*) was wrongly taken by W. Yumjao Singh due to his mistaken assessment of 1646 *Saka Samvat* as 164 *Saka Samvat*.

The evidence furnished by T.C. Hodson[9] in his book, is not convincing, because he examined the evidence without being equipped with the competence of Numismatists. His own statement, that the coin, which was known to him, bears no marking on it, will suffice to prove that he might have wrongly identified this coin in the second century A.D. In absence of any marking or any inscription on the coin, it is neither possible to identify the name of the king to whom it belongs nor to determine its antiquity to which it is ascribed. Hence, it is very surprising as to how he ascribed this coin to Pakhangba. Moreover, the statement of both Yumjao Singh and T.C. Hodson are contradictory. The former had referred inscription on this coin, whereas the latter denies it, although both claim that the coin belongs to Pakhangba. Finally, we may say here that both the views are not based on scientific discovery of the subject under discussion. Moreover, the views put forward by R.B. Pemberton, T.C. Hodson and S.K. Chatterji can be disproved.

We can quote the views of P.K. Bhattacharyya, who has made a scientific analysis of the subject in an objective manner in a very valuable and faithful numismatic document.[10] His views have not been highlighted so far by any native scholar working on the subject. W. Yumjao Singh believes that this view will strengthen the argument already advanced against the high antiquity of that coin and conclusion drawn in support of Saka 1646. He further states that *'Tarasha'* seems to have been derived from *Tarasha* meaning 'Thirst', 'Sun' etc. and the word *'Vara'* has locally changed into *'Vada'* on the coin.[11] Some scholars preferred to read the line as *Tarasha* 2. But in that case it would be difficult to explain the meaning of 2 in the legend. Moreover, on some other coins we have *vada* instead of 2. However, the said coin (*Samvat* 164) did not belong to Pakhangba. Rather it belongs to Garibaniwaj (1646 *Saka*). Hence the reading of Je-Rama (i.e. Jai [Jaya]-Rama) 2 or Je-Rama-vada (i.e. Jai [Jaya]- Rama-vada) would be most appropriate. D.C. Sircar is inclined to accept the later reading. According to Hodson, the coin bears legend but does not mention the name of the king. But Yumjao Singh has tried to show that it was actually struck by Pakhangba and thus he has preferred to read the date given in the third line as Sam, 164 which in his opinion, is equivalent to (164-58) 106 A.D.[12] In other words, the coin was issued in the second century A.D. during the reign of Pakhngba. But it is doubt that there is another digit after 164 and that it is 6, which has, however, been unfortunately overlooked by Yumjao Singh.

So, the third line of the legend may be restored as Sam 1646. Now the *Samvat* starting from the 'Cheitrasudi' should be taken as *Saka Samvat*.[13]

It may also be noted that the traditional literary sources of Manipur, the inscriptions and coins discovered here so far, indicate the popularity of *Saka-Samvatsara* in this region. Besides *Saka* era, Chandrabda[14] seems to have been in vogue in Manipur, but we don't have any evidence of the prevalence of the Vikrama era. Thus sam1646 should be equivalent to 1646+78-9 = 1724-5 A.D., and it coincides with the date of the first expedition of Pamheiba *alias* Gopala Singh or Garibaniwaj (1709-1748 A.D.) against the Burmese, ten years after his successful expedition against the ruler of Tripura.[15] Garibaniwaj may be said to be the founder of the fame of the royal house of Manipur. The intensive orientation towards Hindu culture through Bengal Vaishnavism began through him. Je-Rama (Jai-Jaya-Rama) on the coin legend reminds us of his initiation into the Ramandi order. He became a zealot champion of Ramandi cult.[16] Thus, Bhattacharyya also rejected the view of Pemberton, Hodson, McCulloch, Suniti Kumar Chatterji and Yumjao.[17]

The coins bearing the letters 'Wu', 'A' and 'La' in Archaic Manipuri script stand for the initial letters of the name of the kings Wura Konthouba (568-658 A.D.), Ayangba (821-910 A.D.) and Lairenba (1394-99 A.D.) respectively. Further, it is stated that in Manipur the coinage started not later than sixth century A.D. There are findings to establish that the coinage started from the time of King Wura Konthouba (568-658 A.D.) because such coin bearing the initial letter *'wa'* attributed to Manipuri king Wura Konthouba raises the possibility of Manipuri alphabets being introduced as early as sixth century A.D. In the coins of Manipur, the practice of depicting the initial letter of the king was most commonly adopted. Moreover, all the available coins (except a few) bear the initial letter of the king. When these coins are un-dated, it is possible to confirm through the study of the initial letter of the coin that identification of the particular name of the king is made. The same type of investigation and close study applies to the coins with a letter — 'A' attributed to king Ayangba and 'La' for Lairenba (1394-99 A.D.).[18]

It is not known exactly the date of introduction of the art of writing in Manipur. It is yet to be studied whether the Manipuris knew the art of writing before or after the Christian era. In the opinion of Damant "the old Manipuri alphabet was introduced from Bengal in the reign of Charairongba who flourished about 1700. There are no traces of the existence of writing in Manipur before that time."[19] On the basis of certain local tradition, T.C. Hodson framed a hypothesis that the Manipuris acquired the art of writing from the Chinese who came to Manipur about 1540 A.D.

The views of Damant and T.C. Hodson may be analysed with reference of numismatic evidences available today. The coins of Wura Konthouba (568-658 A.D.), Ayangba (821-910 A.D.), Lairenba (1394-99 A.D.) etc., containing Archaic Manipuri script give valuable information about the introduction of Manipuri alphabet before the sixth century A.D. The addition of some scripts from Bengali and Nagari has been made in the list of the Archaic Manipuri script.[20]

Some larger bell-metal coins have been attributed to Manipur but the attribution is still somewhat tentative. Several other gold coins, two with an image of Krishna playing the flute have also been discovered in Calcutta in recent years, but as their authenticity is not credible, they have not been included in the list.[21] These symbols, figures, letters etc. were deliberately stamped on the coins by issuing authorities probably, to guarantee their genuineness and value. These authorities might be king or state. Apart from conveying some vague religious ideas and artistic conventions these coins don't supply any historical information.[22]

A comparative study of coins between the numismatic history of Tamildesa and Manipur is discussed here. The numismatic history of Tamildesa, from the third century A.D. to about the tenth century A.D. is shrouded in uncertainty. No coins are known of this period and the picture that emerges is not very encouraging. The coins that are known pose a big problem with regard to their attribution. It is generally believed that the chief devices that are found on these coins are the same as the heraldic marks (*lanchhanas*) of the various dynasties of this area but this does not appear to be true in all cases. At times, the devices seen on the coins of one dynasty are found incorporated on those of the others. Inscriptions on these coins are rare; where they appear, they are short. They give only a part of the ruler's name (full name on these coins is an exception).[23] For instance, some tiny silver coins of Rajendra Chola

I (weighing between 1.4 and 30 grains) bear the initial letter *'Ra'* on the coins of smaller one. These coins might have been issued at the time of Chola conquest.[24] On a few of the copper coins of the Pandyas, the names Sundara, Sundara Pandya or merely the letter *'Su'* are found.

Some coins which show the titles of the rulers, but only a few of them, may be attributed to any particular ruler with the help of epigraphs.[25] Likewise, the practice of depicting the initial letter of name of the king was most commonly adopted in Manipur. It is through the study of the initial letter of the coin that identification of the particular name of the king is made. McCulloch considers Khagemba (1597-1652 A.D.), the first king, who struck bell metal coins. The figures of the coins which is round and square, bears the letter *'Ma'* in Archaic Manipur script, and is ascribed to Mayang Ngamba *alias* Kahgemba.[26] Another reference may be made to the coins of King Khagemba and Paikhomba (1666-97 A.D.) depicting the initial letters *'Ma'* and *'Pa'* in Archaic Manipuri script.[27] An account about the introduction of first Manipuri coins by king Khagemba has been refuted by numismatic evidences. Quite earlier to Khagemba, Wura Konthouba (568-658 A.D.), Ayangba (821-910 A.D.) and Lairenba (1394-99 A.D.) had issued coins.[28] Since the time of Wura Konthouba, the practice of depicting the initial letter of the name of the king began and continued till the period of King Kulachandra (1890-91 A.D.).

The epigraphic features on the coins help in the identification of the periods of the coins. The coins issued during the pre-Hinduism period differ from that of post-Hinduism. Before the spread of Hinduism in Manipur the initial letter of the name of the kings depicted in the coins were in Archaic Manipur script.

Paikhomba (1666-97 A.D.) was the last king who issued the coins depicting the legend in Archaic Manipuri script. King Garibaniwaj (1709-48 A.D.) for the first time introduced to depict Nagari and Bengali script on the coins. The initial letter of the name of the issuing king raised a question about the similarity of the initial alphabet of the seventy two kings given in the royal chronicle, Moiramba (1278-1300 A.D.) and Mungyamba (1562-97 A.D.) who ruled before King Garibaniwaj. Madhuchandra (1801-03 A.D.) and Marjit (1813-19 A.D.) after Garibaniwaj were the only exceptions having similar initial alphabets in their names. However, they depicted the initial letter of the names differently.

It can identify the issuer easily, e.g. the coins of Madhuchandra are depicted as 'M' and the coins of Marjit as '*Ma*'.

The antiquity of coinage in Manipur on the basis of the above references and the material evidences available to us can establish that it was the sixth century A.D. which witnessed a new era in the history of numismatics in Manipur.

Notes

1. W. Yumjao Singh, "Report on the Archaeological Studies in Manipur", *Bulletin*, No. 1. Imphal, 1935, p. 45.
2. In Manipur, *Sel* is known as money as well as coin (bell-metal). The word *Sel* is found as the suffix in the names used in the royal chronicle as early as 1142 A.D. See, R.B. Pemberton, *A Report on the North Eastern Frontier of British India*, Calcutta: Mittal Publications, 1935, p. 20.
3. Mutua Jhulon Singh, *Vijay Panchali*, Imphal, 1986, p. 30.
4. T.C. Hodson, *The Meithies*, Delhi, 1975, p. 37.
5. S.K. Chatterjee, *Kirata-Jana-Kriti*, Calcutta, 1950, p. 151.
6. W. Yumjao Singh, *Report on the Archaeological Studies in Manipur*, Imphal, 1935, pp. 46-47.
7. P. Gunindra Singh, *Manipuri Numismatic*, Imphal, 1983, p. 3.8.
8. L. Kunjeswori Devi, *A study of Archaeology in Manipur since pre-history time* (unpublished), Imphal, 1988, p. 69.
9. T.C. Hodson, *The Meitheis*, Delhi: Neeraj Publishing House, p. 37.
10. *J.N.S.I.*, vol. XXXIX, 1977, pp. 182-85.
11. W. Yumjao Singh, *op. cit.*, pp. 47-48
12. W. Yumjao Singh, *op. cit.*, p. 22.
13. D.C. Sircar, *Indian Epigraphy*, pp. 256-60.
14. In 1760 A.D., King Bhagyachandra entrusted Maniram Pandit Sidhanta to prepare a calendar. The calendar was prepared by the pandit and his associates based on an era known as Kangleipak Sak or Manipur era which was renamed as Chandrabda. The era was started counting year from 789 A.D. It was again used during the time of Gambhir Singh, see Chandrabada on the coin of Gambhira Simha, *J.N.S.I.*, XXVII, pp. 110-11.
15. W. Yumjao Singh, *op. cit.*, p. 73.
16. "An interesting coin of Manipur", *J.N.S.I.*, vol. XXVII, p. 85.
17. W. Yumjao Singh, *op. cit.*, p. 74.
18. G.A. Grierson (ed.), *Linguistic Survey of India*, vol. III, pt. III, Calcutta, 1905, p. 21.
19. *Ibid.*

20. Kangjeeya Gopal, *Kanglei Eyek*, Imphal, 1972, pp. 1-2.
21. R. Collin Nicholas Johns, F. William, Deyell Bruce, *Rhodes Spengler, The Standard guide to South Asian Coins and Paper Money since 1566 A.D.*, Krause, 1983, p. 85.
22. R.C. Majumdar, *History and Culture of Indian People: The Vedic Age*, Vol. I, Bombay, 1951, p. 57.
23. P.L. Gupta, *Coins*, New Delhi, 2000, p. 92.
24. *Ibid.*, p. 99.
25. *Ibid.*, p. 100.
26. M. McCulloch, *An Account of the Valley in Manipur*, Delhi, 1980, p. 39.
27. N. Khelchandra Singh, *"Manipuri Language: Status and Importance"*, Imphal, 1975, p. 6.
28. P. Gunindra Singh, *op. cit.*, p. 4.

6
Pre-Colonial Economy of Manipur
An Overview

K. Ruhinikumar Sharma

To write about the pre-colonial economic history of an ancient kingdom situated in an area sandwiched between India and kingdoms and countries of a region called Southeast Asia is not an easy task since literate culture or written literature developed at a much later stage more or less only during the seventeenth century AD. Yet despite the limitations an attempt is made to reconstruct the economy of pre-colonial Manipur and its contribution in social formation. Here the term 'pre-colonial' refers to the period prior to the British conquest of Manipur in 1891. Historians and economists considered economy as the primary determinant of any social formation.[1] But, since every historical situation has its roots in the past, for a proper understanding of the economic practice as it evolved during the eighteenth and nineteenth centuries, the period in which the kingdom of Manipur reached its zenith of power and glory and eventual decline as well, first, we have to trace its roots in the early history of Manipur. We shall also make an attempt to trace the changes and continuities if any, in its growth and the level of development it reached during the eighteenth and nineteenth century, the period with which we are more concerned here.

Economy of Ancient and Medieval Manipur: a bird's eyeview

Extensive information on important aspects of the economy of ancient and early medieval Manipur is not available. However, from the few available archaeological and literary sources we are able to reconstruct a rough feature. The archaeological finds from the prehistoric cave sites situated at Khangkhui, Tharon and Napachik indicates the use of neoliths and bone tools in the region. These findings established beyond doubt the existence of a hunting and food gathering economy in early Manipur. The excavation at Napachik site points to the prevalence of agriculture which again implies the possibility of the establishment of a settled life and economy in Manipur valley. The introduction of agriculture and its accompanying technology have drawn the attention of both the archaeologists and historians in order to understand the economy of a community. The Manipuri chronicles and literary texts in Meitei language record the accounts of the discovery of paddy in wild, invention of agriculture, practice of shifting cultivation, development of bronze and iron technology for making of implements and tools like *dao*, axes and hoes for agricultural and allied purposes. Tradition and myths as recorded in a number of literary texts of the land have clearly shown that the ancient Meiteis practiced shifting cultivation in early period of her historical evolution from tribe and chiefdom to a full-fledged feudal monarchy. Before developing the knowledge of wet rice agriculture, they carried out the shifting cultivation on the hill slopes or dry land forest areas. The northern and eastern parts of Imphal valley which were a thickly forested dry land provide the environment for the development of this type of agriculture. The agricultural implements adopted were axes and *daos* for felling down trees and clearance of jungles and small iron hoe for digging up the soil. There is evidence of Neolithic Celts which suggests the possibility of being used in the primitive agricultural system long before the introduction of iron hoes. References are made in some early literary texts of the discovery of a variety of rice called Morshi Thangyi in the proto-historic period. However, the first literary reference to paddy cultivation in the plains of Manipur valley is made in some texts.[2] But there is no reference of employing plough animal or plough in the literary accounts dealing with pre-Pakhangba period, acknowledged the first historical ruler of the emerging chiefdom in the first century A.D. It is probable that agriculture was further improved during the time of Poireiton, a contemporary of Nongda Lairen Pakhangba as reference are made of the use of iron and introduction of domesticated animals like the cattle.[3] The chronicles refer to initiation of irrigation works by dredging the rivers and making drainages to drain out the water from the low lying marshy areas of central Imphal Valley.[4] *Naothingkhong Phambal Kaba,* a text dealing with the coronation of *Naothingkhong* as ruler of his domain (663-763 A.D.) refers to the system of shifting cultivation being practiced by the Shelloi Langmei tribe of Nongmaiching hill and adoption of wet rice cultivation by the valley dweller Meteis, *Loiyumba Shilyen,* (edict of king Loiyumba, 1074-1122 A.D.) and *Mashil* (an archaic text in Meitei language) refer to the rates of revenue imposed on agricultural fields by the state on the peasants. This implies definitely the distinct prevalence of wet rice cultivation in the valley of Manipur from the middle of the first millennia.

There is no definite mention of the use of iron plough pulled by bullock in earlier accounts. There are several myths which refer that tigers were yorked by serpents and back of stork used as plough by gods. Because of the development in knowledge of metallurgy especially iron and existence of regular trade between Manipur and neighbouring countries of Ava and India (especially Tripuris, Cacharis and Ahom states), there is a possibility that leads us to suggest that plough must have been used during Naothingkhong's time, *i.e.* the eighth century A.D. But here, it must be clearly stated that agriculture in Manipur was greatly improved during King Khagemba's (1597-1652 A.D.) reign and the Muslim peasant immigrants who were also mercenaries from Bengal introduced improved agricultural technology including transplantation of paddy seedling thereby putting an end to age old practice of broadcasting.[5] *Nongshamei Puya* a semi historical account refers to the contribution made by Muslim peasants to agricultural development in Manipur kingdom but it also mentions the practice of wet rice cultivation and use of plough drawn by bullocks. Contact with neighbouring countries over a period of time made it possible the introduction of improved varieties of paddy in Manipur. Thus, the surplus from the paddy production could be collected by the state and the surplus production was made possible by wet rice cultivation in Manipur. The state acted as facilitating agent for agricultural activities by taking up the works like dredging of rivers and draining away water deposits from swampy areas and marshes. It shows the control exercised by the state over its resources which clearly strengthened the view that land belonged to the state and over distribution and re-distribution of land and other allied resources. The royal chronicle of Manipur refers to innumerable instances of state undertaking the works of creating bunds and dykes to check inundation.

The Meitei kings, originally a tribal chief thus successfully played its role in the organisation and continuation of wet rice cultivation, stabilised and strengthened the institution of kingship. The king, by virtue of his position and as representative of the agricultural community exercised the control over distribution of land as vested to him, who was theoretically the owner of all land, cultivated and waste along with all natural resources. Because of the scarcity of labour owing to smallness of the population and wet rice cultivation being labour intensive, the possession of wet rice lands by peasants were subject to their rendering periodic labour service to the state. In return for labour service, such a peasant, who was known as *Lalloi* or *Loumi* was granted the use of one *Pari* (2.5 acre) of land subject to the payment of regular tax in kind. The residential homestead (*Ingkhol*) lands were free from tax. The rate of tax levied per *pari* of cultivable land is varied from two pots to twelve pots. Normally, a *pari* of land annually produces around 150 pots. Except for certain cases the wet rice land known as *Lou* was considered the property of the state and theoretically it was neither hereditary nor transferable.

We do not get much information about the nature of land tenurial system, land holding, different rates of revenue and rent, extent of cultivation in the valley etc. However, ninetieth century colonial writers and officials connected with or posted in Manipur in the form of official reports, accounts and memoirs left behind have provided useful information on the subject. According to these reports and accounts, the land areas of the valley are generally divided into two categories, viz. *Ingkhol* (homestead land) and *Lou* (cultivable/agricultural land). These *Ingkhols* are distributed in a number of villages. The agricultural lands available in the valley and types of tenurial system are classified as—(i) *Taonaro*, (Tounarou), (ii) *Sarkari* (Raja's own or Ningthoulou), (iii) *Phumlo* (Phamlou), (iv) *Sepoys* (Siphailou), (v) *Manaro* (Manalou), (vi) *Brahmins* (Lugun-lou), (vii) *Royal family*, and (viii) *Maharani* and *Temple* (Lairou) etc.[6] Of these *Lous* only *Tounarou, Raja's own Lou* (agricultural land) *and Phumlou* are taxed which varied from two to sixty basket per *Pari* and the remaining are tax free lands. About one-fifth of the total cultivated area was covered under *Tounarou*. The rate of revenue per *Pari* under *Tounarou* was fixed at six *Chengkoks* of rice (three maunds approximately) which was paid in kind and sometimes in cash and calculated on the rice of price at the time.[7] *Tounarou* holding are of two types—(i) holding through purchase and (ii) holding through clearing of jungles on receiving permission from the state. Those who possessed *Tounarou* through the later mode are exempted from payment of tax for one year. Except in case of default in payment of tax, the king cannot evict the land holders without paying proper compensation. The land holders can either inherit or disposed of the lands falling under *Tounarou* category.

The Raja's own lands (*Sarkari*) are cultivated either by the slaves or free man and the rate of rent were quite high as compared with other tenures. Each slave was given one *Pari* of land along with plough, cattle and implements and he had to pay sixty baskets of paddy as rent. In case of the land being let to free man, they were supposed to pay twenty-four baskets of paddy. However, the free men were not supplied cattle and other implements.[8] Another category of land which was held by officers and nobles in lieu of their salary was *Phamlou* and these lands were cultivated either by the slaves of the official or free men. The rate of rent per *Pari* was twenty-four baskets of paddy and the officers in turn gave revenue of two baskets to the state.[9] Failure in payment of revenue resulted in the confiscation of *Phamlou* and was given to others.

More than one-third of the cultivable area falls under *Siphai-lou* (Sepoy's land) categories which were given to the sepoys and officers of the native army. The sepoys who were in the service of the state were not paid in cash and in lieu were given lands, the size of land holdings varied according to their ranks. A Major who headed a number of companies got one *Pari* each calculated on the basis of number of companies under his supervision. A *Poila* got six *Pari*, a *Subedar* (subaltern) four *Pari*, a Jamandar got three *Pari* while a sepoy got one and a quarter of a *Pari* etc. and was revenue free. In case a sepoy died-in-harness and left behind a male heir, his family was given half a *Pari* and the remaining land reverted to the state. If the son joined army after attaining majority, he was given the same amount of land to which a sepoy was entitled. Sepoy who had surplus land could sublet it with at the usual rent of twenty-four baskets per *Pari*.

There were certain instances in which the king also granted lands to his favourites and to individuals who performed/rendered valuable service to the state. Such type of land grant was called *Manalou* (land given as reward) and was granted only for the life time of the grantee. If his heirs desired to continue possession of these lands they had to pay revenue at the rate of twenty-four baskets of paddy per *Pari*. Otherwise the land used to be reverted to the Raja. The Meitei kings also granted land to the Brahmins. Every Brahmin on taking the sacred thread (*Lugun*) is entitled to receive one *Pari* of land from the Raja. When the Brahmin died his widow was allowed to possess half of it to maintain her and the children, and the rest was reverted to the state. The land so received under this system cannot be disposed of or sold out to any other person. Brahmin lands are usually known as *Lugun-lou*. The practice of giving land to the Brahmins became widespread after the Meitei kings were converted into Hinduism in the eighteenth century. Another interesting feature of the land tenurial system in Manipur was assignment of lands to the Hindu temples and pre-Hindu sylvan deities. The lands assigned under these categories were revenue free and never reverts back to the king. For example, 'Govindaji,' an important deity of the royal family was assigned one hundred *Pari* of land and these were cultivated by the *Keis* (slaves) of the temple who lived in the villages of Charangpat, Thinunggei, and Uyan.[10] Lands belonging to members of the royal family including the *Maharani* and those lands whose ownership descended from father to son were exempted from payment of revenue but the size of each holding was fixed. Those who were in possession of more than the fixed ceiling were liable to pay revenue in the usual rate. Lands were also granted to individuals who rendered distinguished service in war and such land grant was known as *Pangal-lou* (land acquired through merit and strength). These land grants are inheritable and revenue free. The successive Meitei kings used to exact royalties for the sale of timber, bamboo and other forest products from Jiri and thus maintained their rights over them which formed part of the state revenue in the nineteenth century and the same was followed during the colonial era too. Access to common lands such as forests, grazing grounds and fisheries were open to all subjects. To regulate the realisation of revenue in a systematic way, two officers known as *Phourungba* and *Lourungba* were appointed by the king. Maintaining proper record of land holding by the subjects was introduced during the reign of King Garibaniwaz (Mayamba), 1709-1748 A.D.

The introduction of *Lallup* system in a systematic manner by King Loiyumba in the early part of the twelfth century A.D. had drawn the kingdom towards a more stable and organized polity. Literally, *Lallup* (*lal*=war, *lup*=organisation) means war organisation. A rudimentary form of the evolution of this organisation had been seen during the reign of Taothingmang (264-364 A.D.?), while he engaged the labour service of his subjects in dredging the Imphal river. Lallup covered all state works both military and civil. Though originally started as a military service, it was extended to non-military or economic activities of the state. Loiyumba's introduction of six administrative units called *Lup* strengthened the working system of the *Lallup* service. The system was very often criticised by the colonial writers as forced labour, the development of *Lallup* system was the manifestation of the emergence of feudalism and feudalization in the social, administrative and economic structure of the kingdom. Considering the backward nature of the economy of the kingdom, characterised by absence of large-scale trade and commercial activities, absence of a monetised economy and ever reliance on barter system made the system of *Lallup* more meaningful and a necessity for development of the country. The *Lakpa*, who supervised the regulation of *Lallup* service, enjoyed revenue free from the state as his salary. Most of the hill tribes did not attend *Lallup* and in lieu they pay annual tributes to Meitei kings failing which punitive actions were very often inflicted upon them.

From the preceding discussions it is clear that the successive Meitei (Manipur) kings exercised an overall control over the distribution of land and allied resources. The king being addressed as *"leimaba"* (owner of land) was regarded as owner of the land. Establishing control over such an important resource increased the power and authority of the successive rulers. It also enabled the state to keep a check on the growth of large-scale land holdings by individuals. At the peasant level, the peasants who had taken to wet rice cultivation, the compulsory feudal service restrained the peasant's initiative to enlarge holdings of land. The nobility were granted larger agricultural lands in comparison with what the peasants were entitled to be cultivated either by the slaves of the official or free men. The rent which the nobles got from their tenants (free men) was twenty-four baskets of paddy per *pari*. These officers in return usually pay revenue of two baskets of paddy per *pari*. However, if a noble fail to pay his share of revenue in time the *phamlous* were confiscated and given to others. To a certain extent, it checked the growth of large-scale land holdings concentrated in a few hands and enabled to check their unrestrained power and authority. Thus, the nobility owing to its close links with the throne and having enjoyed the agricultural lands at the pleasure of the king could not emerge as independent and powerful landlords. Ostensibly because of these measures, there was absence of landlordism in the kingdom of Manipur.

Role of the State in Production and Distribution Process

In Manipur, the state played an important part in production activity by acting as facilitating agents in organising and supervising dredging activities, constructing bunds to check inundations and clearing of drainages. However, the role of state in production process and organisation of production was not much apparent. But labour being the most crucial factor in production the state by the beginning of the twelfth century, had evolved a highly ingenious system of mobilisation of labour through the *Lallup* system about which references have already been made. This system was made more effective by successive Meitei kings evolved over the years and it transformed the whole nature of the economic activity by bringing it under direct state control. The introduction of this feudal service and improvements made upon it over the years converted the loosely organised militia into a centralised militia pool with a regular gradation. An officer known as *Lallup Chingba* was appointed to oversee the functioning of this system. Reacting against the system being termed as 'forced labour' by some colonial writers.[11] James Johnstone observed, "The system was a good one, and when not carried to excess, pressed heavily on nobody. It was especially adapted to a poor state, sparsely populated. In such a state, under ordinary circumstances, where the amount of revenue is small, and the rate of wages often comparatively high, it is next door to impossible to carry out many much needed public works by payment. On the other hand, every man in India who lives by cultivation, has much spare time on his hands, and the Lallup system very profitably utilises this, and for the benefit of the community at large.[12] He further commented, "Many of the great works of the former ages in other parts of India,.... we have still to learn that the native system has much good in it, much to recommend it, and that it is in many cases the natural outgrowth of the requirements of the people.[13]

In such state control over the mobilization of labour for production not only enhanced the prestige and authority of the Meitei kings but also enabled the state to intervene directly in the production process. The vital control over labour meant that economic activity was shaped and dictated by the states interest and policies.

Agriculture

From a small chiefdom, the growth and development of Manipur kingdom had its basis on the wet rice culture which sustained the state apparatus. Hence, the success of wet rice cultivation was crucial to the stabilisation of a agrarian economy. But wet rice economy not only required a large base of manpower to clear the swamps and marshes and level the soil but also a system of efficient water control and management to irrigate the fields. In this case, seasonal rainfall being abundant, the state was largely successful in providing the basic infrastructural facilities for extension of wet rice cultivation. Through its control over the supply of labour, the state played a dominant role in land reclamation. It may be noted that in wet rice cultivation availability of water is most important as it basically supplies all necessary nutrients required for healthy growth. In Manipur, rainfall being abundant, small scale irrigation facilities could be organised by the peasant community at the village level.

To a large extent the nature of wet rice cultivation is dependent upon varying ecological condition and depended mainly upon its elevation and in the capacity to retain moisture. For this purpose the field was first levelled and low ridges or *Louri* were raised in a criss-cross pattern to retain water in the fields and the excess water being drained out whenever necessary. These ridges were generally not higher than a foot. This technique suited the alluvial plains of Manipur valley and wet rice cultivation was mostly carried out in this alluvial plain. Not less than nineteen varieties of rice are grown in Manipur which are divided into early *(Anganphou)* and late crops. The early crops ripen in about three months and are ready for cutting in September. *Sajikhong, Tumai, Kabaw Phou* and *Phourel Anganphou* are the favourite varieties of early crops. The great bulk of rice which is grown in the valley is of late variety which ripens in about six months and is ready for reaping in November, the most popular and of finest quality among them are *Phourel, Luining (Huining?)* and *Yenthik*. However, by the close of the nineteenth century a large quantity of the early variety has been sown.[14] It is possible that peasants are more attracted towards cultivation of the early variety as it took lesser amount of time and labour in comparison with the later variety. The successful operation of agricultural activity was depended upon the construction of river embankments. The rainfall in normal years was so abundant that the danger of cultivation arose from floods rather than the scarcity of water. To prevent the annual flooding of rivers resulting in inundation of vast tracts of cultivated lands, high embankments were constructed on state initiative besides periodic dredging activities were taken up. These embankments served alike bunds and high roads of the region.

The overall impact of the introduction of wet rice cultivation resulted in increased productivity which helped to sustain the growing state apparatus and the rising population. Though population of the country was greatly reduced during the Burmese occupation of Manipur (1819-1826), known as *Chahi Taret Khuntakpa*, many of the valley dwellers left the country and took refuge in the neighbouring areas such as Cachar, Sylhet and Dhaka for safety, there was definite signs of a growing population as evidenced by the establishment of new villages. The population of Manipur as it stands in 1881 were 2,21,070 out of which 1,35,782 comprised valley population[15] and it increased to 2,84,465, in 1901.[16]

Industry and Manufacture

It is axiomatic view that the level of technological development is an indicator of development of material culture and civilisation of a country. From the earliest times down the seventeenth century, there was a slow but steady development of technology in Manipur as already proved by archaeological findings and historical evidences. As cited earlier, the prehistoric man in Manipur used both stone and bone tools. But the development of pottery which was coterminous with technological development was found to have flourished since early times as well. The material remains of

Napachik are a testimony of it. Other archaeological sites at Sekta, Khamran, Khangabok, Irengbam, Phunan etc. prove the antiquity of pottery in Manipur. It has been suggested that some of the potteries found at the Napachik site have affinities with the potteries of ancient north China. The Chakpas who were dispersed in different parts of Manipur valley are described as the earliest pottery makers of Manipur.[17] Some of the Chakpa villages, *viz.* Andro, Phayeng, Chairel etc. are still engaged in pottery making and produces good quality potteries which could be used for cooking, preserving and storing foods, in the hill areas, the Tangkhul and Paomei tribesman knew and practiced the art of pottery making since the early time.[18] Potteries were widely used throughout the centuries in the kingdom. The Muslim immigrants during the reign of Khangemba introduced improved technology of pottery making by using wheels besides making different types of vessels. The Muslim family engaged in pottery making was given local surname known as *Phusam* (pottery making family) by the king and giving in marriage a local woman.[19]

In comparison with pottery making metallurgy appears to be not well developed in early Manipur. There are historical references to iron, copper bronze, silver, gold and tin. According to popular tradition King Khuyoi Tompok (154-254 A.D.?) was regarded as a technological innovator. During his reign iron was found at Kakching, gold at Kongba Meirembi and copper at Sibong. The myths associated with local deity Khamlangba of Kakching gives an interesting account of discovery of iron in the area.[20] Widespread use of bell-metal gong for religious and cultural activities leads us to suggest that bronze metallurgy was developed within Manipur itself or perhaps, it might have been brought to Manipur by way of trade from upper Burma and Thailand. Use of iron implements in agriculture, weaponry (swords, spears, *daos* and other tools) was clearly proved by the development of blacksmiths in the kingdom. The account of Poireiton refers to the use of iron implements for the first time in the history of Manipur. Accounts of the coronation of Naothingkhong mentions iron made weapons and metals like tin, silver and gold. The introduction of guns, gun making and use gun powder in Manipur is of later origin. The Meiteis learned the art of gun making from the Muslim war captives in the seventeenth century during the reign of King Khagemba (1597-1652 A.D.).

The creative impulse of the people of Manipur especially of womenfolk was best represented in the handloom and handicraft products. Though metal technology was not highly developed in the kingdom, yet in the field of handicraft Manipur could claim a proud heritage. It was in the field of weaving and related works like dyeing, printing, embroidery and appliqué art, Manipur excelled among all her neighbours. Queen Laisna, wife of Nonda Lairen Pakhangba was believed to have introduced several designs of clothes based on the pattern of python, *Phanek Phibal, Samchin,* and border of shawls. These designs are called *Namthang-khulak, Khamen-chatpa* and *Ningkham* which were used by the royal family and nobility. The mulberry silk-worm locally known as *Leimatil* was discovered by Nongmainu Ahongbi, wife of Khuyoi Tompok. There was a village known as Leimaram which specialized in production of high quality silk. Handicrafts, including weaving and dyeing were greatly engaged in this trade. It might have compelled King Loiyumba to issue his famous decree known as *Loiyumba Shilyen* to assign weavers' families to produce particular types of cloths, the case being same in dyers' families too. Thirty families were assigned to weave different designs of clothes. It is very interesting to know that in the twelfth century A.D. Manipuri weavers developed such a rich variety of weaving patterns which were patented with the state. As many as thirty-two different designs of cloth were found. The dyers families were assigned to produce different colours based on the colours of flowers. Eight families were assigned to dye specific colours. *Loiyumba Shilyen* has projected picture of a well organised economy of Manipur. The wet rice agrarian economy was supplemented by the growing handloom and handicrafts industry. It was in such a situation that the state had to intervene and regulate the organisation of these industries. The people, who primarily were peasants, had now become artisans.

Thus from the above discussion, it is apparent that weaving that prevailed in Manipur was an indigenous one; spinning, weaving, and dyeing were fairly developed in Manipur. Later on, the handloom industry was further developed with the introduction of fly shuttle known as *Pangandem* (perhaps fly shuttle might have been introduced in the kingdom by the Muslim immigrants).

With the success of wet rice cultivation and the surplus that followed, industrial activity witnessed slow and gradual changes to meet the basic requirements of the state for metals and scarce goods. Because of its specific importance the extraction of precious metals like iron for boat building for transport and defence, handloom and handicrafts and allied manufacturing activities received particular interest from the Meitei State. As in agriculture, the above industries were dependent on the labour of the *Lallois*.

As salt being a scarce commodity, the state made systematic arrangements to procure the precious commodity. Salt was mainly obtained from the brine wells situated in the valley; principal salt wells in the kingdom were situated at the villages of Ningel, Chandrakhong, Sikhong and Waikhong.[21] The whole of the salt wells are considered property of the king/state and are worked for his benefit. The men employed in production of salt are remunerated for their labour, and a certain amount of salt is set aside for their benefit. The king collected as revenue thirty per cent of the produce and remaining seventy per cent is distributed among the salt manufacturers. Though there are seasonal variations in production but at an average about 150 *maunds* of salt (estimate of 1867-68) are produced per month from these wells which almost met the requirements of the state. A small quantity is occasionally imported in times of scarcity from Burma and Cachar.[22] The wholesale price of salt was rupees six per maund in 1873.[23] The Ningel inscription of King Garibniwaz forbids people of other areas committing offences in the area, if any, are liable to be inflicted heavy punishment clearly shows the importance attached to the protection and preservation of salt wells.[24] Salt produced from these wells are of high quality and free from smell. The villagers employed in salt production are from the Loi community and their *Lallup* duty is for six months in a year, i.e. three months of more labour than that of the Meiteis. However, their longer period of engagement in *Lallup* is well remunerated by the state.[25]

In a region where water afforded a ready and universal mode of transport, boat building was a popular industry under state supervision. The industry was sustained by the easy availability of timbers and free labour of the Lallup. They made excellent boats large and small. The *Hiyangloi Hangjaba* and *Hisaba Hanjaba* oversaw the whole operation of construction and maintenance of boats.[26] The boat building technique was simple. The locally available boats were hollowed out until only an outer skin about an inch and quarter thick remained. The inhabitants of Hiroi-Lamgang village (a Loi village), in the south of the valley not far from Sugnu made boats for the Raja.[27] Widespread use of boat is evidenced by the annual boat race competition known as *Hiyang Tannaba* which are regularly held in the September every year. About seventy rowers occupied one boat in this competition.[28]

The economy of Manipur being basically agrarian, industry did not emerge as a popular occupation of the people. The limited industry that developed on state initiative was based on the easy availability of natural resources and to meet certain basic needs of metals and scarce products. Being a land of rivers and streams which intersects the valley like a network, boat making developed. The salt industry was an important one for the very reason that home reserve was meagre. Amongst the few manufactures produced silk was considered important, it also constituted an important article of export. Silk weaving was an ancient art and hence its manufacturing was a continuation of the popular tradition. A relatively stagnant technology and rather rudimentary implements was characteristic feature of production. No scientific or technological change formed part of the eighteenth and nineteenth century historical experience. Technology in general was backward. The uneven development of technology over a range of crafts resulted from a semi-tribal economic base, a small quantum of surplus in circulation and a relative scarcity of basic metals like iron in the country.

An overview of Micro-economies of Peasant Production

The *Lallois* whose labour service sustained the state apparatus of the kingdom was also peasants and direct producers. While not on active state service the *Lallois* carried on their subsistence activity mainly by cultivation. Alongside the cultivation of wet rice in the state allotted plots, they were also involved in petty production mainly for domestic consumption.

On the sides of the hills and undulating grounds which was not easily reducible to a plain level, or in deeply flooded plains, swamps and marshes, the peasants cultivated a wide variety of vegetables and *Anganphou* which includes *Sajikhong, Tumai, Kabaw Phou* and *Phouren Anganba* which ripens in three months and is ready for cutting in September.[29] This was followed by the cultivation of later varieties of paddy. The later crops being transplanted one, the grains after being sown in nursery beds for about two months, the seedling were transplanted in June or July to carefully manured beds, which had been ploughed as much as four or five times till the soil was reduced to a fine puddle of clay. The transplantation of the seedlings to the field was mainly done by women. The harvest was reaped by December. Each *pari* of land yielded as much as one hundred sixty to two hundred baskets. The annual average yield per *pari* is about one hundred and fifty baskets and each basket contains about sixty pounds.[30]

The dry field cultivation of the peasants included pulses, potato, brinjals, pumpkins, onions, and pepper, tobacco of good quality and white sugarcane which has medicinal property. English vegetables, peas, and English cabbage, cauliflowers, beans etc. were also gradually brought in and cultivated in the nineteenth century.[31] A small quantity of opium was also grown by the Muslims.

The most important crop grown for manufacture was cotton. The cotton plant was generally cultivated in the periphery of Manipur valley and its adjoining hills, but more specifically by the tribes. Small quantities of Indigo, Bixa, Alba etc., used for dyeing were also cultivated by the peasants in the vicinity of their villages and homesteads.[32]

In addition, a rich variety of garden crops such as tobacco, opium, several kinds of plantain, vegetables and a few varieties of spices were grown by the peasants. The richness and variety of the crops grown indicated not only the fertility of the soil but also a secure and cultivated life enjoyed by the peasants. A number of fruits such as mangoes, plantains, pineapples, apples, peaches, bramble, wild raspberry, jack, guava etc. were grown in the valley and the hills. Ginger, India corn and *pan* leaves are widely grown in the hills of Manipur.

Besides the agricultural and horticultural crops noted above, the region being richly endowed with forest products, the basic requirements of the peasants for shelter, fuel etc. were met without much effort. The forest provided valuable timbers chiefly adapted for constructing houses, furniture, boats etc. The bamboo which grew abundantly was utilized by the peasants for their houses, furniture, implements of agriculture etc. such crafts constituted subsidiary occupation of the peasants.

Organisation of Labour

Though King Loiyumba in his edict of 1110 A.D. had initiated distribution of economic occupation among various *Yumnaks* (families), the close unity between agriculture and handicrafts was reflected in the distribution of labour. Most of the peasants needed for crafts and artisans services being satisfied within the household there was no strict division of labour. Except for some Loi villages and few Meitei families who were assigned specific occupation like pottery making, sword making, there was no sharp division of labour between agriculture and industry. Every peasant or rather every household built its own hut, grew its own vegetables and tobacco, scoop out its own canoe and weaved its own mats. In most cases, the crafts constituted a subsidiary occupation of the peasant and his family.

Thus blessed with a favourable geography and environment, the Manipuri peasants could sustain and reproduce themselves without much labour and hardship. The micro-economies of the peasants were largely of a subsistence nature. The peasants produced up to the extent where their household needs could be met and self-exploitation was minimal. Some references have been made about the indolence of Manipuri peasants and their frequent involvement in festivities round the year. But, in the fertile valley of Manipur, forcing a living did not require much labour and prolonged physical exertion. Besides, the lack of incentives for surplus production which was linked to the mode of appropriation and the restrictive nature of state service did not encourage peasant activity. In the absence of incentives, peasant's enterprise for enhancing productivity of crops by adopting new techniques was lacking. There was practically no rotation of crops apart from the system under which the winter rice was followed by pulse or oil seeds. As wooden plough with a iron tipped share, wooden rakes, a rough wooden harrow, sickles, knives, winnowing fan, a large mat and baskets comprised a peasants tools even by the end of nineteenth century.[33]

Mode of Appropriation

By the eighteenth century, the Meitei state had evolved elaborate and systematic machinery for purposes of appropriation. But generally appropriation took in the form of labour services which the peasant Lallois offered to the state in various capacities. The cash revenue collection of the state from all sources including the Kabaw valley compensation which the British government paid to Manipur since 1834 according to an estimate of 1873 is about twenty five to thirty thousand rupees annually.[34]

Collections in kind were mainly realised from the land grants to officials in lieu of salary, tributes from the hill chiefs and brine wells. Revenue in kind was also collected from the Loi villages. Sufficient data are not available for revenue collected from import and export of goods. According to information furnished by the state administration to the British officials in Manipur, the cash revenue realized from import and export of goods for the year 1868-69 stood at rupees 1,975, 7 Annas and 9 paise and rupees 3,533, 1 anna and 9 paise respectively. Revenue collected from export of silk to Burma accounted for a mere rupees one hundred only.[35] The Manipuri officials estimate of revenue collection from export and import trade came around rupees twelve thousand per annum.[36] Some sort of tributes though on limited scale was also appropriated from the tribes. The hill tribes such as the Kabui, Mao, Maram, Tangkhul, Anal, Maring, Khongjai etc. came annually to the Meitei court bringing with them a number of articles such as cotton, ginger, pepper elephant tusks etc. failing which retributive actions were carried out. The exaction from the hill tribe was limited being exacted mainly for vindication of Meitei suzerainty. The idea was not so much to collect revenue as to bring and keep the indigenous hill tribes under complete or some sort of allegiance to the Meitei king. Annual congregation of tribal chiefs under Manipur kingdom was regularly held at the palace since 1700 A.D. during the reign of Charairongba (1697-1709) which later on came to be known as *Mera Haochongba* festival. About the festival it is reported that, "This festival in October lasts only for one day; it is a gathering of the hill tribes under the Manipur government, and is a curious sight on account of the great number of different tribes assembled, with their curious dress and weapons, differing from each other in feature and language, but all unanimous in one particular, to get drunk as speedily and remain so long, as possible. The hillmen indulge in feats of strength before the Raja, such as carrying heavy weights etc. They also indulge in war dance and sham fights. The sports of the day conclude with a feast, at which they are regaled with the flesh of cows, buffaloes, dogs, cats etc., which may have died in the valley. The flesh is dried and preserved for this feat.[37] Organising such events by the king helped in bringing about integration among the hill and valley people and also the safety and security of the kingdom.

The above discussions suggest that the extent of appropriation by the Meitei state was not as extensive as compared to the strength of the population and resources. Though the successive rulers attempted to cover all the probable source of revenue available within the region, the royal receipts were comparatively small owing to the cumbrous nature of the system and loose control over the receipts. Though the number of revenue receipts was increased to meet the growing need of resources, especially after Manipur-Burma conflicts, yet the amount collected was far less of the potential resources of the kingdom. Allegations are made about the revenue officials involved in corrupt practices while collecting revenue and in measurement of land allotted to the peasants. There are instances of punishment meted out to officials for taking bribes.[38]

Trade and Commerce

The mode of appropriation by the state in the form of labour service not only determined the level of production and the development of a marketing network, also eventually determined the level of trade and commercial activity within and outside the state. Because of the limitations imposed by the mode of appropriation, the range of trading activities at various levels was greatly limited. The available evidence suggests that the state not only gave in kind but also received mostly in kind and service. Surplus, therefore, largely took the form of labour rent for direct appropriation by the ruling class. Besides most of the basic requirements of the peasant and his family for food, clothing etc., were satisfied within the household. However, self-sufficiency in its totality appears to be a myth. A minimal surplus production was necessitated by the scarcity of essential items within the state. Theoretically, production of surplus would be necessary to acquire artisans and craftsmen services. But in case of Manipur, the division of labour on caste specific profession was yet to emerge as there was no caste system existed in the kingdom. Hence, though the peasants did exchange their products, a substantial surplus production on their part was not necessary. Moreover, the artisans and craftsmen still retained their link with agriculture. Since, surplus production was minimal a marketing network and trade that developed were essentially rudimentary in structure. At local markets exchanges were made of scarce products. Private trade not only did not appear in any substantial form, it was also not as it appears encouraged by the state. Not that private trade was totally absent. But considering the magnitude of the trade which in fact, was meagre, it appears that private trade was very limited and highly susceptible to the vagaries of the political situation of the day. Besides, most of the traders never cut-off their link with agriculture which constituted their primary occupation.

A special feature of marketing network within the country was the existence of local markets (*Keithel*) where most of the exchanges took place. Exchanges was mainly intra-local on petty scale and at a peddling level within the limitations of a basically barter and cowrie economy. Important marketing centres were at *Sana Keithel, Kha Keithel, Moirang Keithel, Khuman Keithel, Phaibung Keithel, Chairen Keithel, Nambol Keithel, Konglang Keithel, Andro Keithel and Phayeng Keithel.*[39] The markets contiguous to the hill areas were generally frequented by the neighbouring hill tribes. In these markets where regular trade was carried on between the plain and hill tribes, a variety of goods mostly perishable were exchanged. Particularly during the winter seasons a large number of hill people frequented the main markets. Most of the items sold or exchanged in the markets are dry fish, rice, vegetables, *pan, supari,* clothes, ornaments for the hillmen and sweetmeats. One very interesting feature of these markets of Manipur was it being exclusively run by women. About three thousand women assembled in the afternoon bazaar. Men with the exception of foreigners were not allowed to enter the market place; all the buying and selling was conducted by women.[40] The most important and essential item which the hillmen collected/buy from these markets is salt. They brought cotton, ginger, pepper, baskets and wax etc. for exchange or sold of for cash. Trade with the hill tribes was conducted on a small scale. Exchange was carried out mainly for use value or consumption. Exchange of the most part was on a personal level and the goods usually bartered. Though the markets were established by the state since a long period it appears that the state did not exercise much control over them.

Though sketchy references have been made in the royal chronicle of the long distance trade routes between Manipur and neighbouring kingdoms, like Tripura, Cachar, Assam and Burma a fair picture could not be drawn about the nature and quantum of trade carried out between Manipur and these countries for want of sufficient data. However, some important items of trade as suggested by the chronicle included among others elephants and horse. It appears that elephant trade was exclusively a royal monopoly. Manipur silk which was of fine quality was in great demand by the Burmese. However, by the eighteenth and nineteenth century. Manipur's trade and commercial relation with the neighbours were at its lowest ebb as frequent wars broke out between Manipur and her neighbours especially with Burma. In 1873, a sum of rupees one hundred only was levied as tax by the state as export duty of silk from Manipur to Burma.[41] However, British colonial intervention in Manipur owing to Anglo-Manipur War of 1891 had substantially altered the economy of Manipur as monetisation was vigorously enforced by the colonial authorities.

Notes

1. B. Hindess and P. Hirst, *Mode of Production and Social Formation: Pre-Capitalist Modes of Production,* London, 1975; John G. Taylor, *From Modernisation to Modes of Production,* London, 1979, p. 107.
2. The first reference to paddy cultivation in Manipur is made in texts like *Soubol Lairembi Loutarol* (MS.), *Ningthou Maputhiba* (MS.) and *Soubol Yairel* (MS.); M. Chandra Singh (ed.), Poireiton Khunthokpa, Imphal, 1967, p. 3.
3. *Cheitharol Kumbaba,* the royal chronicle and *Tutenglon,* an archaic text (N. Manaoyaima, ed.) refers to dredging of Imphal river by Meitei king Taothingmang (264-364 A.D.?) along with his brother Yoimongba.
4. B. Kullachandra Sharma and Badr-ud-din, *Meitei Pangal Hourakpham,* Imphal, 1991, p. 146.
5. A.A. Howell, *Short Account of Land Revenue in Manipur,* Imphal, p. 9, 1907.
6. *Ibid.*
7. *Ibid.*, pp. 5-6.
8. *Ibid.*, p. 4.

9. *Ibid.*, pp. 3-4.
10. William. McCulloch, *Valley of Manipur*, Delhi, 1980; R. Brown, *Statiscal Account of Manipur*, Delhi, 1975, pp. 11, 13, 83 and T.C. Hodson, *The Meitheis*, Delhi, 1989, p. 31.
11. James Johnstone, *Manipur and the Naga Hills*, Delhi, 1987, Rept., p. 14.
12. *Ibid.*, pp. 114-115.
13. R. Brown, *Statistical Account of Manipur*, Rept. Delhi, 1975., pp. 83-84.
14. E.W. Dun, *Gazetteer of Manipur*, Delhi, 1981 rept. p. 15.
15. T.C. Hodson, *The Meitheis*, Rept. Delhi, 1975, p. 2.
16. *Chakpa Khunthok Khunda* (MS).
17. Kshetri Kumar, *Manipurda Chaphu*, Kakching, 1984, p. 12.
18. R.K. Sanahal (ed.) *Pangal Thorakpa*, Imphal, 1985, p. XV, and B. Kullachandra Sharma and Dr. Badr-ud-din (ed.) *Meitei Pangal Thorakpa*, Imphal, 1991, p. 27.
19. Gourachandra, *Manipurda Yotshung Yotsha* (Traditional Iron Smelting and Forging in Manipur), Kakching, 1997, p. 9.
20. Kh. Chandrasekhar Singh (ed.), *Loiyumba Shilyen*, Imphal, 1974.
21. R. Brown, *op. cit.*, pp. 9-10.
22. *Ibid.*, p. 10.
23. Mutua Bahadur and P. Gunindra Singh, *Epigraphical Records of Manipur*, Imphal, 1986, vol. I, pp. 8-13.
24. T.C. Hodson, *op. cit.*, pp. 33-36.
25. N. Khelchandra Singh (ed.), *Phamlon* (Imphal, 1987), pp. 4,14.
26. T.C. Hodson, *op. cit.*, p. 33
27. *Ibid.*, p. 52.
28. R. Brown, *op. cit.*, p. 83.
29. *Ibid.*, p. 86.
30. *Ibid.*, p. 84.
31. B. Kullachandra Sharma, *Meiteigee Machugee Manat*, Imphal, 2000, pp. 34-41.
32. R. Brown, *op. cit.*, p. 87.
33. *Ibid.*, p. 88.
34. *Ibid.*
35. E.W. Dun, *op. cit.*, p. 66.
36. *Ibid.* pp. 24-25.
37. R. Brown *op. cit.*, p. 86
38. Gangmumei Kabui, *History of Manipur*, V. I, Delhi, 1991, p. 220.
39. R. Brown, *op. cit.*, pp. 90-91.
40. *Ibid.*, p. 88.
41. *Ibid.*

SECTION II
Anti-Colonial Movement

7

Beyond Her Role as an Anti-Colonial Freedom Fighter

The Cultural and Religious Legacy of Rani Gaidinliu

Som Kamei

Rani Gaidinliu, as we all know, was a legendary freedom fighter of whom India is really proud of. An Indian historian writes, "Any nation or country would be proud to have such a gifted woman who sacrificed everything for her people and for the cause she believed was good and true. She became a living legend in her own lifetime." Pandit Nehru eulogized her as the "Rani" of the hills. Prime Minister Shri Atal Bihari Vajpayee describes Haipao Jadonang as a martyr and Rani Gaidinliu as a freedom fighter of India. During her Birth Centenary Celebration in New Delhi in August 2015, Prime Minister Narendra Modi recalled her contribution to India's freedom struggle and gave her credit for spreading the message of Mahatma Gandhi in North East India.

In this chapter, I would be going beyond her role as an anti-colonial freedom fighter and highlight her impact on the highly misunderstood and misinterpreted cultural and religious aspect of Rani Gaidinliu's contribution in the strengthening of indigenous religion in North East India, more specifically on her Zeliangrong community which occupy a geographically contiguous area spread over the three states of Assam, Manipur and Nagaland.

Before that, I am going to go into a little background of Gaidinliu as a young girl born on 26th of January, 1915 in a Rongmei village of Nungkao in Tamenglong district of Manipur.

Gaidinliu's father's name was Lothanang and her mother's name was Karotlienliu. She belonged to the influential Pamei clan of the village. Her father was not the chief of the village but young Gaidinliu was the pampered child of the clan. Gaidinliu showed her extraordinary quality and talent right from a young age. She grew up as a little mystic. She was always independent, determined and courageous in whatever she did. Needless to say, she was a born leader.

According to her supporters, her life took a new turn when she met a kindly deity who looked exactly like her in the forest near her village. Later on, she learnt that the goddess was the daughter of God Bisnu of the Zeliangrong pantheon of gods and goddess. They established a lifelong friendship. Her parents thought that their daughter might be a shaman priestess. Later on, the Political Agent of Manipur, Mr. G.C. Higgins describes her as a 'Maibi': a medicine woman.

But she came to know of Jadonang through her dreams and she went to Kambiron to meet her future master. Since 1926-27, the relation between the Master and Disciple developed between Jadonang and Gaidinliu. Jadonang recognised the god given talent of the young girl who also volunteered to join his movement. Ultimately, she became the most trusted Lieutenant of Jadonang.

Gaidinliu upon her return from Kambiron performed the prestigious house ceremonial of 'Taraạng Kai' at the village of Nungkao. She also devoted a home of worship where common people might worship Tingkao Ragwang or Tingwang (Almighty God). Gaidinliu participated in the acts of reformation of the age-old Zeliangrong religion, abolition of taboos and gennas, organisation of religious congregation, performance of dances and singing songs or hymns as carried out by her master, HaipaoJadonang. A new cultural and religious awakening was started amongst the Zeliangrong.

Young Gaidinliu was opposed to the oppressive rule of the British, particularly the forced labour of the poor villagers and imposition of house tax. She came into contact with large number of people through her association with HaipaoJadonang mostly in the religious reform movement. During the last joint pilgrimage to the holy cave at Bhuban hills of lord Bisnu, young Gaidinliu came to know of the future of her struggle as was revealed to HaipaoJadonang and Gaidinliu.

During this time, she also learnt about the impending death of Jadonang. When Jadonang was arrested by the Assam police at Lakhipur, she escaped into the forest. She was accompanied by 40 youth including girls. She went into hiding awaiting the outcome of the trial of Jadonang. She knew that Jadonang was innocent and he was framed on a concocted charge by the British.

However, after the unfortunate execution of Jadonang on 29th August, 1931, Gaidinliu took up the cudgels to organise the people. A historian writes,"The real revolt occurred after the martyrdom of Jadonang. Gaidinliu, the charismatic, spiritual and political successor of Jadonang, took over as the leader of the rebellion. The revolt was a violent protest against the British imperialism and a logical consequence of the ideology and strategy of Jadonang which would have taken shape but for the unfortunate British clamp-down on the protagonists of the "MakamGwangdi" which can be translated as the kingdom of the Makam meaning Zeliangrong or Nagas which have been described as 'Naga Raj' by the British Political agent of that time. This was a new concept introduced amongst the tribes which more or less existed like an independent village units.

The arrest, trial and execution of Jadonang stunned her followers with fear and anxiety. His own villagers even disowned him. Jadonang's role was in a preparatory phase and real action came during the time of Gaidinliu, a brilliant and determined disciple. Success or failure did not deter her. Fight she must, she was determined to put her master's ideology into practice.

However, apart from her obvious political movement to free her people from the foreign/alien rule, her real contribution to her community was the reform movement in both socio-cultural and religious domains. We will briefly discuss her contribution here.

Socio-religious Movement

The movement of Rani Gaidinliu was intertwined with socio-religious and political objectives. Socially and culturally, her movement aimed at the integration of 3 Naga kindred tribes (Zemei, Lingmai, Rongmei), commonly known as Zeliangrong. She wanted to preserve the traditional/indigenous Naga culture. Hemmed in by pressure from the Naga nationalists movement to declare her allegiance who was espousing "Nagaland for Christ" as its defined goal and rapid loss of her own indigenous religious followers to the western/alien proselytizing religion like Christianity, strongly supported by the colonial power, Rani Gaidinliu had to devise a double purpose movement to save her socio-religious identity and also fight for the political rights of her people. Hence, she not only fought against the British rule but also was opposed to any alien religion. With this objective in mind, she established the Heraka religion.

Heraka

Heraka is a religious reform movement devised from the ancestral practice known as Paupaise (Zeme) or Pupouchapriak (Rongmei). It has been known by various names such as Gaidinliu movement, Periese (old practice), Kelumse (Prayer practice) and Ranise (meaning in praise of the queen referring to Gaidinliu as people's queen) and finally to Heraka in 1974.

What is the meaning of Heraka? According to Shri N.C. Zeliang, the past president of Zeliangrong Heraka Association, "Heraka literally means 'Pure' in Zemei." The Heraka religion, according to him, is a pure and reformed religion of the Zeliangrong people comprising of three kindred tribes—the Zemei, Liangmei and Rongmei (1998).

What N.C. Zeliang refers to is attributed to the Heraka's adoption of one God, Tingwang, and the subsequent ban on animal sacrifices. Thus, the purity is the metaphor for no blood sacrifices and the adoption of a single God who is omnipresent, omniscient and creator of the universe.

Impact of the Reforms of Gaidinliu Movement

The Rani Gaidinliu movement appealed to the people by combining emotional appeal with the devising of practical reform with focus on Zeliangrong religious practices and economic problems. Thus, the reform focussed on rituals connected with the agricultural cycle, comprising a series of animal sacrifices, non-working days (NREI) or "Neimei." The old practices involved many sacrifices to be made to appeal the various deities and ensure a good crop.

Another old practice was the "Feast of Merit" for social status which became a huge burden on the villagers. Rituals of NREI or Neimei led to restriction on the movement of people outside the demarcated geographical area which may be a family home, village zone or entire village. Such restrictions limited the movability of the villagers.

The Gaidinliu movement responded to this problem by eliminating the tradition of animal sacrifices and with it the restriction on people movement. This was one of the reasons that people adopted "Heraka."

Now in Heraka, people could venture out of the village, get educated and find jobs. There were also economic benefits of banning animal sacrifices which were attractive to the people. Substituting or altering the sacrificial practices like adopting sacrifice of chicken and smaller birds made it more practical.

Old traditional social ranking which were mostly connected with displaying material wealth through animal sacrifices and 'feast of merit' on a massive scale led to huge drain in the economy. After the abolition of the old social order, a new non-heredity practice called "Peipou/Peipue" or 'village elders' based on seniority and wealth of the individual replacing the old land owners (Kadepeu) and the priest (Tingkopeu) came into existence.

Heraka as a Modernising Religion

The new Heraka religion made the cosmology a simpler one and give primacy to one universal God who inherited all the attributes of the other lesser gods. This led to the marginalisation of the traditional priest in favour of the Paipeu, the village elder leading to both social and economic change. It moved towards a more monotheistic way of perceiving the almighty through "Tingwang or Tingkao Ragwang."

Heraka as a reforming religious movement and to some extent Christianity, proved more suitable to deal with the change the outside world was bringing. Hence it also became a competing change agent giving rise to hostilities and propaganda against each other in the Zeliangrong countryside which can still be felt in the State of Nagaland and other places. The movement not only adapted a more monotheistic understanding of the cosmology but also adapted certain rules of do's and don'ts for its followers called the Heraka Hingde.

Heraka Hingde

'Heraka Hingde' is a systemisation of the religious belief and practices and becoming a modern way of acting. To understand the philosophy of the Heraka religion, it is necessary to examine the Hingde book. The Hingde book of the Heraka speaks of 8 (eight) steps to lead a pure life:

(i) Tingwang created the earth and will destroy again but believe in him saying his praise and pray to him;
(ii) Respect your parents and elders and preserve the Zeliangrong culture;
(iii) Have a disciplined mind and clear body and emphasize on Heleuraube (Selflessness);
(iv) In all your speech and work, your mind must be truthful. Search for knowledge and light but breed not jealousy and enmity;
(v) Love all Tingwang's sons and daughters and search the way for happiness and peace;
(vi) Observe Jalua (Full moon day) well;
(vii) Set up Kelumki (Prayer house) and pray with an empty hands (Stop animal sacrifice); and
(viii) Have faith in re-birth.

The above reform movement of Heraka led by Rani Gaidinliu was more appealing form of religion to deal with the modernisation process. However, many obstacles were faced by the movement. As mentioned earlier, it was actively competing for the same space with Christian missionaries which led to many misunderstandings and it continues to bicker even to these days especially in the Christian dominated areas of Manipur, Nagaland and Assam.

In this scenario, helping hands from other social and religious organisation from other parts of mainland India such as Vishwa Hindu Parishad and Kalyan Ashrams led to strengthening of the movement and at the same time, retaining its own identity. It is to be mentioned here that Heraka does not form a part of the Hindu cosmology, but its support by various Hindu organisations has led to this understanding which the protagonists neither denies nor accept openly.

The immediate impact and areas of influence of the reform movement was felt amongst the Zemis of north Cachar hills (Haflong) in Assam and Peren district of Nagaland. However, the cascading affect was felt in Manipur also and inspired the reform movement such as Tinkao Ragwang Chapriak (TRC) movement in Manipur which has the same cosmology in adopting Tingkao Ragwang as the omnipresent and omniscient God and with the same set of philosophy as practiced by the Heraka.

Another important impact was the growth of the already rich cultural heritage of the Zeliangrong people through the encouragement given to traditional songs, hymns in praise of Tingwang, dances performed in honour of the Gods and traditional dresses which were worn during various religious and cultural festivities. These helped in the preservation and continued propagation and growth of the rich Zeliangrong traditional cultural practices.

Today we can proudly say that Zeliangrong tribe is one of the richest in terms of advancement in cultural heritages amongst the tribes of India. Folk songs composed by Jadonang and Rani Gaidinliu continue to be sung and new compositions continues to be adopted, hence making it a living culture and not a museum piece as is the case with other tribes.

Hence, the reform movement such as the Heraka and TRC can be seen as an expression in responce to the changing world amidst the cacophony of the dominant religious groups like Christianity and other religious groups.

Maintaining a balance between the influences of various religious traditions like Christianity and Hinduism and while drawing attention to their own traditions, make the Heraka a marginal yet significant religious movement of India.

In conclusion, we can say that Rani Gaidinliu movement was a socio-religious movement intertwined with political objectives. Its impact continues to be felt across the Zeliangrong region in Assam, Manipur and Nagaland.

References

Arkotong Longkumer (2016), *The poetry of Resistance—The Heraka movement of North-East India*, NESRC.

Prof. Gangmumei Kamei (2015), *Rani Gaidinliu (1915-1993)—Freedom fighter, social and religious Reformer.*

Prof. Gangmumei Kamei, "A brief note on Rani Gaidinliu (1915-1972)", in Dr. S.P. Sen, (ed.), *Dictionary of National Biography*. Indian Institute of Historical Studies, Kolkata.

Gangmumei Kamei (1997), *Jadonang—A Mystic Naga Rebel.* G. Lanshailu Kamei, Majorkhul, Imphal, Manipur.

8
Anglo-Kuki War 1917-1919
The Forgotten Great War Theatre

Jangkhomang Guite

How many of us are aware that Manipur was one of the First World War theatres where the longest armed rebellion and the 'largest series of military operations' in the region took place, and perhaps the longest military operations against any armed uprising during the Victorian era. Officially known as 'Kuki rising' or 'Kuki rebellion', the Anglo-Kuki War 1917-1919 (which we prefer to use here) witnessed one of the fiercest tribal resistance movement and one of the most military brutalities against any uprisings. This was also one of the important events in Manipur history where both the Kuki and Meitei revolutionaries joined hands to fight the British. The war was triggered by the labour recruitment for the WW1 but the grievances of people of Manipur against the British, who had controlled Manipur administration since 1892, had also already grown into proportion by this time. People were fed up of British dominance over Manipur and just wanted to get rid of it. The circumstances of the Great War provided the trigger. Thus, when the Great War broke out in Europe, there was 'the wildest rumours' of British defeat and withdrawal in the valley of Manipur that, for a time, there was fear of rebellion so that the government had to immediately intervene and 'satisfactorily allayed' after much effort. Similarly, when the Maharaja of Manipur, as the puppet of British Empire, promised to supply Sappers and a Double Company of soldiers to the British for the Great War, hundreds of young men escaped to the hills or other places in the name of trading or otherwise. When the Maharaja also promised to contribute 6000 labourers, 4000 from the hills and 2000 from the valley, the response was also completely against it. Only 2000 hillmen could go to France under duress whereas others took to arms to expel the British from Manipur. The 'Kuki rebellion', which broke out in response to the forced labour recruitment, was dominated by the Kukis but all the other communities of Manipur also took part in different ways. I will briefly discuss in the following sections how and why the Anglo-Kuki War is an important event in the history of Manipur and why we cannot pretend to forget in our state commemoration of freedom.

The Event from the Archives

The origin of the Anglo-Kuki War can go back into the changing relationship between the Kuki chiefs and the British since the latter took over the administration of Manipur in 1892. Kukis were opposed to the imposition of house-tax, *pothang*, *begari*, and finally the colonial sedentarization policy which had hugely challenged their independence in the hills. However, their opposition to the recruitment of labour for France since March 1917 was one major factor which eventually compelled them to take up arms. Kukis were opposed to the idea of going to France for some genuine reasons. Like all the other tribes in the region, the Kukis feared death and told to the government in clear terms "that they feared to go so far from their homes and that if they had to die they preferred to die in their own country and would be prepared to meet force with force."[1]

They reasoned to the British officers that "it is the custom of the Kukis to bring the head of the dead man wherever he died", the meaning which the latter could not understand.[2] Two factors had explained why the question of death was so strong in the minds of tribal people. First, the rumour that was current in the hills during that time was that British were losing the war, Germans were so powerful and terrifying, and that whoever goes to the warfront (like France) will never return alive. Second, and sequel to the first, was the cultural factor. Most tribes in the region by this time were still a strong believer of their traditional religion and culture, in which the idea of crossing their hills, their *kalapani*, as it was often said, was still shrouded with multiple dangers of life and lore.

The Kukis particularly were a strong believer of their traditional religion and culture (only very few of them were Christians by this time) and felt that their gods (*pathen*, expressed in the form of *indoi/seldoi*) were not in a position to protect them in far away land beyond their hills. The lack of protection from their gods or the lack of healing when sick or injure in the absence of their *seldoi*, besides the fear of German terror, was a serious matter. Death was, therefore, sure in their worldview. That is not enough. Kukis had two concepts of death, *thise* (bad death) and *thipha* (good death). Death in accident, warfare, killed by wild animals, and so on was considered as bad death. Bad death did not deserve the normal death ritual, which means, they were deprived of the coveted *mithikho* (the village of the dead) in next world. The worst part was that the souls of those who died in the war would become, in the next world, the 'slaves' of the victor/those who killed them. Therefore, to the Kukis, the war that promised death was something they can never accept at all cost. In this context, their opposition to labour conscription was not without substance; it was a non-negotiable subject to them. Hence, despite rounds of negotiation with the colonial officers, who assured them life and several material gains, the Kuki chiefs stuck to their gun, 'they preferred to die in their own country'.

Thus, already by the early weeks of March 1917, the Kuki principal chiefs had issued orders to all Kuki villages (through traditional *sajam-lhah* or sending out pieces of meat) not to send any man for France. While other tribes who had also initially opposed sending their men to France, had eventually gave in to government under the pressure of threat, blandishments, and repeated assurance for their safety, the Kukis continued to oppose and demanded exemption.[3] Rounds of negotiations with them fail. However, the trigger point for the armed resistance was the burning of Mombi (Lonpi) Kuki village by J.C. Higgins, the Political Agent (PA) in Manipur (in-charge) on 17 October, 1917. On 10-11 October, 1917, the PA was having a round-table conference with 40 Kuki chiefs. No agreement could be reached but the PA promised to convene another meeting shortly.[4] However, after going back to Imphal, he took 50 rifles to Mombi village and burned it down on 17 October, 1917, barely five days after the Oktan meeting.[5]

The burning of Mombi provoked the Kukis so much that they

have decided to go for an armed resistance. A series of war councils were held in different parts of the Kuki hills, concluded at the grand war council at Chassad in the end of November or early December 1917.[6] J.B. Marshall, Deputy Commissioner, Upper Chindwin District, Burma, reported that about 150 Kuki chiefs were present in the 'Assembly of Chiefs' at Chassad where they took a resolution to go for a war. He reported: "At this meeting, it was resolved not to obey any orders or summons from Government and to fight if Government tried to enforce orders."[7] The Chassad chief, Pache, then circulated bullets to all the Kuki chiefs informing about the resolution taken and ordered them "to resist forcibly any attempt to impress coolies or to burn villages."[8] The declaration of war was followed by preparation across the Kuki hills. Foods were gathered and stored in 'hidden granaries', guns were collected from all sources, and in all villages gunpowder was manufactured, leather cannons (*pumpi*) made, village fortification, stockades, stone traps, and so on were constructed. While such preparation was going on, the war broke out when the first British military column under J.C. Higgins (now assuming Political Officer) was ambushed at the Thangjing ranges on 28 December, 1917 in south-western hills, when the first shot was made and the first blood was shed on the troops. Very soon, the war broke out over an area of 6-7000 square miles covering the rugged mountain ranges surrounding Manipur Valley, extending up to part of Naga Hills (in Assam), part of the Chin Hills, Somra Tract and Thaungdut State (in Burma). It lasted till April 1919.

The Kuki method of war was popularly known as 'hit and run' or 'guerilla warfare' in which they ambushed with sniping the marching military columns from their secreted hideouts in the jungles and then remain elusive from the troops. Such strategy was perhaps the most effective way to engage with a well equipped state army, the efficacy of which the modern insurgents also still appreciated. To the trained troops fighting such elusive enemy was, as Lieut. Col. French-Mullen, DIG, Burma, has rightly put, the 'thankless, disagreeable jobs'.[9] Besides, the Kukis also met the military columns at different strategic points where they erected their stockades. Here, normally exchange of fire with the government troops took place for hours. At Khailet (Gotengkot) stockades, for instance, the military column from the Chin Hills under Lieut. Stedman was confronted by the Kuki fighters from a series of stockades erected by them and the column was eventually 'repulsed' or 'reversed' after several hours of exchange of fire involving seven pounder mountain gun. Stedman was 'seriously/ dangerously wounded' with many casualties in his column; 8 sepoys were killed and 8 wounded. He retired to Lenacot for a refit.[10] At Hengtam, the military column was attacked from a 'very strong forts behind a long and substantial stockade'. Cosgrave reported that the 'enemy kept up a brisk and well directed fire from the stockade' and they could not be dislodged from it until several shells from seven-pounder mountain gun and bullets from magazine rifles were deluged into it at close range. He said that his 'column had to fire some 1300 rounds of .303 [rifles] and Martini Henry ammunition'.[11] In all these stockades and in other places, the Kukis also used, besides their familiar muskets, their leather cannons (*pumpi*), stone traps (*songthang*) and sharp bamboo stack or panjies (*sou*) in great numbers.

The military operations against the Kukis were carried out into two phases, December 1917 to April 1918 and November 1918 to April 1919. During the first phase, following mainly the 'flying/ mobile column' method, altogether 15 military columns were sent out against the Kukis in different parts of the hills. During the second phase, the operation was carried out by 6234 combatants, 696 non-combatants, 7650 transport carriers, and other camp followers. A notorious military strategy of 'posts and flying columns' was deployed when only 'mobile column' principle was ineffective to suppress the rising. It was, in practice, the military occupation of the hills, where the Kuki hills (covering an area of 6-7000 square miles) was divided into 6 areas, each area being enclosed by military outposts (of 50 rifles each) as blockhouses to hem the movement, and within which stronger mobile columns were deployed to pursue the Kukis and to 'do all damage possible'. In both the phases, the military operations were carried by the combined forces of Assam and Burma provinces.

The instruction of government was to go easy: "no force should be used except for the purpose of preserving order."[12] However, the military operations against the Kukis turned out to be one of the most brutal and inhuman operations in colonial history. As the usual principle of 'mobile column' in the region, the military forces, in the first phases, burned down all the rebel villages, destroyed all their food supplies, livestock and other properties, in the villages and hidden granaries, and returned to the plain. The destruction was completed. The objective was to punish the rebels in this way so that they may eventually surrender where there is no food and so on to live on. Reporting on the consequence of the operation, J.B. Marshall, DC, Upper Chindwin District, informed: "Consequently, the destruction of grain and cattle was very thorough, the punishment of villages by burning was systematic, and the rebels were driven out and had to take refuge further north."[13]

The thoroughness of destruction was, however, not able to break the spirit of Kuki resistance. Lieut. Col. French-Mullen, DIG, Burma Military Police, felt that such a scorched-earth policy "has always subdued rebellious savages and semi-civilized races" but it could "not break their [Kuki] morale as we did elsewhere."[14] W.A. Cosgrave, the PA in Manipur also frankly admitted that "the suppression of the Kuki rebellion is too big a matter for our Assam Rifles and that the operations next cold weather should be made over to the Military Department."[15] This was the view shared by all the frontier officers that the second phase of operation was, therefore, carried out under Army Department of Government of India (GoI).

In the second phase, the military operations, under the new method of 'posts and flying columns', had caused maximum damage to the Kuki villages than it was in previous year operations. Now, the Kukis were enclosed and fortified by the chain of military outposts into 6 areas, it was much easier for the flying columns not only to do all damage possible to their villages, granaries, livestock, and other properties but also to pursue the Kuki rebels from hills to hills and deep into the jungles. Being unable to run very far now as they have been encircled by military on all sides, the hot pursuits against them by the strong mobile columns were very effective in rendering the wholesale surrender of the rebels and civilians or killing them if they fought back. In the process, there was wholesale devastation of the rebel villages, granaries, livestock, and other properties. They were also prevented from cultivation and rebuilding their villages. The whole populations were driven into the forest without food and clothing during the chilly winter of the mountain massif. Hundreds of people died due to starvation, cold, epidemic diseases, and so on. The sepoys also killed hundreds of them in the hot pursuits.

Those who were captured or those who had surrendered were kept in detention at the 'prison of war' at Imphal and different 'Concentration Camps' in the hills until the war was completely suppressed. Some villages have been raided and civilians being burned alive or killed by bullets. Many people also died in the concentration camps and prison of war due to bad food, hard works and diseases. The sufferings of people were, therefore, immeasurable. In this way, the stubborn Kuki resistance was finally suppressed by April 1919. The official figures of damage and casualties on the Kukis (in second phase) are: 120 persons killed, 126 Kuki villages burned down, 16 villages deserted, 140 villages surrendered, and 576 mithuns destroyed. Unofficial figures are much larger than this. No figures are available for damages caused to food grains, properties and other livestock which were wholly destroyed by the troops. Casualties on British troops were 60 dead (including one British Officer), 142 wounded (including 3 British Officers), and 97 dead due to epidemic diseases; a total of 393 coolies died during the operations due to pneumonia epidemic.[16]

While their leaders have been trialed and deported to Sadiya (Assam) and Taungyi (Burma), others have been released only to work on the 'communal penal labour' punishment imposed on them and also to pay war reparation of one lakh seventy-five thousand, much of which was also to be paid in labour. By May 1919, the hills of Manipur, Somra Tracts and part of unadministered areas inhabited by the Kukis were handed over to the civil administration. In Manipur, three subdivisions were established in the north-eastern, north-western and south-western hills where the northern and south-eastern hills were brought under direct Sadar subdivision of Imphal. This is the story of a small tribal community challenging the most powerful Empire of the world and the way a merciless colonial army had to suppress the rising with the brute 'force of arms'. The military brutality was something not unknown in colonial world, but something quite rare in British empire which Indian nationalists termed it as the 'brute force in all its hideous nakedness'. I would like to close this section with as quotation from an American Baptist missionary lady at Haka, Chin Hills, Mrs. Laura Carson, who had witnessed the British brutalities and called it as 'shameless', 'brutal' and 'inhuman':

"The relief column remained behind to do a shameless

> thing. They went to Hniarlawn, which has been the leading village in the rebellion, and shot the cattle and hogs, confiscated the grain and fowls and burned the village a thoroughly German performance and quite unworthy of the British government. The poor women and the children will have to sleep in the jungle and we are having freezing weather. I do not see what is to prevent many of them starving to death. It is brutal and inhuman and *I resent it with all the strength of my soul.*"[17]

How it was known in Colonial Officialdom?

Lt. Gen. H.D'U. Keary, GOC, Burma Division, and the Command of Kuki Operation, for instance, commended the Kuki fighting spirit in the following way:

> "The Kukis, who numbered at least 8 to 1, were fighting in country that *neutralized* to a great degree our superiority in modern weapons. Moreover, they were *not lacking in courage or skill.*"[18]

The experience gained in the first phase, the introduction of Stokes mortars, rifle grenades and Lewis guns was, according to him, decisive in their defeat.[19] He, therefore, recommended to the Army Headquarters that Kukis should form part of the colonial armies in the future.

There is fine soldierly material in the Northern Chin, and I have every reason to anticipate that they and the Kuki will in time make a useful addition to our local irregular forces, and ultimately to the Army.[20]

Col. L.W. Shakespear also similarly wrote on the Kuki war in his book:

> "The rapidly spreading rising amongst the Kuki clans was disconcerting and most difficult to deal with.... It grew therefore into the largest series of military operations conducted on this side of India since the old expeditionary days... eclipsing them all in casualties and arduousness of active service."[21]

An 'extract' from the proceedings of the Chief Commissioner of Assam puts as follows:

> "The Kuki rising of 1917-1919... is the most formidable with which Assam has been faced for at least a generation... In all, the rebel villages held... over some 6,000 square miles of rugged hills surrounding the Manipur Valley and extending to the Somra Tract and the Thaungdut State in Burma."[22]

Sir Robert Reid, another official historian of North East India, also wrote in his book:

> "The most serious incident in the history of Manipur and its relations with its Hill subject was the Kuki Rebellion. Commencing in the closing days of 1917, it cost 28 lakhs of rupees to quell, and in the course of it many lives were lost."[23]

J.H. Hutton, Deputy Commissioner of Naga Hills, and one of the Political Officer of Kuki Operations and well versed with Kuki life and lore, also wrote, later:

> "The operations against the rebellious Thado of the Manipur State in 1918 and 1919 led to a very much better acquaintance with him, and from then onwards the more I have seen of the Thado, the more I have respected him and the better I have liked him."[24]

Various field reports also show how fighting against the Kuki tactic of 'hit and run' or 'guerilla warfare' was most tedious and demoralizing to the troops. In this respect, the ground-driven experience of the sepoys, as has been described by Lieut. Col. J.L.W. Ffrench-Mullen, become instructive:

> "There is nothing more disheartening to troops than chasing the elusive savage through his dense jungles never really scoring off him, on the contrary suffering daily casualties with the very remote chance if lucky of 'downing' a sniper. Always every moment of the 24 hours,

> whether in the camp or on the march, [they were] in danger of a shot from the surrounding jungle. Nothing to show for weeks and months of effort, no rest and no relaxation of mind or body, bad food and an entire absence of the amenities of life. These operations have no glamour for those engaged, far from it. They are thankless, disagreeable jobs which have to be got over and which involve a serious risk to life and health."[25]

Seeing the performances of the Kukis in various encounters, Lt. Col. Ffrench-Mullen also provided some of his general estimations of the Kuki warriors.

1. They 'are born snipers and can creep up to a camp at night without a sound'.
2. They 'are certainly to be called brave as they take big risks in these efforts to shoot our people especially British Officers'.
3. They 'have been known to stand the scorching fire of seven-pounder mountain guns and Lewis guns at close range and then pop up and snipe at our columns from the very place on which the scorching fire had been directed'.[26]

He called them as the 'crafty jungle fighters on their own chosen terrain'.

Finally, Kuki Operations was accepted by the British War Office as part of the Great War and Manipur as one of the Great War theatre. Accordingly, the two IWW medals, British War Medal 1914-1919 and Victory Medal, were given to them, making it the 'humble part of the Great War'. Therefore, we have the forgotten Great War theatre in Manipur.

How this important world event in the region remain unknown and unremembered till today then? There are some important factors for the invisibility of it which we intend to bring out in the following sections. Before we do that, let us see how this event has been not an exclusive affairs of the Kukis. It would be too difficult to accept by both the Kukis and other communities that the Anglo-Kuki War has been the war where all the communities of Manipur had a share in it in one way or the other, which the present ethnic contestation would find it very difficult to accept. While some Meitei revolutionaries had actually fuelled and participated in the war, many Nagas had actually helped the Kukis (interpreted by British as under duress and extortions, and being accepted in the present as it was) in construction of stockades, fortifications, supplying provisions, guns, ammunitions etc.

This is not to deny also the fact that all the people of Manipur suffered from the war. Kuki community, as the target of British forces, suffered most. Many hill villages (of both the Kukis and Nagas), considered to be 'friendly villages' by the British, have also been destroyed (causing several deaths) by the British (to prevent being used by the Kukis for procuring their supplies) and by the Kuki rebels (due to their support to British forces and denying help to them or in certain cases in revenge of attacking the villages of certain Kuki chiefs, taking advantage of their weak position under the colonial military violence). While killing of innocent people in any form cannot be justified by history, history also has it that beyond such killing under the war circumstances there was also ample evidence to show that there was a very strong sense of anti-colonial feeling among the people of Manipur. This, they actually poured out, in secret or explicit manner, by helping the Kuki rebels who had actually fought the established colonial regime. In the following section, I will show the case of collaboration between the Kuki and Meitei during the war.

Kuki-Meitei Connection: Chingakham Sanachaoba Singh and the Kuki Rising

Soon after the Mombi Kuki village was burned by the British troops, and seeing the war cry among the Kukis against the British in the hills, a group of Meitei revolutionaries, under Chinga Khamba Sana Chauba Singh (Chingakham Sanachaoba Singh) climbed up the Thangjing ranges and held a meeting with the Kuki chiefs at Ukha.[27] Chingakham Sanachaoba Singh told the Kuki chiefs that the British rule is coming to an end and that it was time to expel them from Manipur by force. He told them that the Kukis should fight from the hills and his men (the Meiteis, of which he said he had 3 companies of sepoys) should fight from the valley. He assured them safety from the bullets through his mystical power. His objective of the war was to expel the British from Manipur and uproot the Maharaja of Manipur, who was there as a mere puppet of British. Thus, he told the gathering Kuki chieftains that he will take only one rupee as house-tax (instead of 3 rupees they were paying at that time) when he becomes the Maharaja of Manipur. After such agreement was reached with the Kuki chiefs, Chingakham Sanachaoba Singh then circulated bullets and other articles among the Kuki chieftains with the intention of stirring up armed rebellion against the Government. He sent *dao* to Tintong, Khutinthang, Ngulbul, Ngulkhup, and Pache with an order to wage war on the Government and cut the telegraph wire.

The above agreement and other activities are evident from the joint 'memorial' of 12 Kuki political prisoners to the Advisory Committee (a civil tribunal set up to trial the case):

> "About 15 days after burning the Mombi village, Chinga Khamba Sana Chauba Singh Manipuri came to Wokha [Ukha] and called the following villages, *viz.* Hinglep, Mombi, Lungja, Sangphu, Nevil, Jingkai, Khabang, Phaibong, Jownai and Gowthang, and said that the Kingdom of the British is coming about an end now and wants his people to be killed at the same place with them. Chinga Khamba Sanachauba Singh also told us that he had got three companies of sepoys and 8 men who are very expert in using swords. If any Kuki villages do not obey my orders he is my enemy. Government takes Rs. 3 per house as house-tax but I will take only Re. 1 per house. You the Kukis to kill the Chaukidars of Dak-Banglow and cut off the telegraph lines and I will attack the Government at Imphal, then the Government cannot do anything to us."[28]

This was also confirmed by J.C. Higgins report during the time:

> "I also received report from Moirang that the Haokips of the south-west were under the leadership of a Manipuri named Chingakhamba Sanachaoba Singh, whom they believed... to be a scion of the old ruling branch of the royal family."[29]

The agreement to fight together against the government first turned into a reality on 19 December, 1917 when, under the leadership of 4 or 5 Meiteis, the Kukis attacked Manipur State forest toll station at Ithai. It was planned by Chingakham Sanachaoba Singh. The report described the incident as follows:

> "Before any action was taken on our part, on the 19th December Kukis from Ukha, Hinglep and neighbouring villages, headed by 4 or 5 Manipuris, raided the Manipur State forest toll station at Ithai. This raid is found to have been planned by Chingakhamba Singh, a Manipuri of bad character with reputed magic powers, living by his wits."[30]

However, due to this attack the British forces had immediately clamped down on all the Meitei revolutionaries and very soon broke the spine of the revolution in the valley. Thus, on 8 January, 1918, nine of the Meitei revolutionaries, who were associated with Chingakham Sanachaoba Singh, were arrested from Kumbi. They were sent to Imphal for trial and imprisonment.[31] Chingakham Sanachaoba Singh however managed to escape and took shelter among the Kukis in the hills. With the help of Kukis, he managed to reach up to the Thaungdut State of Burma, possibly for seeking its support. However, to his amazement the Thaungdut State ruler, which was also loyal to British, arrested him and gave him up to British authority. He was then transferred to Manipur where he stayed in Imphal jail until the Kuki rising was suppressed in 1919. Along with 12 Kuki chiefs, he was trialed at Kohima under Bengal Regulation III of 1818 and incarcerated at Dibrugarh jail (Assam).

The cases against Chingakham Sanachaoba Singh before the Advisory Committee are as follows:

1. That he falsely proclaimed himself as the elder brother of the Maharaja of Manipur.
2. That he instigated Kukis and others to make war on the Government with a view to establishing himself as Maharaja.
3. That he visited Ukha with this object.
4. That he circulated bullets and other articles with the intention of stirring up armed rebellion against the Government.
5. That he sent a *dao* to Tintong, chief of Laiyong and Khutinthang chief of Jampi; another *dao* to Ngulbul, chief

> of Longya and thence to Ngulkhup, chief of Mombi, and a third to Ngulbul chief of Longya and thence to Pachei, chief of Chassad, with orders in each case to make war on the Government and to cut the telegraph wires.

The Committee found that "the evidence on record and the statements of many of the chiefs, leave no doubts as to the part which Chinga Khamba played in the rebellion." It went on remarking that "his claim to supernatural powers seems to have been readily accepted by the rebel chiefs, while the false stories that he spread about the straits to which the British Government had been reduced, greatly encouraged them."[32]

Due to his health, Chingakham Sanachaoba Singh was later transferred to Shillong jail in 1920. As there was a strong objection for his release from the Darbar and the Maharaja of Manipur, he stayed back in jail when the Kuki chiefs were released in 1922. Government wanted to release him in 1925 but due to opposition from Maharaja and Darbar that he continue to serve in prison. In 1927 another proposal for his release was moved by government and the Darbar also agreed on condition that he should not enter Manipur ever. However, when Chingakham Sanachaoba Singh refused to go to any place other than Manipur, the government continue to detain him in jail. In October 1929, he was finally released when he was willing to settle in Dimapur and promised not to enter Manipur ever on condition that he should be recommitted to jail for disobedience. Therefore, he was settled down at Dimapur, on his wish and with the approval of the Darbar of Manipur. However, having no source of livelihood, he was literally begging for a living. Therefore, he very soon escaped from Dimapur and secretly entered Manipur again, staying there as a fugitive for about four months, possibly among the Kukis. He was arrested again in March 1930 and trialed at the court of the Political Agent in Manipur who had sentenced him to 3 months rigorous imprisonment for 'disobedience' under section 188 of IPC.

Meanwhile, the Government of India sanctioned the detention of Chingakham Sanachaoba Singh at Sylhet Jail for another one year, following the expiry of his three months RI at Imphal jail, for disobeying the earlier order not to enter Manipur. He was released from Imphal jail on 4 June, 1930 and straightaway taken to Sylhet jail where he was committed on 6 June, 1930. After one year of detention there, he was again released on 5 June, 1931 and finally settled down in Cachar among the Meitiei community there. Colonial records are completely silent on him after this. It is not possible from our present knowledge whether he had continued to engage with his revolutionary movement there or not. We can only assume that he did so secretly considering the air of revolution in Cachar in the 1930s and 1940s.

Chingakham Sanachaoba Singh movement had been so badly coloured by the British that it continues to remain unknown to us until today. He was said to be priest, 'pretender', 'magician', 'unscrupulous and clever adventurer', and so on. The Advisory Committee, for instance, declared that 'though his name contains the appellation "Sana" which is usually confined to members of the royal family of Manipur, he is of common birth and no social position, and that he is merely an unscrupulous and clever adventurer, who saw an opportunity of bettering himself in troublous times'.[33] J.C. Higgins also reported of Chingakham Sanachaoba Singh as:

> "This man is a notorious Manipuri who lives by his wits. He is credited with various occult powers, such as the raising of spirits. It is reported that he gained influence over the Kukis recently by allowing them to fire at close range at a pig, which escaped unharmed—probably a variation of the old bullet conjuring trick, which Houdin played on the Arabs."[34]

Regardless of his lineage, Chingakham Sanachaoba Singh was certainly a revolutionary with exceptional quality. It was said that he migrated from Imphal to the southern margin of the valley, probably when the WW1 broke out, in order to start a revolutionary movement there. He possessed the art of performing some strange magic, which played immense role in his campaign, taking a sort of millenarian movement. The so-called 'occult powers', 'conjuring trick', 'supernatural powers' or 'false stories' that he had used, how shabby it could have been to the British, were certainly to play magic among the downtrodden and infuriated ordinary people of the valley and the hills. Because of his mystical power, he had actually assumed a millenarian figure among the people who knew him to restore the old glory of Manipur and thus showed a great hope in his movement. He took his base at Kumbi from where he started the movement among the local populace and had a great influence among the people, including the hill people who had frequented the valley for trade or otherwise. It is obvious that any revolutionary minded people would take the opportunity created by the WW1 in order overthrow the established authority. The marching of soldiers and officers to the warfront was visible before everyonen's eye and rumours of British withdrawal, as we noted, had been already in vogue in the valley at the outbreak of the war, in 1915.

As a scion of the old royal household, Chingakham Sanachaoba Singh would surely had disagreement with the prevailing system where the king was reduced to a mere puppet under the colonial power, the idea which many royal bloodlines would share at that time. As an ordinary person, the prevailing regime, which had become so corrupted with power and wealth, has generated much resentment from the mass. The growing taxation regime, extortions and intolerance within the power clichés *vis-à-vis* the growing poverty and hardships in the state would certainly form the sources of disenchantment to many people. The rise of Chingakham Sanachaoba Singh would, therefore, be much welcomed by the people had it not been immediately nipped to the bud by the colonial repressive forces.

Yet, despite stringent laws against any support to the rebels, we can still see section of valley people supplying food and other items to the Kuki rebels. For instance, it was reported that 'the Kukis are in touch with some sections of the Manipuris themselves, and that certain villages of Lois... have contributed rice and rice-beer to the Kukis'.[35] At the height of the war, W.A. Cosgrave, the Political Agent in Manipur, also reported that the Manipuris in Moirang area were 'helping rebel Kuki villages with supplies of food'. He had arrested four men of village Nganka Lowai who 'had been selling large supplies of food to rebel Kukis'. He sent them to Imphal where they were tried for 'trading with the enemy'.[36] Col. L.W. Shakespear, who commanded Assam Rifles and was involved in the operations from the beginning, also reported during the height of the war that the Kuki rebels continue to received provisions from the valley through the 'friendlies': 'Kukis obtain supplies etc., by commandeering from friendly villages and also still trade with the Valley through "friendlies" too weak to refuse, cotton for clothes we know passes to them from the Shuganu side to south'.[37] He, therefore, suggested the policy of what he called 'blockade and detention camps', which, however, was not accepted due to high cost of doing it. The point is that, Kukis continue to receive supplies from the valley population during the war, of course with utmost secrecy, which could not have been possible unless there was any tacit understanding between them.

The secret understanding between the hills and valley people was also visible from the fact that the Kuki revolutionaries had not harm any Meitei civilians although the British propaganda hyped the dreads of Kuki attack across the valley. W.A. Cosgrave, for instance, reported that the Manipuris of Palel remain calm and peaceful because they said that the Kukis do 'little or nothing to harm the Manipuri villagers'. He went on saying that three large parties of Manipuri traders returned from the Kabaw valley (Burma) through the Tamu bridle path and without meeting any sort of molestation from the Kukis. He remarked:

> "This confirms my opinion that the Kukis are not up against Manipuris but only against the sahebs and their subordinates. The Kukis were clever enough to understand that the administration of the hill tracts of Manipur is not in the hands of the Manipuris but of the sahebs whom they regard as responsible for all their troubles about recruitment for the labour corps."[38]

It was true that the hills was not in the hands of Meiteis but the fact that Meitei civilians were not harmed by Kukis was not without any substance related to their relationship during the war. We have already noted that the agreement between the Kuki chiefs and Chingakham Sanachaoba Singh to fight together against the government, the Kukis from the hills and Meiteis from the valley. Although Meitei forces were very soon decimated due to the large presence of colonial forces in the valley, the Kukis, who continue to fight the British, adhered to such agreement. We have already noted how the valley populations secretly transited food and other items to the Kuki revolutionaries, which was not possible unless there were some friendly attitudes toward the rising. Overall, one can say that the Kukis and Meiteis, certainly not the population who had supported the Maharaja, were friends and allies in the war against the colonial regime during the Great War.

Why Anglo-Kuki War Remains Unknown?

Why and how this longest anti-colonial uprising and largest military operation in the region became invisible, unknown and unremembered today? This event was not known much until scholars buried their heads into the deep, dark and decomposed files of the colonial archives in recent time. Under the world war circumstance, the frontier operations were carried out in complete secrecy from press and Indian public. The operations were carried in so secrecy that even the British Parliamentarians were not aware of its existence during the time. Only in later period they started questioning about the medals to be granted to the combatants and non-combatants participating in the Kuki Operations. For instance, on 1 June, 1921 Sir C. Yate asked the Secretary of State for India (in British Parliament): "whether the Indian frontier medal is to be granted for the operations in the Kuki Hills?" Mr. Montagu, the Secretary of State answered: "The question of an award for the operations in the Kuki Hills is under consideration with the War Office, and it is hoped that a decision may be reached shortly."

Again, on 30 April, 1923, Sir A. Holbrook asked the Under Secretary of State for War (in British Parliament): "when the Indian general service medal will be issued to troops engaged in the Kuki Chin operations on the North East Indian Frontier in 1918?" The Under Secretary of State for War (Lieut. Colonel Guinness) answered: "The India general service medal is not issuable for these operations. The troops in question are eligible for the British war and victory medals, which are being issued to them in ordinary course." Sir A. Holbrook then questioned: "Were not special medals issued for the North West India operations of a similar character?" Lieut. Colonel Guiness answered: "In any case, they could not possibly get both the special medal and Great War medals for the same operation, and the grant of the two great War medals would seem to have been the more favourable alternative."[39] Sir A. Holbrook did not realised, and for that the British Parliament, that 'Kuki Operations' was considered by the British War Office as part of the First World War operations and for that the officers, soldiers, camp followers and labourers have been already granted, and issued, the two Great War Medals—the British War Medal 1914-1919 and the Victory Medal.[40]

Some important factors also make this event unknown to the world. First, it was relatively insignificant to the First World War fought in Europe. This was particularly due to its geographical remoteness. Second, the inhuman military operations were secreted from press and world public, and then classified in the colonial archives, partly, to evade public outcry from Indian nationalists, and partly, to save the image of British Empire from any criticism that could come from the rival empires like Germany. Such secrecy becomes particularly necessary when Government of India was criticized from the Indian nationalists due to the only press report at the beginning of the operation. As usual, the Assam Government had issued a press communiqué in February 1918 and received a sharp reaction from Indian nationalists. For instance, *The New India,* mouthpiece of the India's Home Rule Movement, made a scathing attack on British government, saying:

> "The Bureaucrats in India have been, with respect to these hill tribes [of Assam], behaving in a way not quite different from [Germans] atrocities in Belgium... The brute force in all its hideous nakedness is found perpetrating its havoc in both places.... To destroy villages on such a systematic scale and to harass people until... they surrender to any conditions of life...—are these practices to be tolerated by a civilized Nation like England?"[41]

It condemned British military actions as barbaric, brutal and inhuman and warned the British government that its 'tragic inhumanity' will be revealed to the world if it did not stop the inhuman operations. It urged the Viceroy and the Secretary of State to 'order an immediate cessation of the brutality' and to institute 'a searching enquiry to find out who are actually responsible for initiating them'.[42]

Similarly, the *India* newspaper in London, the mouthpiece of the Congress, also condemned the actions as impulsive, intemperate and brutal:

> "What actually provoked these ignorant people to adopt this desperate remedy is not disclosed. Instead of endeavouring to allay their fears and suspicions, measures of reprisal were taken at once."[43]

It questioned on the very method of 'pacification' and demanded that this 'ought to be elucidated in the House of Commons' (in British Parliament). Thus, to avoid such embarrassment and criticism, and also save the image of British Empire, the Kuki operations were eventually carried out in complete isolation. It was under compulsion that the operations were carried out in isolation.

How do we Remember the Anglo-Kuki War?

When Manipur was a Union Territory, the Central Government granted a plot of land and war memorial hall to the Kuki war veterans to commemorate the Kuki rising and their participation in INA movement. However, after Manipur got statehood in 1972, no memorial was constructed or no grant was given for construction of any monument, not to speak of according any state commemoration to the Anglo-Kuki War. The state government had given its full attention to the Anglo-Manipur War 1891, constructing monuments and memorials, and commemorating the event with two state holidays. For a statewide commemoration of the event, it declared 23 April and 13 August every year as 'Khongjom Day' and 'Patriot's Day' respectively. Both the public holidays are still celebrated with statewide celebration every year. To this was later added 'Nupi Lan' and 'Hijam Irabot' days. However, despite its importance in Manipur history, the Anglo-Kuki War continues to remain unnoticed by the state of Manipur as if it never existed. While the event is known to everyone, all pretended to remain ignorant about it. The conspiracy of silence and forgetting on the part of the state government reduced this major event in North East Indian history as the forgotten episode in the history.

The politics of remembering is very easy to comprehend. History has become victim of narrow ethnic politics and contestation of the present. Since the state government is dominated by the valley population, the history of Manipur is considered to be only the history of the valley people, in which the history of Manipur kingdom has assumed a prime position. In this, the history of the hill people, how important and large it would have been, has become unimportant, inappropriate and even extraneous to Manipur history. An interesting episode, in relation to Jadonang, is instructive of how history has become victim in the whirlpool of ethnic politics. His death anniversary was once declared as state holiday when a Naga chief minister was there. However, it was immediately withdrawn when a Meitei chief minister came in power. Interestingly, the withdrawal was on the ground of Jadonang being capitally punished by British for murdering 3 Meiteis for a human sacrifice. The projection of him as 'freedom fighter' by his community could not actually sit well with the ethnic sentiment of the politically dominant Meitei community who held the state government. No wonder, ethnic sentiment continues to determine history writing and public discourse in history in the state. It was within this strand of ethnic politics of remembering that the Anglo-Kuki War has become one major victim.

Kukis had given representation after representation to successive government of Manipur for state recognition of the Anglo-Kuki War as one of the important events in the history of Manipur and hence accordingly commemorate with one state public holiday. However, it continues to fall on the deaf ear of state. No particular reason was ever given for the denial nor was it even taken up for discussion in the state assembly. The silence of state is unique. It amounts to what Eviator Zerubavel has called the 'conspiracy of silence', a phenomenon which highlights the fundamental tension between personal awareness and public discourse. It was the condition in which everyone is personally aware of the facts but which they ignore it collectively. It revolves around undiscussable, let alone unmentionable, truth that is generally known but cannot be spoken. It was the 'uncomfortable truths hidden in plain sight'. Here, the muteness, the silence of state may be plainly see in terms of the prevailing ethnic politics in the state. Since the anti-colonial movement was seen to be the 'Kuki war of independence', as the Kuki themselves has claimed, and the hill tribal subject, it rarely sit well with the historical imagination of the Meitei dominated Manipur state.

It is true that the backbone of the Anglo-Kuki War was the Kukis. But it is also true that many other non-Kuki people also joined them in the war, directly or indirectly. What is still truer is that the Anglo-Kuki War was:

1. disconcerting and most difficult to deal with and the

largest series of military operations conducted on this side of India;

2. the most formidable with which Assam has been faced for at least a generation; and
3. the most serious incident in the history of Manipur and its relations with its Hill subject.

Either we like it or not, this is what history has it. It is 'the elephant in the room', too big to deny to post-colonial freed society whose objective was to build a new society on the ruins of colonial rule. It can only be denied any state-sponsored public spaces in the state in the form of what Jay Winter has called 'banned speech' or what Paul Connerton has called 'repressive erasure' or 'prescriptive forgetting'.

Conclusion: What would Manipur benefit from remembering the hill chapters?

Scholars around the world have shown that remembering, as a living social process, help the present society to integrate or disintegrate. Integration takes place when all members of the society can have a shared memory and historical imagination. Disintegration takes place when different groups in the society have different and contested memory. Eviatar Zerubavel has, for instance, said that remembering, as a social process, is a means of:

> "...acquiring a group's memories and thereby identifying with its collective past is part of the process of acquiring any social identity, and familiarising members with that past is a major part of communities efforts to assimilate them."[44]

State can play a major role in this process of acquiring and integrating public memory and familiarizing its members with the objective of assimilating or integrating them to acquire a similar social identity. This is particularly so in a multi-ethnic multi-cultural societies like Manipur. This will be possible only when the state recognizes all the major historical events of the state, possessed by different groups and brought together under state commemorative ceremonies and memorials.

What Manipur state did so far is rather the reverse of what we have seen from the experiences of other countries in the world. I have written on this aspect few years back but nothing has happen even after that. Like many other states in India or many countries around the world, the urgent need of Manipur state is integration of the state, which means integration of the people. Physical integration would be impossible until there is an emotional and mental integration. This emotional integration can best be done by integrating the historical imagination of the different groups within the state. The fact that *only* the history of valley people (that too only the dominant Meitei community) is recognized by the state and commemorated in state-sponsored public spaces had generated the sense of neglect and forgetting in the minds of the hill people who also wanted to participate in politics in their own vernacular. This act of forgetting and silence on the part of state and the sense of neglect and abandonment produced a dangerous course of fissiparous tendency in the mind of the hill people. The inability of state-sponsored public history (the 'official memory') to climb up in the hills and the growing numbers of 'vernacular or unofficial memory/memorials' in the hills produced a situation of competing memories, politics and identities which is presently driving the state politics on a slippery slope.

It is within the above noted situation that Manipur state must willy-nilly act on what is written on the wall. These are the emotional needs of different groups in the society and state must strive to satisfy them or else run the hazard of contesting hopelessly with the counter-memories of the groups in question. This would be unwelcomed proposition to some people, many valley people may dislike the idea, many hillmen may not wanted to sacrifice what they consider as 'theirs', but state must act for the common interest of the people who are ready to go with the state project if their aspiration of participating in politics in their vernacular is ensured. This is the writing on the wall, which the state government cannot continue to ignore them. This is necessarily the first step towards the integration of Manipur.

And *lest I forget*, let us not forget the Anglo-Kuki War and the Meitei revolutionary Chingakham Sanachaoba Singh who gave all his for Manipur and who had joined hands with the hill Kukis in fighting the government with the objective of abolishing the oppressive British government in the region and *restoring* the old traditional governments.

Notes

1. British Library (BL), London, Asian and African Collections, Indian Office Records and Private Papers (IOR), IOR/L/PS/10/724: 1917-1920, File No. P-383/1918: J.E. Webster, CS Assam to S.R. Hignell, Secy. to GoI, 7 Nov. 1917.
2. See the 'Memorandum' of Kuki political prisoners to Commissioner, Surma Valley and Hill Districts', as appended in the letter of Webster to Hignell, 27 June, 1919, BL, IOR/L/PS/10/724: 1917-1920, File No. P-6933/1919. See also National Archives of India (NAI), Foreign and Political Deptt. (hereafter FP), Secret-External, July 1918, Nos. 7-131: Webster to Hignell, 7 Nov. 1917.
3. More than 8,000 'able bodied men' had eventually went to France. 750 Kukis had also indeed went to France.
4. Manipur State Archives (MSA), Imphal, R-2/230/S-4: *Higgins Tour Diary*, 10-11 Oct., 1917; BL, IOR/L/PS/10/724: 1917-1920, File No. P-6933/1919: Webster to Hignell, 27 June 1919.
5. See MSA, R-2/230/S-4, *Higgins Tour Diary*, 13-18 Oct. 1917.
6. See MSA, R-2/230/S-4: *Higgins Tour Diary*, 1 and 8 Nov. and 1 Dec. 1917; D.L. Haokip (ed.), *Documents of Anglo-Kuki War*, pp. 65-74.
7. BL, IOR/L/PS/10/724: 1917-1920, File No. 2686/1919: 'Report on the Rebellion of the Kukis' by J.B. Marshall, DC, Upper Chindwin District. *n.d.*
8. *Documents of Anglo-Kuki War*, pp. 65-74.
9. BL, IOR/L/PS/10/724: 1917-1920, File No. P-2686/1919: Lt. Col. JLW Ffrench-Mullen, DIG, Burma Military Police to IGP Burma, 17 Sept. 1918.
10. Assam State Archives (ASA), Dispur, File No. M/64-P of 1918, Pol. B, March 1919, No. 132: Telegram from Imphal to CS, Assam, 2 Feb. 1918; see also BL, IOR/L/PS/10/724: 1917-1920, Telegram from CS, Burma to Foreign Secy. GOI, 4 Feb. 1918; BL, IOR/L/PS/10/724: 1917-1920, File No. P-2686/1919: Lt. Col. JLW Ffrench-Mullen to IGP Burma, 17 Sept. 1918.
11. MSA, R-2/230/S-4: *Cosgrave Tour Diary*, 18 March 1918.
12. BL, IOR/L/PS/10/724: 1917-1920, File No. 5115/1917: Foreign Secy. GoI to Webster, 26 Nov. 1917.
13. BL, IOR/L/PS/10/724: 1917-1920, File No. 2686/1919: 'Report on the Rebellion of the Kukis' by J.B. Marshall, DC, Upper Chindwin District. *n.d.*

14. BL, IOR/L/PS/10/724: 1917-1920, File No. P-2686/1919: Lt. Col. JLW Ffrench-Mullen to IGP Burma, 17 Sept. 1918.
15. ASA, File No. 9C/M-61P of 1918, Pol. A, March 1919, Nos. 1—255: Cosgrave to Webster, 18 May 1918.
16. BL, IOR/L/MIL/17/19/42: 1919: 'Despatch on the Operations', Macquoid to Keary, 27 April 1919, Appendix—II and III.
17. Laura S. Carson, *Pioneer Trails, Trials and Triumph.* New York: Baptist Board Publication, 1927, p. 182.
18. BL, IOR/L/MIL/17/19/42: 1919, 'Despatch on the Operations Against the Kuki Tribes of Assam and Burma, November 1917 to March 1919', Lieut.-Gen. Sir H.D'U. Keary, GOC, Burma Division to Chief of the General Staff, Army Hqtrs. June 1919.
19. BL, IOR/L/MIL/17/19/42: 1919, 'Despatch on the Operations', Lieut.-Gen. Sir H.D'U. Keary to Chief of the General Staff, Army Hqtrs. June 1919.
20. *Ibid.*
21. Shakespear, *History of the Assam Rifles*, pp. 224, 235-236.
22. BL, Mss. Eur E 325/13: 1920, 'Extract from the proceeding of the Chief Commissioner of Assam in Political Department' by A.W. Botham, 27 Sept. 1920.
23. Robert Reid, *History of the frontier areas bordering on Assam from 1883-1941*, Concept, New Delhi, 1997 [1942], p. 79.
24. J.H. Hutton in Shaw, *Notes on the Thadou Kukis*, p. 23, fn. 1.25.
25. BL, IOR/L/PS/10/724: 1917-1920, File No. P-2686/1919: Lt. Col. JLW Ffrench-Mullen to IGP Burma, 17 Sept. 1918.
26. BL, IOR/L/PS/10/724: 1917-1920, File No. P-2686/1919: Lt. Col. JLW Ffrench-Mullen to IGP Burma, 17 Sept. 1918.
27. Chingakham Sanachaoba Singh (rather than Chinga Khamba Sana Chauba Singh as used in colonial records) is apparently the better appellation as used by the Maharaja Chura Chand Singh in his letter.
28. Manipur Secretariat Library (MSL), Cabin No. 26, Office of the Pol. Agent in Manipur, File No. 388: 'Correspondence about release of Chinga Khamba Sana Chaoba Singh and Kuki rebellion': Memorial of 12 Kuki political prisoners at Kohima Jail to the Comm. Of Surma Valley and Hill Districts (through the DC, Naga Hills), 18 May 1919, p. 86.
29. MSA, R-2/230/S-4: *Higgins Tour Diary*, 22 December 1917: Imphal to Bishanpur.
30. BL, IOR/L/PS/10/724 (1917-1920), File No. P-6933/1919: Webster to Hignell, 27 June 1919.
31. ASA, File No. M/64-P of 1918, Pol. B, March 1919, No. 99: Heggins to Webster, camp Moirang, 8 Jan. 1918.
32. MSL, Cabin No. 26, Office of the Pol. Agent in Manipur, File No. 388: 'Correspondence about release of Chinga Khamba Sana Chaoba

Singh and Kuki rebellion': J.E. Webster, Secy. to CC Assam to Secy. GoI, F&P Dept., 27 June 1919.

33. MSL, Cabin No. 26, Office of the Pol. Agent in Manipur, File No. 388: Correspondence about release of Chinga Khamba Sana Chaoba Singh and Kuki rebellion: Webster to Hignell, 27 June 1919.
34. MSA, R-2/230/S-4: *Higgins Tour Diary*, 22 December 1917: Imphal to Bishanpur.
35. BL, IOR/L/PS/10/724 (1917-1920), File No. 3931/1919: Webster to Secy. GoI, F&P, 14 (15) Dec. 1917.
36. MSA, R-2/230/S-4: *Cosgrave Tour Diary*, 26-27 Feb. 1918.
37. ASA, File No. 9C/M-61P of 1918, Plo. A, March 1919, Nos. 1-255: Shakespear to Herbert, 27 Feb. 1918.
38. ASA, File No. M/64-P of 1918, Pol. B, March 1919, No. 141: *Cosgrave Tour Diary-II*, 24 Jan. 1918.
39. See 'Kuki Hills Operations (Medal)', Hansard, 1 June 1921, http://hansard.millbanksystems.com/written_answers/1921/jun/01/kukihillsoperationsmedal (accessed 5/6/2017) and 'Indian Frontier Operations (Medals)', Hansard, 30 April 1923. http://hansard.millbanksystems.com/commons/1923/apr/30/indianfrontieroperationsmedals (accessed 5/6/2017). 'Indian Frontier Operations (Medals)', Hansard, 30 April 1923. http://hansard.millbanksystems.com/commons/1923/apr/30/indianfrontieroperationsmedals (accessed 5/6/2017).
40. See, Assam State Archives, Dispur (hereafter ASA), File No. 142/1925, Military Branch, Mil-B, June 1925, Nos. 83-175: 'War Medals in connections with Kuki Operations'.
41. See the extract of *New India* in BL, IOR/L/PS/10/724: 1917-1920, File No. 1880/1918: 'Burma-Assam Frontier: Disturbances among Kuki Tribesmen in Manipur'.
42. *Ibid.*
43. *Ibid.*
44. Eviatar Zerubavel, *Time Maps: Collective Memory and the Social Shape of the Past* (Chicago: University of Chicago Press), 2004, p. 3.

9
Analysing the Anglo-Manipur and Anglo-Assam Wars

Understanding the British Colonial Military Strategy in the North East India

L. Nishikanta Singh

Introduction

The importance of North East to the British was not only for natural resources but also as a land route to China. Geographical proximity of the North East India to China provided a closer route, i.e. through Yunnan, instead of going through the treacherous high altitude snowbound Tibet route. By the end of the nineteenth century, the British were deeply involved in the "Great Game." At this point, North East India became a new theatre of a new gambit. The British plan was to set up a buffer between China-Central Asia-Russia, and British India.

My topic is 'Colonial Military Strategy' in North East India. Before going into the nuances of colonial military strategy, let us first look into what exactly is 'Military Strategy'. For conduct of a war, planning on what is required to be achieved at the national level is done based on 'national strategy'. The military strategy derives from the National strategy and is the basis of overall military of planning. On the other hand 'Tactics' are basically the conduct of the individual soldiers or body of soldiers, units and formations during the actual fighting. The difference being strategy (military strategy) is at higher level, involving the planning, coordination, and general direction of military operations to meet overall political and military objectives. On the other hand, tactics pertains to implementing the strategy by short-term decisions on the movement of troops and employment of weapons on the field of battle, so it is at lower level. According to the great military thinker, Carl von Clausewitz "Tactics is the art of using troops in battle; strategy is the art of using battles to win the war."

We all are aware that there is a difference between wars, campaigns, battles. Since my subject pertains to military strategy, I would like to briefly touch and differentiate these three. War is between two or more countries or nations to achieve a national aim etc. A battle is between two or more armed forces. The aim and scope of battle is limited. Even geographically it is confined. Battles are usually short. It may last few hours to few days or even months. Examples are the battle of Imphal, battle of Kohima, battle of Bulge etc. When there are many battles for a long time, for control of a particular region it is called campaign, examples are the Burma campaign, North Africa campaign etc. But in a short war there may be no campaign but only battles. Many battles and campaigns make up a war. A battle/campaign achieves only tactical victory or maybe even a strategic victory. But winning a battle may not necessarily result in winning the war. For example, during the Second World War, both Germany and Japan, initially won many battles but they eventually lost the war. Similarly in Vietnam, the Americans won a number of battles but lost the war.

I will bring out the British Colonial Military strategy mainly through analysis of their military actions in Assam and Manipur. 360 fighting soldiers under a captain were involved in Assam whereas nearly 6500 soldiers under a Major General were required to tackle Manipur.

Assam

By the end of the eighteenth century, the Ahom kingdom had become unstable. The British East India Company was waiting to see the Ahom kingdom disintegrate and annex it. Major opportunity for the British came when a rebellion known as the Moamariya rebellion broke out. Gaurinath Singha, who was then king of Ahom approached the Governor General Lord Cornwallis for assistance. Here the British followed the strategy of 'intervention on invitation'. In 1792, Captain Thomas Welsh of the Bengal Army was dispatched with six companies of native soldiers, each having 60 fighting men, thus following the strategy of using natives. The total strength did not exceed 550 men which included logistic elements, a doctor with his medical team.

Their first military encounter was in November end 1792 with the king of Darrang who had occupied North Kamrup. The British first followed their military strategy of 'winning without fighting', i.e. diplomacy with show of force or simply put the carrot and stick policy and demanded the king to disband his army. This was not agreed. There were two battles and the Darrang king was defeated.

About a year later in early 1794, Captain Welsh dealt with the Moamariyas in upper Assam. Once again, to win without fighting, Captain Welsh began negotiations with them but failed, and in an armed encounter the British defeated them and reinstated Gaurinath Singha as king.

Let us examine the reasons for this small strength of approximately only 360 fighting native men of British East India Company being able to defeat a much larger native force?

The British East India Company's Infantry soldiers were better trained, better led and had superior weapons. This probably made all the difference.

They fought as a unit and knew how to use their guns, here I mean, the cannons effectively in battle.

For the actual fighting they adopted various tactical formations. A typical basic formation is line formation, here the soldiers would fire their muskets one after the other. If the line had 30 men, then 30 shots would be fired in a minute or less. When the last man had fired his weapon, the first man would be ready for his next shot. This continuous fire made the enemy advance very difficult. In the row formation, troops would form two rows, and the front row would kneel. All would fire at the same time. This tactic was called volley fire.

However, against a superior force, they deployed four rows of infantry. After the first two rows had discharged their guns, they would fall back and two fresh rows would take their place.

Regarding their weapons, by the 1790s, the soldiers of East India Company were armed with high-performance easier to load and quite accurate 0.75 calibre flintlock musket popularly known as the Brown Bess. It was used with great success in the Napoleonic Wars too. A soldier carried about 60 rounds of ammunition and could fire four rounds in a minute.

In contrast, the Moamariyas were poorly trained, poorly armed and poorly led. Besides, barring a few matchlocks which were obsolete, they did not have any worthwhile firearms. Most Moamariyas fought with whatever weapon they could find: swords, pikes, pick-axes, spears, and even bamboo sticks.

In 1794, the expedition of Captain Welsh was recalled.

Manipur

The Manipur campaign or what is commonly described as Manipur Expedition amongst the British is one of minor campaigns fought by them during the reign of Queen Victoria. This short conflict with the Manipuris was very typical of most of the colonial campaigns in Asia of that period, often beginning in similar circumstances and ending with British victory.

Even in those days to reach Imphal, there were only three axes (roads). The first was a cart track over the Naga Hill that connected with the then under construction Assam-Bengal Railway at Dimapur; another bridle-path connecting with Cachar; and the third one was connecting to the Chindwin Valley in Myanmar. Militarily the last one was considered to be important to the Manipuris as they were in perpetual conflict with the Myanmarees ruler. The Manipuris called the Myanmarees as 'Ava' and the Myanmarees called the Manipuris as 'Kate'.

Manipur and its Army: Post 1st Burmese War

The British were possibly interested in maintaining Manipur as a frontline country against Myanmar. Since the 1st Burma War, the British set about arming the Manipuris. This small Manipur army actually originated from the 'Manipur Levy', raised by Maharaja Gambhir Singh at the request of the British during the 1st Burma War, in 1824, with strength of 500 men. In subsequent years, this levy was increased to 2,000 men and British officers were deputed to train and supervise the men. The British officers were withdrawn by 1853. However, the Manipuri army continued to grow. They assisted and helped the British with troops in 1879 during the local war fought under, Lieutenant-Colonel James Johnstone. In return, the British gifted the Maharaja a large number of weapons and ammunition, and again the Manipuris contributed troops to the British in 1885 during the Third Anglo-Burmese War. Anglo-Manipur relations seemed good.

According to Mark Simner, in 1889, the strength of Manipuri Army was estimated to be about 6,200 including regulars and irregulars. It was purely infantry based army with no cavalry. For fire support, it was believed, that they had eight 3-pounder brass cannons which could fire only balls.

There was political instability even after its liberation from the Burmese. The ruling-elite of the state were squabbling over power. There was a revolt against Maharaja Sur Chandra Singh on 21 September, 1890. This led to his abdicating and fleeing the kingdom. Sur Chandra appealed to Lord Landsdowne, the Viceroy of India, for assistance. Since he had technically abdicated voluntarily and also considering Manipur's contributions to the British efforts against the Burmese, the British Indian Government declined to help Sur Chandra instead chose to recognise Kula Chandra as the rightful regent. However, they felt that there was a need to neutralise Tikendrajit, who was the *Senapati* of the Manipuri Army to ensure a lasting peace, as they felt that he was the main instigator of the revolt.

Manipur War

The Manipur war or what the Britishers call the Manipur expedition could be divided into three phases.

Phase One: Diplomacy with Show of Force

In this phase, the British conducted a typical diplomacy with show of force or coercive diplomacy. James Wallace Quinton, the Chief Commissioner of Assam, was sent to Manipur with 400 soldiers of the 42nd and 44th Gurkha Rifles (local troops) under the command of Lieutenant-Colonel Charles Skene. They arrived at Imphal on 22 March, 1891. The Manipuris extended a warm welcome. The plan was to capture Tikendrajit at a durbar. However, Tikendrajit, having been tipped off, was aware of the conspiracy. Citing ill-health, he did not attend the durbar. It was re-scheduled for the next day but he again did not come. Quinton gave an ultimatum to Kula Chandra for handing over of Tikendrajit or losing the support of the British Indian Government. The demand was declined.

Battle of Residency: Application of force commenced in the early morning of 24th March. The Gurkhas tried to arrest Tikendrajit at his home but serious fighting with the Manipuri troops broke out. Lieutenant Lionel Wilhelm Brackenbury mortally wounded. Eventually, the Gurkhas entered the house but did not find Tikendrajit. The Manipuri soldiers succeeded in pushing back the Gurkhas into the British Residency. Manipuris now attacked and fired upon the British defences inside the Residency. By 8 PM, Quinton, sensing his precarious position, requested for an armistice. Tikendrajit invited Quinton for talks. The Commissioner accepted the invitation and went for talks with four other officers. As they came out of the Residency, there was a commotion by an angry mob whose kith and kin have been killed or injured during the indiscriminate action of the British native troops and all five men killed. This perhaps was one of the very important moments in the history of Manipur. What could have happened to Manipur if the British were not killed? Would Manipur remain as a frontline country for the British?

Phase Two: Withdrawal, Link up and Rescue

Withdrawal and Link Up

The killing of the British officers was not known to the soldiers inside the residency, but there were unconfirmed reports and indicators suggesting that the Chief Commissioner was unlikely to return; for instance the firing on the residency resumed after mid-night. Those inside the residency realised that the five men were indeed unlikely to return. Because of heavy pressure from Manipuri troops, the chances of being defeated and overrun were large hence, and the British decided break contact and withdraw towards Cachar. On 26th, Captain Cowley and 200 men of the 43rd Gurkhas from Cachar **linked up** with the withdrawing party at Laimatak.

Attempted Rescue, Battle of Thoubal and Seige of British Forces

Reports on events in Manipur reached Tamu on 27 March, but the

British were not aware was that the officers had been killed. Lieutenant Chares James William Grant of the 2nd Burma Infantry volunteered to lead a group of men to **rescu**e the British prisoners. He started the following day with thirty soldiers of the 43rd Gurkhas and fifty of the 12th Madras Infantry.

On 31 March, when he reached Thoubal, he encountered about 800 Manipuri soldiers stretched out on a long front. As they advanced, the Manipuris brought down heavy fire on them, but by surging forward in a number of rushes, they eventually pushed the Manipuris to the bank of the Thoubal River. The British crossed the river and took defensive positions in a nearby village. Having been possibly reinforced, the Manipuris strength went up to around 2,000 with two guns (cannons). The Manipuris were very determined and relentlessly attacked the British force over a period of ten days till 9th April. The lieutenant, however, was equally as determined as his adversaries and demanded the release of the prisoners in return for his withdrawal. Shortly afterwards, a civilian, by the name of Williams, was handed over to Grant. He informed Grant that no other Europeans were being held at Imphal. Grant withdrew as Captain Edward Presgrave with seventy-five men relieved him. As Grant withdrew he was closely pursued by the Manipuris.

Lieutenant Grant was later awarded the 'Victoria Cross', the British highest gallantry award equivalent of our 'Param Vir Chakra' for his actions in Manipur, the citation for which was published in the London Gazette of 26 May, 1891; it read: "For the conspicuous bravery and devotion to his country displayed by him in having, upon hearing on the 27th March, 1891, of the disaster at Manipur, at once volunteered to attempt the relief of the British Captives, with 80 Native Soldiers, and having advanced with the greatest intrepidity, captured Thoubal, near Manipur, and held it against a large force of the enemy. Lieutenant Grant inspired his men with equal heroism, by an ever-present example of personal daring and resource."

The Plan Phase Three: The Punitive Attack

The Plan

The British assessed that a major operation with a much larger force with proper planning would be required to defeat the determined Manipuris and inflict proper punishment. Three brigade group task forces were to advance into Manipur on three different axes starting on different dates to converge on the same date, i.e. 27 April at Imphal. The aim was to disperse the Manipuri forces but enable concentrated application of the British forces on the Centre of Gravity, *viz.* Imphal. Accordingly troops were moved and concentrated. A task force with a strength of 1,200 with the overall headquarters under the command of Major-General H. Collett, commenced advance through Kohima on the 20th April. One task force advanced from Cachar with strength of 1,900 under Colonel R.H.F. Rennick on 15 April. They were expected to experience delays due to terrain friction hence the early start. The third task force advanced through Tamu with a strength of 1,800 under the command of Brigadier-General T. Graham on 23 April. In addition to these 5000 odd troops, the 5th battalion of Madras Infantry was earmarked as the reserve, in addition to guarding the lines of communication.

Battles

The first emcounter for the Kohima column was on 21st, at the village of Mao. Captain Macintyre and 200 soldiers overcame the Manipuri resistance. This short but sharp clash effectively opened the axes (road) from Kohima to Imphal, enabling easy move. There was hardly any resistance till Imphal. Another minor action was also fought by Colonel Browne and 300 soldiers during the advance from Cachar at a point halfway to Imphal.

Battle of Khongjom

However, the task force under Brig Granham from Tamu was very bitterly contested by the Manipuris. The British had intelligence report that a large force of Manipuris were had taken up defences in and around Khongjom. The British plan was to dislodge the Manipuris, who had entrenched themselves and open the road. The force employed for this task was 250 soldiers of the 2/4th Gurkhas, 50 more soldiers of the 12th Madras Infantry and another 43 mounted infantrymen; a total of nearly 350 soldiers and four guns (cannons). Captain Frank Montagu Rundall was to lead the assault. Manipuris had constructed an oval shaped defence which basically trenches, ditches, snager (parapet) along a stream full of water

The British commenced their attack by using the guns (cannons) to shell the Manipuris position. This was followed by concentrated aimed small arms fire. Believing the morale of the Manipuris to be sufficiently dented, Rundall ordered his infantrymen to advance, but the British were surprised by the ferocity of the Manipuris resistance who fought very stubbornly and refused to abandon their position. Even after some British soldiers had captured part of their defences, the Manipuris continued to put up a very stiff resistance. In fact, the contest had become a hand-to-hand fight. However, superior weapons and better training eventually ensured that the Manipuris could no longer resist the British troops and they broke. The mounted British infantrymen pursue the withdrawing Manipuris.

The task force did not encountered any more resistance, finally reached Imphal on 27th. By then all Manipuri resistance had effectively ended and the Union Jack was raised above the Kangla Fort. The British effectively disarmed the Manipuris, seizing an estimated 4,000 firearms.

Conclusion: British Colonial Military Strategy in the North East India

The British colonial strategy and tactics have been brought out during my talk on their fight with Assam and Manipur. To recapitulate them I will just run through these as given below.

They followed the 'divide and rule' policy as was being followed all over the country. Another strategy for war initiation was based on the policy of 'intervention on invitation' through which they used to initiate conflict. Knowing the cost of military ventures they always tried the carrot and stick policy of 'diplomacy with military might—winning without fighting', i.e. diplomacy with show of force. Fighting through the son of the soil concept strategy, i.e. employing local troops was the norms. The most well-known example of this strategy is the annexation of Assam and Manipur.

They also aimed at providing geographical depth or a buffer by creating inner line zones.

Another strategy was what can be termed as military explorations/expansion and expeditions. These military expansions and expeditions turned some unknown territory into colonial territory e.g. Naga Hills. Expeditions were organized to exhibit the British military might and determination, punish and send a message to all concerned. In October 1844, a British outpost along Naga Hills was attacked, presumably by Nagas belonging to Khonoma village. As a response, a British Military expedition was sent and a portion of the village of Khonoma was burnt. They demanded the delivery of the persons who were responsible for the attack on the outpost at Lunkae. In 1846-47, another expedition was sent to assess the establishment of an outpost in the Naga Hills with the aim to deter the Nagas from conducting some 'raids on the plains'.

The British East India Company's Infantry soldiers were better trained, better led and had superior weapons.

Wherever it was required they carried out punitive attacks to inflict proper punishment. They relied on intelligence report. For attack, they advanced to contact and sought battle, preferably in ground of own choosing. To disperse the enemy forces and prevent concentration of force, they used different axes but concentrated simultaneously at the point where they wanted. Proper reserves were earmarked. Opening of the axes (road) and guarding the lines of communication was considered important.

During the actual fighting they adopted line formation or row formation, this tactic was called volley fire. However, against a superior force, they deployed four rows of infantry. If required they took defensive positions including use of built up areas, i.e. village.

They would begin the physical attack by using the guns (cannons) to shell the enemy position. This was followed by concentrated aimed small arms fire and subsequently infantrymen to advance. This could be done by surging forward in a number of rushes, finally resorted to hand-to-hand fight. When the enemy gave up they used mounted infantrymen to chase and annihilate the opponents.

When faced with possibility of defeat they would seek armistice, break contact and organize a proper withdrawal and eventually be linked up or rescued.

Finally, after the fight they disarmed the enemy and seized the remaining weapons.

Lessons Learnt: Manipur War

Political instability due to squabbling and lack of unity amongst Manipuri leaders was there even those days. On 24th March, if the mob had been restrained then the spiraling of the events out control could have been avoided and perhaps history might have been different. The Manipuris literally had no allies; even now we need to cultivate allies. Preparations for such an eventual showdown are a long tedious and continuous process and have to be anticipated, visualized, more detailed and elaborate. Manipuris won the first two phases including the battles of Residency and Thoubal but eventually lost the war.

10
Women's Movements in Colonial and Post-Colonial Manipur

Bhabananda Singh T.

The love for independence and their martial ability to safeguard their freedom against repeated incursions by her neighbours is the history of the Manipuries. A martial race always on war and every able-bodied man was a *lalmi* (soldier). In social, political and economic activities women played an indispensable role as men were mostly out in military campaigns. Thus, Manipur is endowed with a rich history of women's Movement, as it was up to them to relieve the men folk of the social, political and economic requirements of the day. And till date the women's Movement in Manipur is the continuation of that legacy, the new and ever emerging problems and their endeavour to solve it.

The chronicles of women's movement in Manipur are of bravery, courage and self-sacrifices. They have played a very significant role in the history of the state. Throughout the ages, women have contributed in the socio-political and economic developments of the state. They have responded to the many different and divergent issues and crisis, whether it was political, economic or socio-cultural. This chapter examines women's movement in Manipur when new attitudes to polity, economy, and society were forming in the years of colonization process. As a prelude, this work also attempts to relocate the courage and strength from where the women carried to face the emerging challenges, the changing nature of the colonial state and economy. The concluding part discusses the changing post-colonial state and changing nature of women's movement. It examines the phases of women's movement and examines whether the women have been able to transform their movements in this smart age of information and technological marvels.

The Roots of Women's Movement

Historical account of women's movement in Manipur can be relocated in the concept of women represented in the myths and legends. This predates the sanskritization process that followed in the seventeenth century, when bulk of Manipuries were converted to Gourya Vaishnavism faith. In myth and legends, the *Lairembies* (female deities) occupy a prominent and respectable place. The indispensability of Thong-ngak Lairembi, the episode of Tangkhul Nurabi, Haoreima Sambubi, Panthoibi or Phouibi says it all. Coming closer towards history, the *Leishemba* myth (creation myth) and coronation of the mythological ruler Pakangba and the role of his mother are not just a mythical representation, for "it (myth) is not an idle tale, but a hard worked active force; it is not an intellectual explanation or an artistic imaginary, but a pragmatic character of primitive faith and moral wisdom."[1]

During the monarchical times, mention may be made of queen Laitonkhu, wife of Pengshiba, who was responsible for the conquest of a tribal village with one hundred people, the ingenuity of Queen Yaourei Leiyathi Khunkam Leinamung in the settlement of heir to the throne between the princes, Naophang Ahanba and Naophangba, and the love story of Pitanga, a Selloi Langmai girl and the Ningthouja prince Naothingkhong. It was the love of Pitanga that saved the life of Naothingkhong, who later ruled the Meitei kingdom. The episode of king Thawan Thaba Hiran where Chingkhei Thanbi his daughter sacrificed her life in order to save her father's. Mention can also be made of the valour of Queen Lingthoingambi who faced the Tangkhul raid by disguising herself as the King and her maids as soldiers in the absence of the King, Ninghtoukhomba (1432-1467). She captured Puringba, the Tangkhul chief of Tuisen. [2]

Outside the state of Manipur, the history of Manipuri princess Karunganayani daughter of Gourshyam who was married to Swargadeo Rajeswar Singh, the Ahom king is well known. After the death of Swargadeo Rajeswar Singh, Karunganyani was remarried to Swargadeo Lakshmi Singh, the younger brother

Swargadeo Rajeswar Singh. But the rebellion of Mayamaria in 1783 denied the throne of Ahom to Lakshmi Singh. Raghav Moran, the Mayamaria leader had usurped the throne, "but Karunganayani fought hard to kill Mayamaria leader Raghav Moran and thus the rule of Ahom dynasty could be restored," which is another example of valour of Manipuri women.[3]

In political sphere, the influence of common women in the administration cannot be ignored. It was customary for the women folk to gather in groups and present their grievances before the king. Even death sentences were reprieved if women pleaded on behalf of the accused. "In Raja's days, a criminal sentenced to death was occasionally reprieved if a sufficient number of women appeared to intercede for him."[4] During the reign of Maharaja Chandrakriti (1834-1844), the trapping of royal elephants was ordered during the harvest season. But men could not be spared for it would greatly affect the harvest. So the women collected themselves and presented their problems to the King requesting him to postpone the trapping of the elephants till harvest season was over. The King agreed and changed his decision and postponed it till the harvest considering the welfare of his subjects.

The legacy of women being represented as leaders/forerunners and equal partners to men in social, political and economic responsibility can be the important factor for nurturing women's movement in Manipur. With this legacy they could face off with the might of the British Empire, where the sun never sets. Their sense of justice and their reaction to injustices can be traced to the existence during monarchical times, women's own court to try and dispense their own justice.

The British Occupation of Manipur

The internecine quarrel among the princes between the two divided houses of ten sons of the late Maharaja Sir Chandrakriti Singh by his six queens, for the throne of Manipur, led to the Palace Revolt of 1890. The interference of British, through their office of the Political Agent, in the internal affairs of Manipur led to the death of five British officials; Grimwood, the Political Agent of Manipur; J.W. Quinton, the Chief Commissioner of Assam; Col. Skene, Lt. Simpson and Cossins. They were speared to death by an angry mob in front of the Palace at Kangla. In retaliation the British administration declared war on Manipur. Thus, the Anglo-Manipuri war of 1891 was fought in the month of April. "It was a short but momentous contest between a small land locked Asiatic country and the mightiest empire of the world."[5] The Anglo-Manipuri war of 1891 marked the end of sovereign and independent existence of the Manipur for ever; it was the beginning of the British rule of Manipur, as a part of British Indian administration.

Once the British took control of the kingdom, Manipur was administered as a princely state. The administration of the valley (dominated by the Meiteis) and Hills (dominated by the Nagas and Kukis) were separated. The valley was indirectly controlled through the Durbar headed by the Maharaja of the state. The Hills were directly administered through the office of the political agent.

On July 6, 1904, the Khawairamband Bazaar (Sana Keithel) with its 28 sheds that housed about 300 market women were razed to the ground. And on August 4th, the new state bungalow purchased by the government from Mr. Mitchell, the executive engineer and occupied by Mr. Nuttal and Dunlop was again burnt down.[6] At the site of the burnt bungalow, a bamboo stick with an oil rag attached to it was discovered. The nature and timing of the fire, substantiated by the stick convinced the British authorities that the fire was not an accidental one, but the handiwork of an organized group.

The endeavour of the British authority to arrest the culprits failed. It led to the announcement of collective punishment on the people of Manipur. In this regards three consecutive orders were issued. The political agent issued the first order on 12 September, 1904 to temporarily resuscitate the lallup system in Imphal town.[7] It was an effort to rebuild the burnt down bungalow and an exemplary punishment for the crime committed on the Colonial Master by the subjects. The people of Imphal were ordered to collect teak wood from Kabow Valley, now in Myanmar, and to rebuild the state bungalow.

People felt that the punishment was very harsh for a small crime and they sent a petition to the political agent to repeal the orders. However, he issued the second order that mentioned, "if the people decline to carry out the order an application will be made to the local government for permission to quarter upon them a force of punitive police force at their own expense."[8] There was a sharp reaction from the people, and on seeing the momentum of the agitated masses; Maxwell issued the third order on September 30th that prohibits gathering of five or more persons in a place. And having no alternative, the able-bodied male population of Imphal began to subscribe the building materials and prepared to rebuild the houses that were destroyed by the fire.[9] Then, it was left to the women to fight against the punitive measures of the British administration

Defying the orders of Maxwell, thousands of women gathered and staged a big demonstration against the orders of the political agent. The women of Khwairamband Bazar led the demonstration. Later they went to meet the political agent and the superintendent of the state. Khwairamband Bazaar was closed. The agitation continued for several days affecting the normal day-to-day life in the state. Additional forces were called in to suppress the uprising. Some of the prominent leaders were: Smt. Irengbam ongbi Sanajaobi Devi of Nagamapal, Lamabam Leikai; Smt. Lieshangthem Kwathabi Devi of Thangmeiband; Smt. Irengbam ningol Leimapokpam ongbi Dhabli Devi of Wangkhei Ningthem Pukhri mapal; and Smt. Laishram Ningol Juboti Devi of Nagamapal etc.[10]

The event of 1904 popularly known as First Nupi Lal can be taken as a landmark in the colonial history of Manipur and more specifically in the history of women's movement in Manipur. Though the uprising was for a short span, the result and impact it created on the British administration far outweigh the time period. The intensity of the backlash forced the political agent to rescind the rebuilding orders[11], though there were also reports that few people supplied bamboo and building materials for the reconstruction of the bungalow. It was the success story of women of Manipur against the order of the mightiest empire of the world.

The women's agitation was seen again in popular Bazaar Boycott Agitation of 1920-21. This agitation, though, not directed by women, saw a very high participation and involvement of women. The women were instrumental in running, and operation of the bazaar. Thus, their role in the agitation was very crucial. This agitation from the memorandum submitted to the judicial member on 25th September[12] reveals that it was against the exploitation of native traders by the Marwaries. The agitators were drawing the attention of the Maharaja and the British authority to look into the matter. The movement subsided by the end of

December. Still as an expression of their strong discontentment, the women retailers continued to boycott the Khawiramband Bazaar till the early parts of January 1921.[13] In 1925, another movement was launched against the increased water tax, where women led the agitation.

The most important event in the colonial history of Manipur was the "Women's Agitation of 1939" more popularly known as the second Nupi Lal.

In 1939, the state was heading towards a near famine situation due to poor harvest of December-January 1938-39. The scarcity of rice as well as paddy in the state led to hoarding of rice by the rich Marwari traders. They sent out their men to far and near places of Manipur to collect all the available harvested paddy and rice. Meanwhile by this time, the introduction of rice mills run with electricity posed a direct threat to the livelihood of local *cheng taibi* (local women who retails in rice). They still used the traditional pounding method to convert rice from paddy. As such they could not compete with the Marwari traders who had the advantage of more money, more stock of paddy, and efficient and fast production of rice by using electric run rice mills. So the *cheng taibis* were left high and dry. On the other hand export of rice, in spite of scarcity in the state, was increasing.

Added to this, the pressing problem of misadministration, finally led to the outbreak of second women's agitation of 1939. On Monday, 11 December, 1939, a group of women went to the owners of rice mills and asked them not to hoard rice by buying them in increased prices for it had created a lot of hardship on the people due to its scarcity. Later they confronted the president of Manipur state durbar Mr. T.A. Sharpe (ICS). They pulled him down from his vehicle and asked him to stop the export of rice immediately from the state.[14] Mr. T.A. Sharpe gave his word that he would announce the ban order the next day and pacified the women folk.

The next day, 12 December, 1939, a group of women went to purchase rice from the *godown* of Kasturi, a Marwari trader. The shop was closed but women demanded that it should be opened. Mr. Kasturi denied it. Failure to comply on the part of Kasturi, about 1000 women of Khwairamband Keithel gathered at the market place and later they hijacked the bullock carts of paddy that were heading to the Marwari godowns. The bullock carts were then taken in front of the Manipur State Durbar and piled upon the street as a sign of protest.

For the welfare of the masses and to prevent their hunger, the women asked the president and officials inside the durbar to immediately cancel the permits to export rice from Manipur. Many officials ran away but the president was cornered. He pleaded his helplessness for without the order of the Maharaja who was away at Nabadweep (Bengal) he could not cancel the orders. Unconvinced as he had already cheated the women the previous day they forced him to the telegraph office so that he could send a telegram to the Maharaja. As soon as the president entered the telegraph office he sounded the double bugle and called the 4th Assam Rifles (AR).

Major Bulfield the commander of the 4th AR and civil surgeon Major Cummins came to the rescue of the president. The 4th A.R. swung into action; they tried to disperse the women who had surrounded the telegraph office. However, the women did not move and the siege continued till quite late in the evening. By this time the number of women had increased from about 1,000 to around 4,000. They had become more militant and aggressive. In spite of repeated attempts, on the part of the administration, the women refused to leave the office. A clash between the women and the 4th A.R. resulted in the confrontation bayonets and rifle butts injured 21 women. Out of the 21 women 5 were seriously injured and later taken to civil hospital for treatment.

The news of the 12th December spread far and wide. It created a lot of unrest particularly at Imphal. On 13th December, the women of Khwairamband Bazaar called for a *hartal* and the Bazaar was deserted as a protest against the violence meted out on them. The Khwairamband Bazaar was completely deserted and since that day the boycott continued for almost a year.[15] By this time the Political Agent of Manipur Mr. Gimson had returned hastily from a tour. He was a person who had the knowledge of the socio-political structure of Manipur. On the same day he announced that he had received a telegram from the Maharaja. The telegram informed him that except for the supply of rice to the battalion of Kohima and the 4th A.R. stationed at Imphal all other supply of rice should be stopped immediately. It further directed that the Political Agent and the president of the durbar should follow the wishes of the *imas* (mothers). This was the first major success of the Nupi Lal.

Bands of women about 20 to 30 went on a campaign to shut down the rice mills belonging to both Manipuris and non-Manipuris. From many of them they got chits of agreement signed assuring the women that they would stop running their mills. Mill owners were given stern warning. On 14 December, 1939, the women with the political agent along with one engineer went to Mantri Pukhri on receiving the news that a mill was still operating despite the ban orders. They ransacked the mill.[16] The Maharaja also arrived at Imphal on 16th of December from Nabadweep.

A meeting was organized on 27th December at Cheirap compound. The agitated women lodged a formal complain to the political agent. They requested him to punish the Assam Rifles responsible for the atrocities caused on them. However, the reply of the Political Agent on 30th December dismissed the complaint on the ground that the police personnel were provoked by the agitated crowd thus action against the A.R. would be unfair. Meanwhile on 28th December, 13 bullock carts of paddy that was on its way to the market were intercepted by women and brought to the palace.

On 14 January, 1940, a meeting was organized at police lane market in defiance to the words of Maharaja Churchand not to hold any meetings. The agitation, which started for a ban in export of rice from Manipur, later, took the form of anti-Monarchial and anti-imperialist uprising.

The intensity and strength of the women agitation was getting stronger. They started confronting the administrative officials directly. In one such incident the forest officials at Sawombung, west of Imphal, was collecting heavy taxes from the local women for carrying forest products for sale in Imphal. On getting the information, the womenfolk gathered and ransacked the forest office at Sawombung. Such incident increased and many women leaders were arrested. On March 19, 1940, Wahengbam ongbi Tonkhombi, Nonghtombam ongbi Khongnang, Khetrimayum ongbi Oinam ningol Mukhi, Thongam ongbi Amubi were sent to prison. There was chaos everywhere and markets were closed for a long time.

Many of those who participated in the movement were sent to jail and their arrest subsided the intensity of the movement. The very foundation of the British rule in Manipur could be shaken by a band of women is a landmark in the history of anti-colonial movement in Manipur. Due to this many reforms were introduced and changes were made in the administration of Manipur. Chief court was established in Manipur. A council replaced the Durbar in 1946-47. Acts, like Manipur Constitution Act, Manipur State Election Act, etc. were passed. Election rules were constituted and election was also held in the state. In 1948 Manipur Assembly was established.

Today, those who participated in the Nupi Lal of 1939 are respected as freedom fighters and the Government of Manipur were paying pension in honour of their bravery and contributions made for the future Manipur.

In the movement against the colonial empire, one woman stood apart, and she was Rani Gaidinliu, from Longkao (Nungao) Village, Tousem of Tamenglong District. She joined the resistance movement against the British rule in the western hills of Manipur at her tender age of 13, under the leadership of Haipou Jadonang in 1927. However, when the revolutionary movement against the British was gaining momentum, Haiou Jadonang was arrested and hanged by the British on 29th August, 1931 at Imphal Jail.

Rani Gaidinliu took the mantle to lead the revolution after the death of Haipou Jadonang and went underground with her followers. In one of the encounter, "a fierce gun battle took place at Hangrum Village in the North Cachar Hills with the British army and the big village was later set ablaze by the colonial soldiers. A prolonged and hot pursuit took place and Rs. 500 reward was announced for information leading to her arrest."[17] Later she was arrested from Poilwa (Pulomi) Village on 17 October, 1932 by the Britissh Army led by Captain Mac Donald and was transported for life imprisonment for waging war on the British Empire.

After India got independence from the British Rule, Rani Gaidinliu was released on the orders of the then Prime Minister of India, Pandit Jawaharlal Nehru on 14 October, 1947 after serving the prison term of 14 years in various jails in Guwahati, Aizawl, Tura, Shillong and others. But it was not a hero's welcome when she went back to her native village of Longkao, "she could not tolerate the threat to her life and religion Heraka posed by the Baptist based Naga Nationalist Council movement."[18] In order to counter the threat she had to underground again in the year 1960 with her 400 followers and soldiers called Kampai. She had to face the wrath of the NNC where many of her followers were killed at Man-du (Bandu) village in an encounter with NNC cadres.

Rani Gaidinliu finally surfaced in the year 1966 and stayed in Kohima. She was conferred with Tamrapatra Freedom Award in 1972, Padma Bhushan in 1981, Vivekananda Seva Award in 1983. She finally returned to her native village in 1991 and stayed till she passed away in 1993.

In the post-colonial times, the political awareness of women was very high. In 1954 and 1959 women played an active part in demand for responsible government in Manipur. In 1960 women formed 'Women Assembly Demand Committee' to press the Central Government to grant responsible government in Manipur.[19] Women's participation in 'Statehood Demand Movement' was very significant in late 1960s. After statehood in 1973, when the Manipur Peoples Party led government was toppled due to defection in the party, women were first to agitate against it and shouted slogans of 'anti-defections'.

However, in the post-colonial period active politics has become a men's job. There is less participation of women in politics. This may be due to the reasons of increasing expense in elections, threats of violence and character assassinations of the candidates themselves. So women's ability to produce an impact on the political process of Manipur has been negligible. But, their influence as a pressure group has fairly been active.[20]

Since 1978 Manipur has been devastated, there is restlessness everywhere and the situation keeps on getting worse. It has ushered in a new era of armed conflict between the insurgent groups fighting for the right to self-determination and the forces of the state preserving the territorial integrity of a nation. It has witnessed the emergence and operation of a number of insurgent organizations in various forms like the People's Revolutionary Party of Kangleipak (PREPAK), the Peoples Liberation Army (PLA), the United National Liberation Front (UNLF), the Kangleipak Communist Party (KCP), the Kanglei Yaoul Kanba Lup (KYKL) etc. Though varied in forms its main objective was to organise the peoples' support and wage an armed struggle against the Government of India for separation and liberation of the state of Manipur.

To quell the civil unrest of the youth, who are guided by the misfortune of the History, the Indian government on September 8,

1980 declared Manipur a disturbed area. The very next day on December 9, 1980, the infamous "the Armed Forces Special Powers Act of 1958" was imposed. This Act empowers the police and the paramilitary forces to use their powers beyond human ethics and civilization. The worst part of this Act is the misuse of the Act itself. This Act was complemented by the introduction of other extraordinary laws like 'Terrorist and Disruptive Act 1985' (now repealed), the 'National Security Act (NSA) 1980', the 'Punjab Security Act 1953' etc.

The impact on the society is the never-ending reports of gross Human Rights violations. It has resulted in the casualties of arbitrary arrest, executions by fake encounters, torture and punishment by using third degree methods, rape of women, sometimes in front of her children, reports of men being raped, extreme physical and mental harassment of the public in the name of combing operation, unlawful invasion of people's privacy, to name a few. This is not the end; there are reports of heavy extortions allegedly by the underground outfits, highway robberies in the name of revolution, toll tax imposed by the separatist groups on vehicles and goods, rivalries and killings among the separatist groups etc.

A normal and a peaceful life is a long gone story. "Gun Culture" is a way of life; "Right to Life" is a slogan. "The year that just passed by was a gory one with at least 279 people killed in militant related activities. Official sources said of the 279 killed 115 were civilians while militants accounted for 115. Forty-nine security personels were killed while the numbers of militant arrested during the last 365 days were 1,282."[21] The number may be small in appearance, but for a state with a population of about twenty-two lakhs, it is indeed a big one. To counter these threats, the women of Manipur have taken up the lead and responsibility again in the form of Meira Paibi.

Meira Paibi got its name as an organization about two decades ago, but the organization has a long history in another name of 'Nisha Bandhi Uprising' that began around the mid 70s. Manipur became a full-fledged state of the Indian Union on 21 January, 1972. Work culture among the Manipuris that was there was lost. Side by side the number of unemployed persons increased. They resorted to alcohol and other forms of intoxicants like opium, *ganja* etc. The society was plagued with these social evils.

To counter these social evils women formed Nisha Bandhi Associations all over Manipur. This was a spontaneous and voluntary association formed to de-toxicant the society. The association of Nisha Bandhi took its concrete shape from an incident at Kakching on 30 December, 1975. On that day a women had gone to a liquor vendor at Turel Awang Leikai Khunlep part I-II, to call her husband who had gone there to drink. Angered by her arrival, the owner of the vendor beat her up mercilessly. At the same day, the women of that locality had gathered for a grand feast. On hearing the news that a woman had been beaten up, they assembled themselves at the place to protest the beating. As the cause of the incident was liquor they decided to start a campaign against the sale and consumption of liquor. A Nisha Bandhi group was formed which was the first of its kind. This incident marked the starting point of the Nisha Bandhi uprising.

Other women of the neighbouring areas supported this first Nisha Bandhi group. Kshetrimayum Achoubi Devi, a school teacher became its first president and Mr. N. Modhu Singh an advocate was made the first secretary. This association took up the task of enforcing a ban on the sale and use of intoxicants in and around the area of Kakching. They raided the vendors, burnt alcohols, caught drunkards and paraded them in front of the locality as punishment.

Similarly, different Nisha Bandhi groups were operating at different localities, and they needed to be coordinated when bigger issues came up. This led to the formation of the state level Nisha Bandhi organization. Women of Naoriya Pakhanglakpa Kendra organized a mass meeting of the Nisha Bandhi groups of Manipur on Sunday the 21st April, 1976. In that meeting, a resolution was passed that the task of enforcing a ban on intoxicants should be enforced all over the state. With this aim the Nisha Bandhi associations from all over Manipur formed the All Manipur Women's Social Reformation and Development Samaj (AMWSRDS), the parent organization of the Nisha Bandhi groups. Chaobi Devi was elected as the first president, the other office bearers were Indumukhi (adviser), Taruni (vice president), Momon (secretary), Ramani (publicity) and Ibempishak (treasurer). Thus, the Nisha Bandhi groups were well coordinated and more efficiently organized in the state.

In the continuation of the crusade against intoxicants, an All

Manipur Bandh was called on April 4, 1980 by AMWSRDS (All Manipur's Social Reformation and Development Samaj). It was called against the government's permit for sale of liquor in liquor shops as well as an effort to enforce a complete ban of liquor. In '*Prajatantra*', a local daily dated April 2, the AMWSRDS put up their reasons for calling the *bandh* to the government and public as well. "The failure of the Manipur government to put an effort to prohibit the sale of liquor is the reason behind this *bandh*." They made certain demands to the government, "Prohibition orders on the sale of liquor should be enforced immediately. The government should check the increase in the prices of the essential commodities, etc."

Finally, in the year 1991-92, the efforts of the Nisha Bandhi (then transformed into the Meira Paibi uprising) finally paid off. The then Government of Manipur led by Manipur People's Party of R.K. Ranbirsana passed the prohibition order on the sale and consumption of liquor. Manipur was declared a dry state, and is still today. Though it is not possible to totally ban the sale or the consumption of liquor, now sold in black markets and consumed at private places, the efforts and the success of the Nisha Bandhi has reduced the social problems arising out of liquor and other forms of intoxicants tremendously. This is a major success on the part of the women of Manipur.

The transformation of the women's uprising from Nisha Bandhi to Meira Paibi is the logical outcome of the consciousness that arises from the changing socio-political and economic situation of the state. As Marx has aptly said, "It is not the consciousness of men that determines their being, but, on the contrary, their social being that determines their consciousness."

One incident that was instrumental in the outbreak of the Meira Paibi uprising was the infamous incident of Langjing.[22] On April 26, 1980 at around 9:15 A.M. suspected activists of a separatist guerrilla outfit killed two Central Reserve Police Force (CRPF) personnel and escaped with their guns at a village called Langjing about ten kilometers from Imphal. In retaliation, the CRPF personnel posted at the Langjing CRPF camp launched a massive operation at Langjing Patsoi Khunou to search for the insurgents responsible for the attack. It was reported that many innocent villagers were tortured including children and women. There were reported cases of rape, physical abuse also. In that unfortunate incident Smt. Irom Bino Devi, who was hiding herself from the carnage of the angry CRPF personnel at the granary of Mutum Ibetombi Devi was shot dead, then and there, by the CRPF jawans. She was hiding there with a young boy of 10 years, Thokchom Leikham. Then the CRPF jawans dragged the small boy out, tied his hands and shot him dead near the house of Mutum Ibetombi Devi. Angou Singh, a driver at Imphal Municipality office, who was on his way to his office was also shot dead there by the CRPF. And another victim who lost his life to the bullets of the CRPF was Naorem Indrajit Singh. The casualty department at the hospital was packed with wounded villagers. And for days to come the innocent villagers bore the brunt of CRPF's anger. This created a fear psychosis and hatred towards the Indian security forces among the masses of the state.

It was at this time that the women of Manipur realized that they could no longer take this senseless and indiscriminate torture, rape and killings anymore, as this was not the first incident of such kind and it never was the last. The innocent civilians had to bear the aftermath of any skirmish between the separatist and Indian paramilitary forces. Immediately some women from Chingamakha, Imphal went to Langjing Village led by Yumnam Mangol Devi and met the victims. They talked to the frightened villagers, helped them in whatever they could. It was there that the women decided to take prompt action against such inhuman atrocities.[23]

On the next day, after the Langjing carnage, on April 27, 1980, a stray bullet from one of the CRPF jawan killed a market woman, Maishnam ongbi Thambalsana from Kangabam Leikai at Khwairamband Bazar. And the bullet that went through her body hit and seriously injured Mr. R.S. Heithui, a resident from Sanshat village in Ukhrul district of Manipur. It was during the time when the students of Manipur were also waging a campaign against the influx of the outsiders. "Go Back Foreigners", was the slogan of the day. In that uprising shops, godowns, were broken and burnt down, vehicles were burnt especially that belonged to the government. The students uprising against the outsiders, women's uprising against the carnage at Langjing, and the protest at the death of Thambalsana Devi had thrown normal life out of gear in Manipur.

In order to clamp the situation, the government of Manipur

issued curfew orders in Imphal areas on 28th April. The curfew orders were imposed till 6th of May, the following month. This led to the closure of Khwairamband Bazar for eleven days and the bazaar was finally opened on 9th May. As soon as it was opened the womenfolk gathered at the bazaar. They demanded that the CRPF personnel should be removed from the bazaar areas. Pressing their demands they submitted a memorandum to the Chief Minister R.K. Dorendro Singh. On the other hand, the situation of law and order in the state was getting worse. So the Chief Minister announced that if the law and order situation further deteriorated, he would be left with no alternative than to hand over the administration of the state to the Indian Army. There was resentment from the public at the statement. And the women went ahead with their protest and their humanitarian activities. Women with other organizations and clubs extended financial help to the victims at Langjing.

The whole month of May was marred with protest rallies, meetings that ended with numerous memorandums that were submitted to the government. Rallies were held on May 14th and on the next day women gathered at Mapal Kangjeibung and formed the Manipur Nupi Kanglup. Another rally was held at Imphal and its surrounding areas. A mass meeting was organized on 19th at Mapal Kangjeibung and on 21st another mass meeting was also organized where thousands of women participated. A protest rally was organized by Kangleipak Kanna Lup on 26th May. However, the most sensational one was that of 28th May.

The mass rally on May 28, 1980 was organized by the Manipur Nupi Kanglup at Imphal. This rally is very important in the history of Meira Paibi uprising in Manipur. Women from different parts of Manipur numbering around 10,000 joined that rally. It was very significant not just for the huge turnout, but it was also in defiance of the government ban orders on mass gatherings. So the police cracked down heavily on the protestors. Many of them were arrested. They were bundled up in a police lorry and were taken to Pangei, a place at the outskirt of Imphal town. On the way to Pangei an unfortunate incident occurred. Nameirakpam ningol Sinam ongbi Pyari Devi was one of those arrested. She was taken in one of the lorry to Pangei with other protestors. However, on the way at Khurai Salanthong, she fell down from the moving vehicle and died.[24] The saddest part was that she was pregnant and left behind a baby girl of one year. She was a young woman of 25 years. She became the first victim of the women's uprising against the excess of counter insurgency.

After Pyari died, the women's movement grew stronger and stronger. In order to take control of the situation, the Government of Manipur imposed curfew from 8:00 P.M. onwards from that day. But, the women never gave up. Finally, the government announced that a judicial enquiry would take place to the cause leading to the death of Pyari. An *ex-gratia* of Rs. 10,000 was announced to be given to the family of Pyari.

The month of May is indeed very significant in the rise of Meira Paibi. Thus, a Three Day seminar on Meira Paibi was organized on May 8-9-10, 1999 at Kuki Inn, Imphal by the All Manipur Women's Voluntary Association, Poirei Leimarol Meira Paibi Apunba (Manipur), and Meira Paibi Welfare Association (Kangleipak). Scholars, activists, representatives of Meira Paibi associations presented many papers on Meira Paibi. Arambam Lokendra chaired the last day of the seminar. The panel passed four resolutions. Out of that, "to fixed a particular day as 'Miera Paibi Day' the organizers should quickly call for another discussion", was one the resolution passed.[25]

As the follow up of that resolution of May 10, 1999, a seminar was organized at the auditorium of Manipur Dramatic Union, Yaiskul on May 23, 1999. Professor Ksh. Bimola Devi chaired the meeting. It was resolved on that day that, henceforth the 28th of May would be taken as 'Meira Paibi Day' and should be remembered and celebrated every year.

Despite the protest, rallies, memorandums of the women the casualties of the counter insurgency operations increased. So the women started spending nights outside the comforts of their homes, patrolling the streets and guarding their locality against any surprise search operations of the armed forces. They took up the "*meira*", an improvised bamboo torch, and it became the symbol of the uprising, and thus the name "Meira Paibi Uprising" (Uprising of women who hold *meira*). To spend the night the women needed a proper place to rest or stay. This led to the construction of improvised shed, now popularly known as *Meira Shang*. Today, all the localities have Meira Paibi organizations, and almost every locality has their own *Meira Shang*.

The situation of the state worsened with each passing day.

Activities of insurgent increased and in relation the counter insurgency operation of the state armed forces also took a harder stand. With these the activities of the Meria Paibis also increased proportionately. Here Professor N. Joykumar Singh is of the view that the rise of the Meira Paibi Movement is directly related to the rise in insurgency activities in the state.[26]

Some separatist guerrillas had planted three bombs near Tomal Makhong, Liwa Road Singjamei on 29 December, 1980. A combing operation was launched to arrest the culprits. In that ensuing search, Mr. Ibomcha, a resident of Liwa Lambi Maibam Leikai, a place near Tomal Makhong, who was sweeping his courtyard was picked up on the ground of suspicious by the Jammu and Kashmir (JK) army. After he was whisked away to the army camp, women of that area gathered to discuss their plan of action, as his future would be uncertain if prompt action was not taken. And above all he would also be added in the list of those disappeared. The women's organization of "All Manipur Women's Social Reformation and Development Samaj" (AMWSRDS) was informed of that incident. Leaders of that organization K. Indumani Devi, Momon Devi, Chaobi Devi, Ramani Devi, came to Ibomcha's house to help the family. After a short discussion they along with some women of that area went to the JK army camp at Canchipur and asked the officer in charge to release Ibomcha unharmed, and immediately as he was an innocent civilian. Later that evening, a military truck came and dropped Ibomcha at his home.[27]

It was a major success on the part of the women's uprising against the atrocities of the armed forces on the innocent civilians. Thus the 29th of December became another landmark in the history of the Meira Paibi uprising. This was the day when they saved a "*pari*" (son) from the jaws of death. Later it was decided that the day should be observed every year as "*Pari Kanba Numit*" (*pari* = son; *kanba* = to save, protect; *numit* = day). It was also decided that this *Pari Kanba Numit* would be the official foundation day of the Meira Paibi. And the office of the All Manipur Women's Social Reformation and Development Samaj at Konung Mamang, Imphal became the Head Office of the Meira Paibi organizations of Manipur.[28] However, there is a disagreement regarding the exact date when Meira Paibi started among the women groups. Another women group claim that 28th of May ought to be regarded as the foundation day for Meira Paibi. However, the disagreement between the two groups does not affect the activities of the Meira Paibi movement in the state. When it comes to the important issues and crisis they all join together to fight it out. That is the spirit of the Meira Paibi members.

The socio-cultural and political tradition of Manipur has legitimized the women of Manipur in whatever task that they may take up. The legitimacy is based much more on social and moral approval, than on legal sanctions. Manipuri society does not permit men to inflict physical harm to women, at least in public. Even in traditional times, women were exempted from capital punishment. The strength and courage necessary to face any adversary was born from these social and moral obligations of the society towards women.

In the women's movements, the market women of Khwairamband Bazar played an important role. This is due to the vital role the women of Manipur play in the economic activities of the state. And most importantly, the Khwairamband Bazar, more popularly called Ima Keithel is not just an ordinary market place. Besides the economic activities, it is a centre for social and political discussion among the women. Women from all over the state attend this market. There is a free flow and exchange of ideas among these women. Mainly women from peasant and working class background compose them. They are the groups that are most aware of socio-political exigencies of the day. Any problem of the time the impact will fall first fall on them. And they are the first to react.

Throughout the different phases of women's movement in Manipur, they have responded towards multifarious issues ranging from political, economic and socio-cultural issues. But the concept of Manipuri women has not changed much, as the women themselves perceive, except for very few women activist. They are still caught in their traditional collective response and justice. But times have changed. In this global age and cyber world, the whole world is in transition beyond the thought could imagine. Yesterday's (science) fictions have become reality. The traditional collective response and justice has now been termed as mob justice or mob violence, punishable by Indian Penal Code. Recently when 13 women tried to intervene in the court to vent their anger out on a rapist accused, they were remanded to judicial custody and were later sent to jail. Their instinct to react to injustice has not died down, but the way they should respond needs new approaches. When traditional means of response could no longer apply and can no longer serve their purpose, there is the need for new direction and new method to react from the women's movement in Manipur.

Notes

1. Brownislow Malinowski, *Magic, Science and Religion and Other Essays*, cited in Thanaoujam Chanu Ibemhal, *Haoreima Sambubi* (Imphal: Lamyanba Printers, 2000), p. 22.
2. For details please refer Gangmumei Kabui, *History of Manipur: volume one. Pre-Colonial Period.*
3. G.K. Ghosh and Shukla Ghosh, *Women of Manipur* (New Delhi: A.P.H. Publishing Corporation, 1997), p. 8.
4. Manjusri Chaki-Sircar, *Feminism in a Traditional Society*, (New Delhi: Shakti Books, 1984), p. 26.
5. Gangmumei Kabui, "The Anglo-Manipuri War of 1891", in Lal Dena (ed.), *History of Modern Manipur: 1826-1949* (New Delhi: Orient Publishers, 1991), p. 48.
6. Letter from Maxwell to the Secretary to the Chief Commissioner of Assam. No. 373, dt. 1st October, 1904, in Naorem Lokendra, *Unquiet Valley*, (New Delhi: Mittal Publications, 1998), p. 76.
7. This traditional form of obligatory labour, to the service of the king, practiced during monarchy was abolished by Maxwell just after the Anglo-Manipuri war of 1891, for the British thought that it was uncivilized in nature.
8. N. Joykumar Singh, "Anti-British Movement: 1904-1949", in Lal Dena (ed.), *History of Modern Manipur: 1826-1949*, p. 122.
9. *Ibid.*, p. 124.
10. *Ibid.*, p. 125.
11. N. Joykumar Singh, *The 1904 Movement*, in The Third Annual Conference of North East India History Association (Imphal: Manipur University, 1982).
12. Naorem Lokendra, *Unquiet Valley*, p. 98.
13. *Ibid.*, p. 103.
14. N. Khelchandra Singh, Nupi Lal, in *Nupi Lal 1939*, A souvenir produced on the dedication ceremony of Nupi Lal complex on 18th April 1989, Imphal, p. 23.
15. Naorem Lokendra, *Unquiet Valley*, p. 140.
16. N. Khelchandra Singh, 'Nupi Lal', in *Nupi Lal 1939*, p. 24.
17. Freedom Fighter Rani Gaidinliu (1915-1993) Haipei Rani Gaidinliu Birth Anniversary Celeberation Committee, *http://www.manipur*

online.com/Profiles/January2006/raniguidinliu29_1.htm accessed on 11 February, 2009.

18. *http://en.wikipedia.org/wiki/Rani_Gaidinliu* accessed in 11 February, 2009.
19. Dr. Ksh Bimola Devi, "Manipuri Women—A Study", in Naorem Sanajaoba (ed.) *Manipur: Past and Present, volume one* (Delhi: Mittal Publication, 1988), p. 169.
20. *Ibid.*, p. 172.
21. "279 people killed last year", *The Sangai Express* (a local daily), Monday, 1 January, 2001, Imphal, p. 1.
22. This incident can be taken as the flash point of the Meira Paibi Uprising in Manipur. In every interview and almost all the articles published on Meira Paibi, this incident is referred again and again.
23. Yumnam Mangol Devi. *Personal interview with the author.*
24. K. Indumani and Ima Chaobi. *Personal interview with the author.*
25. S. Mangi Singh, Asst. Prof., Political Science Department, Manipur University, *Personal interview by the Author.*
26. Prof. N. Joykumar Singh. *Personal interview by the Author.*
27. K. Indumani and Ima Chaobi. *Personal interview by the author.*
28. *Ibid.*

SECTION III
Colonial Legacy

11
Impact of British Colonial Commercial Policies in North East India

K. Himalay Singh

Introduction

North East India has been and still continues to be one of the under-developed regions in the country. Reasons for the same are varied. Geographical location, historical realities, connectivity issues ethnic fault lines and socio-economic issues are some of important reasons for this state of affairs today. As regards contact with British India with the North East India, it is believed that one Mr. Jean Barister of East India Company came to Goalpara district of Assam for trade in salt, wood, and gold in the banks of river Brahmaputra in the year 1755. It may be mentioned that this is the period when Bengal province of which parts of Assam were also included contributed close to 25 per cent of India's GDP. British and other colonial powers had deep interests in the Arakans due to the port of Chittagong. However, British interest in the Assam region was very limited till Ahom rulers invited the British to upper Assam for assistance against the uprisings of the Mao-Maria tribes during 1792. It is pertinent to mention that the East India Company signed an agreement with Maharaja Jaisingh of Manipur in 1762 which showed British Colonial interest in Empire building and trade in the region. As per this agreement, besides other issues, the British agreed not to hamper operations of the gold mines belonging to the king of Manipur near Sibsagar in present day upper Assam.

British acquisition of Chittagong port in 1760 three years after the battle of Plassey opened the door to look more towards the north east region and to look for a natural frontier of the Raj to the east. The vast plains of erstwhile east Bengal in the Eastern frontiers of the Raj lacked a natural and geographical frontier against the Burmese kingdom as well Chinese influence in the region. With the signing of the Treaty of Yandaboo in 1826, the British concept of eastern natural frontier took some shape. The inaccessible jungles in the Naga Hills, Mizo Hills, Manipur kingdom became a natural frontier. Moreover, trade interest too became one of the preferred policies in the region due to the huge natural resources in the region.

British East India Company commercial policy in India during the period was guided by the need for raw material for the Industrial revolution in their home country. It was, therefore, no different policy when they discovered immense source of raw material in Assam and adjoining country. The administration initially collected huge amount of revenue from the region to meet the requirement of upkeep of the military. Vast tracts of uncultivated land were brought under cultivation in order to impose more land taxes.

Discovery of tea during 1823 in the region gave the impetus towards commercial exploitation in the region. Vast tracts of land were converted to Tea Gardens. With the onset of tea industry, came the immigration of millions of labourers from other parts of the country into Assam. By 1901, it was estimated that more than 1.2 million had migrated to Assam from parts of Bengal, Bihar etc. due to lack of suitable labour force within the region. Soon, there was huge import of rice to Assam to feed the million plus labourers from other parts of the country. Anglo-Burma war which resulted in the signing of Yandaboo treaty was perhaps aimed at commercial interest resulting from huge profits from tea industry as much the need for a natural frontier for British India. By 1854, oil was also discovered in Digboi and the first well was completed by 1885. By 1914, Assam produced 1 per cent of world oil production. Oil began to play a major role for the further British interest in the region. Rail connectivity and steamer services in the river Brahmaputra to connect with other parts of Bengal such as Calcutta, Chittagong took off in a big way to meet the commercial needs of tea, oil and teak industries.

Capitalist economy in the region thrived as a result of annexation of Cachar plains in 1833, Khasi Hills 1832, Karbianglong area 1838, Naga and Mizo Hills 1866. Coal industry grew by leaps and bounds in upper Assam and Khasi Hills during the period. The formation of Assam Railways and Trading Company in 1881 acted as the engine of the commercial activities of the East India Company in the region. The Britishers were thus forced to take up road, rail and other communication systems to meet the ever increasing demand of the trading activities.

Initially, the British wanted the region to become agricultural hub. However, the commercial gains of the tea, teak, oil and coal industry was too attractive option for the British to further attend to agricultural activities. Thus, the local agricultural sector suffered significantly during the period. Native participation in the commercial activities was limited to providing limited labour force. The entire Region became only a resource provider for the needs of the Industrial revolution back home. Local economy was inadequate to meet the needs of the migrants. Hence, import of food from Bengal became a norm during the period. Hill areas such as Naga, Mizo, Khasi areas were only marginally integrated since resources in these areas were very limited. Social impact of the commercialization resulted in further isolation of the tribals from the plainsmen. The colonial economy remained confined to the two valleys of Brahmaputra and Cachar valley with the sole objective of maximization of profit by the British. No dividends of the commercial activities were invested in the region. Immigrants largely spent their income on the non-local produce. Growth of modern sectors did not bring any improvement in the quality of life of the locals. Huge drain of money from the region took place. Mineral and natural resources only served the alien interests. Divide and rule became the new mantra to further their commercial pursuits. The story perpetuated till Independence in 1947. Thereafter, the curse of geopolitical realities such as bifurcation of Bengal depriving the region of the erstwhile regional connectivity prevented the region to be economically fully integrated for considerable period of time even after Independence.

It is hoped that Act East Policy of the Government of India will ameliorate some of the concerns of the region as far the economic integration with the mainland as also with the neighbouring countries. Some of the issues that need to be addressed in order to improve the economic and commercial climate in the North East are expected to be included in the Act East Policy of the Government of India. However, it is imperative that NEC and DONER need to streamline their acts with the region in more meaningful ways. The Economic and commercial climate of the North East is deeply intertwined with law and order and terrorism in some states. It is also linked to the ethno-political realities, besides issues such as connectivity, and investment opportunities, infrastructure, and governance issues. It can only be hoped that centuries of perceived neglect of the region in terms of economic progress will be replaced by hope for progress as 'India Acts East'.

12
Second World War and North East India

N. Lokendra Singh

A significant historical theme, which is crucial for understanding the post-Second World War Naga society and polity is the nature as well as the extent of socio-economic and political changes, which took place in Naga hills during and the immediate post-War period. The inflow of large number of the Anglo Allied forces followed by the arrival of Indian refugees as well as the Imperial Japanese forces coupled with intense war time politico-military tactics and strategies and on both sides brought rapid and profound changes in the consciousness as well as socio-economic life of the people. These changes not only paved the way for the emergence of new social forces but also prepared the necessary pre-conditions for a strong ethno-national movement for bringing about broad economic and political changes in Naga Hills during the immediate post-Second World War period.

Naga Hills on the Eve of the War

The echo of the occupation of Burma by imperial Japanese army in 1943 and the subsequent bombing of Manipur valley in mid-1943 had reached the inhabitants of Naga Hills. Soon after these events, there began the process of an inflow of a large number of Indian refugees from Burma including the retreating Anglo-Allied army.[1]

There were Indian coolies, dock labourers from Rangoon, household servants, Anglo-Indian, Anglo-Burmese, along with British families who had been engaged in oil or timber, and random representatives of many other nations. They were attacked by exhaustion, hunger, disease, and stumbled into the refugee camp more dead than alive. Many did die, and it is said that the columns of vultures wheeling above the camp could be seen for miles.[2] While the incoming refugees which came mostly by Imphal-Dimapur Road were looked after by the Burma Refugee Organisation in different camps at Dimapur and nearby places, the Indian Tea Association and the local administration of Naga Hills also provided every possible relief measures to the refugees in Bokajan and Dimapur. Mr. A.B. Bore as the Chief Refugee Administrator and Director of the scheme for population movement under the Government had been empowered in 1943 to indent for any rations as required. Subsequently, large quantities of food grains, blankets, mosquito nets, medicine were requisitioned to relieve the immediate situation.[3]

During 1942-43, the great road building programme, particularly the metalling and widening of the main Imphal-Dimapur Road into a two-way asphalt road and the improvement of a number of bridle paths into tracks capable of motor traffic for military purposes was carried on at war footing.[4] The new developments had not only attracted a large amount of capital but also employed thousands of local as well as immigrant labourers. While all these rapid developments had begun to stir the consciousness of the otherwise isolated people of Naga Hills, the congestions and the unhygienic conditions created by crowds of immigrant labourers and refugees had provided ideal conditions for the break out of diseases like small pox, cholera and dysentery. The innumerable refugees had also bought in new disease like new strains of malaria. To compound the problem, there was a steep rise in the price of all sorts of consumption items including rice, kerosene, salt etc. Since the military suppliers had brought up all the available foodstuff including vegetable and meat, these items were in many instances found to be unavailable in the market for general consumption. Moreover, what was available was again requisitioned by the Japanese.[5] It was in the midst of such an utter confusion and rapid socio-economic changes that a number of enterprising Naga Businessmen took advantage of the vacuum created immensely favourable condition for the growth of the local contractors and suppliers.

Coming of the War

In the early part of 1944, the Japanese top brass in Tokyo decided to launch an all out offensive against India. The crack 31st division of the imperial Japanese army under the command of General Sato was to attack the British garrison at Kohima, seize vital railways and supply depot at Dimapur and then send forces southwards for the capture of Imphal.[6] The division had in fact split into 8 strong columns and crossed Chindwin on a 40 mile front from Hamalin onwards in the north on rafts and boats on March 17 and at an incredible speed emerged around Kohima earlier than expected. Out of the 8, one main column was heading for Ukhrul with Kohima as its chief objective while the rest moved straight towards Naga Hills. The Japanese plan, as stated earlier, was to cut the main Imphal-Dimapur Road, north of Imphal and swarm through Somra Hills towards Jassami. Then the whole force was to converge upon the British garrison at Kohima. The garrison was, however, warned by some Naga hillmen and as a result defence positions were hastily constructed on a series of hillocks along a mile long ridge. At the centre of these defences were the assistant District Commissioner's bungalow, his pretty garden and his Tennis Court which will subsequently become the centre of intense fights between the two forces.

The first shot in Naga Hills was fired by the Assam Regiment and Assam Armed Police 30 mile east of Kohima at Karasom. Although these forces fell back from position to position and suffered from heavy casualties they succeeded in slowing down the movement of the crack 31st Division, thereby providing sufficient time to the Allied forces for proper mobilization of their army. Kohima has been given tremendous military preparation. Even the 500 convalescing soldiers admitted in the dispensary were armed while the non-combatants and hospital patients were shifted to safer place. With every available man, including some from administrative units the total strength of the garrison was increased to 1,000 personnel who had to fight the no less than 15,000 Japanese men closing upon them. In the nearby Dimapur Garrison, out of 45,000 persons on the list of the ration card holders, only about 500 could handle rifle. The Commander of the garrison, Col. H.V. Richards called in every soldier although he could hardly get sufficient force. But General Slim of the 14th Allied Army ordered

5th and 7th Indian Divisions to be airlifted from Arakan where the operation was halted. He also ordered 2nd Division from India to come for rescue works at Dimapur and Kohima.

Meanwhile, the Assam Rifles fighting bravely but sustaining heavy casualties were almost exhausted and on April 4, some 200 Assam Rifle personnel managed to fall back into Kohima's defence force. Major General Sato who could have attacked undefended Dimapur which was only 30 miles away stuck to the idea of occupying Kohima only and therefore, waves of Japanese force attack scantily manned Kohima.[7] Meanwhile, Major General Stopford took over the affairs of the battle at Kohima and along with this the allied position was stabilised. A force of 5th Indian Division was flown in and deployed to hold the Nichugard pass almost adjacent to Dimapur because it was expected that it would be attacked after overrunning Kohima. The Kohima-Imphal Road was now controlled by the Japanese. However, it was fortunate that the Royal Air Force (RAF) had absolute air control over the region. During the day time fighter air crafts roared down almost to the jungle roof to augment the Allied fire power. They also dropped ammunition, medical supplies and food to the hard pressed garrison.

After some days, however, the position of the Japanese force had deteriorated due to their inability to either capture Kohima or get supplies from their base at Burma as the RAF had already cut off the supply lines. Sato, therefore, reversed his policies and sent the infantry force for attack only at night time while in the day time the British positions were attacked by shells, mortars and machine gun. Although the Britishers suffered tremendously in terms of casualties and exhaustion due to ceaseless fights and sleeplessness, by April 6 they all concentrated at the garrison hill, their man position. The Japanese had also captured their only water supply, thus making them completely dependent on the RAF supply of water filled inner tubes. Despite a number of Japanese casualties, there was continuous attack and as a result of that the Japanese force came closer to the office of the Deputy Commissioner. The battle of attrition finally took place between the two groups and there were hand to hand fight or lobbing of fused grenades at each other across the Tennis Court in front of the DD's main office. Casualties on both sides were very high and Summer House Hill was blood stained. For almost 10 days, Kohima continued to be seize but on 15 April, 1944, a brigade of 2nd Division fought up the road to reinforce the army of the 5th Division at Kohima. Another stronger group of the 2nd Division supported by tanks, artillery and air support broke through the enemy line on 18th April to reach the defenders. Along with this food and water supplies came to the wild eyed bearded survivors of the British force. Two days later on 20th April, some other men of 2nd Division came to their rescue to relieve the rest of the garrison.[8]

Although after 16 days the siege ended for all practical purposes, the Japanese still occupied some bunders on a 7,000 yard forest whose sides were unscalable green cliffs. As long as this force was there Imphal Dimapur Road, the main supply line was still under their control. However, two Brigades of army, one from the 7th Division and the other from the Chindits had come south-east towards Jassami to block possible Japanese reinforcement from the Chindwin and thus completed the process of encircling and isolating the Japanese from their supply lines. Till 30th April, the Japanese control of the ridge was attacked. By 3rd May artillery and tanks were brought from Dimapur for an all out attack against the Japanese force. Although British attack was countered by cross-fire from hidden hill top many Japanese died. Along with this, tanks began to crawl up and by May 13, the surviving enemy fell back.

Ravages of the Local Economy

As indicated earlier, in their push northwards from Ukhrul through the hills on the 27th March, the Japs destroyed Karasora village and so also was the fate of Jessami a few miles further north. By the 18th April due to ceaseless fighting there was a complete disruption of normal life in Kohima and surrounding villages. The Japanese patrol which went along the bridle paths from Kohima reached distant places like Sakhalu on the new Sema Road, Ghukia on the old Sema Road, Wokha on the Makokchung Road and Pedi on the Henima Road. The inhabitants of these places were absolutely terror struck and began looking for safer places. Kohima village which was occupied by the Japanese was completely destroyed by fire before the inhabitants could save their paddy or household goods. The place and its houses were torn and cratered by shells and bombs and hone combed with trenches and bunkers.

It was the centre of bitter fighting for weeks afterwards. Dead bodies of the war littered the place. The village wells had been to a large extent fouled or destroyed. Even some outlying medical dispensaries had either been destroyed or robbed by the Japanese.

The large village of Chedema was completely destroyed during the fighting and the same fate befell the villages of Aradura and Chandmari.[9] The eastern half of Viswema village was blasted by the British guns and gutted by fire. Chizami was bombarded by the Allied air craft and in the process many houses were destroyed.[10]

At the beginning of April 1944, refugees—Kukis from Kanjang, a village in the eastern Naga Hills and Gurkhas from the settlement at Sakhabhama near Kohima appeared in the plains and were housed in the refugee camp at Bokajan and cared for by a nucleus of the Burma Refugee Organisation. Another camp was also maintained by this organisation in Dimapur where the staff fed and despatched to Nepal several thousands of Gurkhas who had been working on the road in labour units. During the months of April, May and June assistance to the homeless was rendered by the Deputy Commissioner, Naga Hills local staff, the Indian Tea Association and the Burma Refugee Organisation.

Since the Japanese forces brought very little food with them, rice was requisitioned in very large quantities for their daily consumption as well as for their mules. They had specific instructions to treat the local people well and pay for all supplies they collected they distributed large quantities of Japanese currency and well forged Rs. 10 Indian currency notes among the villagers in return for food and labour. They also killed and ate enormous amount of chickens, pigs, cattles, mithuns and buffaloes. Although some Angami villagers succeeded in hiding their herds of cattle in the deep secluded villages of Japvo Range, the destruction of pigs was so complete that A.B. Bore noted in his report about the deteriorating sanitary conditions of the Naga Hills villages due to the absence of pigs. Since the villagers fled to the jungles or to the field houses low in the valley, they contracted malaria. The Japanese did not even spare the household goods. Cooking pots once used were smashed.[11] *Daos,* axes and hoes were collected and thrown away in the jungle or into the river. In the eastern Naga Hills were the local people used to manufacture their own salt by using the local brine wells, salt pans which were used were also destroyed. Even the Naga blankets and other clothes which were forcibly taken from the villagers were never returned to the owners.

What was of crucial importance however, was the disturbance in the agriculture of Naga Hills. The cultivation of the hill terraces was seriously interfered with and all the above mentioned villages got little or no crop. Although the Nagas made a great effort to do what they could, shortage of implements and the lateness of planting of crops prevented the rice from setting seeds.

So far as the responses of the local people towards the war are concerned it may be stated that the Nagas were impressed by the Japanese as coolies to carry heavy loads for long distances.[12] The treatment of people at first was on the whole fair but there were also isolated cases of barbarism like rape, maltreatment and murder.[13] The coolies used to be tied up at night to prevent them from escaping. Since the Japanese were suspicious of possible Naga Vengeance they collected systematically all the hoes, axes and *daos* and threw them into the rivers and jungles. Some of the spears and guns were, however, "hidden by the Nagas and were used afterwards with good effect." When the opportunity arises the "Nagas discovered that the Japanese head was not proof against a well placed blow from a billet of wood and many were disposed of in this way."

In contrast to this, the colonial policy of dealing with the hill tribes of North East India was very subtle and slow process of colonisation. The missionaries were also instrumental in laying a smooth foundation for the penetration of colonial administrative and economic forces. Ursula Graham Bower, a lady anthropologist who came to North East India to study Zeme Nagas of North Cachar Hills toured extensively the neighbouring areas and canvassed support for the Allied forces. The V force was also organised and many Nagas were recruited as its volunteers. In their dislike for the collection of supplies and coolies, the Nagas went so far as to give information to the allied group.[14] In many cases the inhabitants of the villages laid down ground signals which indicated to the allied aircraft that the village was occupied by the Japanese troops. In several other cases, many Naga volunteers penetrated the Japanese line and brought back invaluable information. The British authorities were indeed, thoroughly impressed by the Nagas responses to the war. A.B.

Bore noted that the Nagas reactions "in all respects (were) exemplary. The personal and material damage they suffered was much greater as the result of our military against the Japs than any they suffered directly at the hands of the later. Everywhere however, there was a complete understanding of the necessity for measures taken and in spite of their severe material losses there is quite a buoyant feeling that all was just in the days work."[15] H.E. Short also wrote "there was a real pride (among the Nagas) in their loyalty to the British rule. This pride is fully justified because they did not merely passively endure ... but when possible were active helpers against the Japanese in the forms of porter's work, rescue of stragglers, bringing of important and reliable military information and even the giving of wrong information to the Japs."[16]

It was precisely because of such an attitude that the Britishers were in full sympathy with the Nagas and remarked, "All these facts make it a moral obligation on our part to give back all and more than they have lost provided their independence is not undermined by pamperin."[17]

War-Time Relief Measures

In May-June 1944, many places in Nagas Hills had to be provided food, clothing, mosquito nets and blankets particularly the 8,000 Nagas who had abandoned their villages and were living in field houses and in hastily constructed camps within the Allied lines. But in August when the Japanese were finally ejected, the immediate problem in Naga Hills was to house and feed 28,000 people.[18] To provide the homeless with shelter against the monsoon which had just broken, the Government of India was asked for 16,000 tarpaulins and the timely arrival of these did a great deal to solve this immediate and pressing problems. The army was also requested for 2,000 tents and large quantities of unserviceable tentage were obtained from salvage dumps. Thus, within a very short period of Japanese departure, those who had lost house were provided with shelter of some kind and could settle down with some degree of comfort during the remainder of the rainy season and start on the reconstruction of their homes.

As the magnitude of the problems began to be realised, the Government of India sent Sir Charles Ogilvie, Secretary to the

Government of India, Defence Department to Shillong to discuss the initiation of relief measures with His Excellency, the Governor. The immediate result of this move was the commissioning of Assam Relief Measures with Mr. A.B. Bore as the Director. The base camp of the relief measure was set up at Bokajan Rail Head and from here supplies were transported by trucks to the subsidiary camps at Kohima and Imphal. Rice and paddy were obtained through the Assam Government Agents particularly, (i) Messers Steel Brothers in the Assam Valley, (ii) The Food Grains Syndicae, (iii) The Eastern Bengal and Assam Commercial Syndicate (both from the Surma Valley), and (iv) the Deputy Director of Supply Procurement of the Supply Department.[19] Orders for the supply of agricultural implements and aluminium were placed with Messers Shaw Waliace & Co. Agent to the Government of Assam. But as the arrangements for supply and despatch of the firm proved to be unsatisfactory orders were placed with some Indian firms in Calcutta. Blankets were supplied by six firms two of them in Gauhati and the remainder in Calcutta.

By August 1944, even when Imphal-Dimapur Road had been cleared of the enemy, thousands of Naga refugees were maintained by D.C. Kohima at 41 milestones on the main road. Nobody who applied for food was refused. Gradually a system of issue of rice upon ration cards was adopted and a weekly scale of 5 seers of rice per adult and 21/2 seers per child was adopted. With the departure of the Japanese from the Naga Hills, depots were rapidly opened at 12 places, i.e. Kohima, Phesama, Phekerkrima, Chizami, Viswema, Kigwema, Khuzama, Ghaspani, Pfutsero, Phek, Mcrema and Deruma. All of the villages fed from these depots were on the Jap line of communication and suffered severely from losses in rice, paddy and livestock. Although the Nagas made great effort to do what they could, the lateness of the planting prevented the rice from setting seed. All these villages, therefore, were provided food till the harvest of 1945. Altogether a total of 28,796 persons (17,777 adults and 11,019 children) in 57 villages were provided supplies from the above depots. All these depots excepting those at Phikroked Zema (Phek), Pfutsero and Chizami were on the main road or on subsidiary roads over which trucks could run. Whereas the above three depots were on Jeep tract Kohima, 46 miles from Dimapur was the central supply base for Naga Hills and all rice and stores coming from Dimapur were unloaded into godowns and distributed to the outlying depots. The total quantities of rice and paddy imported and subsequently supplied to the different depots were 60,088 mds and 63914 mds respectively.

Immediate Post War Initiatives for Rehabilitation and Reconstruction of Naga Society and Economy

During the War, in Naga Hills, altogether 2780 houses were destroyed.[20] Since it would not be possible to cultivate the fields which had been lying fallow during the whole of 1944 until the villages were properly housed, the government decided to immediately provide monetary assistance to the villagers. The villagers were encouraged to build their own houses with local materials and local aid with a simultaneous promise of a cash payment of Rs. 200 plus a sum of Rs. 200 in saving certificate for each house which had been destroyed in 18 villages, i.e. Kejumatuma, Kenoma, Ponglomi, Dehoma, Chechama, Enholomi, Purr, Yesi, Swemi, Akhywu, Berema, Kanjang, Khabruma, Kekrima, Gokhevi, Kidima, Laruri and Chizami. In these villages, altogether 755 householders were provided cash reliefs. It was considered advisable to give part of the relief in saving certificates since the householder could use in the time of future difficulties. In addition to this, additional materials for construction of houses were provided to as many as 2025 householders in 17 different villages, i.e. Phesama, Veswema, Khuzama, Jotsema, Chedema, Merema, Pfuchama, Keruma (Chazauma), Thizama, Phekekrima, Chandmari basti, Aradura, Kigwema, Chiesama (Khroma), Cheiswema, Kohima town and Kohima village. As a special case, the Government of India granted a sum of Rs. 8400 for rebuilding the four 'morungs' (dormitories) in Kenoma. In order to provide assistance to all these villages many new roads and paths were constructed. The path leading from Kohima bazar to Kohima village was widened by the Nagas themselves. Elsewhere also many subsidiary roads into the villages were constructed to enable the building materials reach the villages.

Since thatch was not sufficiently available in Naga Hills, the Government of India was requested to obtain corrugated iron sheets from the Army. As the available 1,14,509 iron sheets were not galvanised it became necessary to buy red oxide primer and camouflage paints to give protective coating. It was also decided that the butts of the pillar posts which were to be sunk in the earth should have a coating of adequate creosote coating. The requisite quantities of bolts, nails, screws were also purchased.

In order to provide adequate pillar posts a survey of the forest in the Jharnapani valley, south of Ghaspani on the Dimapur-Kohima Road was carried out and realising its rich resources contracts were immediately placed in consultation with the D.C. Naga Hills at price rates which were prevailing in the district. Although these rates compared unfavourably with those of the Forest Department in Sibsagar division of Assam, the area chosen had an advantage of reduced distance of about 30 to 60 miles. Indeed it was only through this source that rehabilitation of Kohima and nearby villages was successfully carried out. By February 1945, 1,70,912 posts and 58,050 bamboos were stacked at Jharpany valley in small depots. But a number of bridges and feeder roads had to be built at great expense to extract the post. By May, the task of transporting all the required materials, even if each vehicle had to undertake three trips between Kohima and Ghaspani, was completed.

The Government of India with a view to facilitate resumption of normal life decided that relief measures should also be provided for either the loss or destruction of household goods during the War. It was laid down that the maximum relief in respect of those who had lost their houses and contents should be Rs. 400 whilst a maximum of Rs. 200 was fixed for those who had been looted by the enemy. Agricultural implements which were either thrown away by the Japanese or destroyed during the war were also replaced to a maximum quota of 2 *daos*, 2 axes, 2 hoes and 1 ploughshare to enable each householder to resume normal life. As the Nagas had to fell the trees and shrubs on the hill fields towards the end of the year axes and *daos* were immediately procured and distributed. Altogether 7401 *daos*, 2642 axes, and 7651 hoes were distributed. About 30 tonnes of broken lorry spring were also obtained from army salvage dumps and issues. The Naga blacksmiths preferred these metals to any other for the manufacturer of agricultural implements.

A large quantity of good blankets was purchased from a number of Indian firms for sale to the Nagas and Manipuris. But later on, all those households which came under the "necessitous case", (all those householders who had lost their house or had been looted by the Japanese particularly on the Japanese lines of communication) were altogether issued 67,000 blankets. Other household items were also provided at a specified quota of 2 aluminium cooking posts, 2 enamel mugs and 4 enamel plates to all those householders who had lost them. Cash relief amounting to Rs. 4,57,152 was provided to the Naga hill villagers for acquiring 45 mithun, 23 buffaloes, 1935 cattle and 5955 pigs. The authorities of Assam Relief Measures had fixed a rate of Rs. 150 for one mithun, Rs. 100 for one buffalo, Rs. 500 per householder as compensation for the loss of their animal.

The distributions of all these supplies were made possible by pressing into service all the available lorries belonging to Burma Refugee Organisation. A number of new lorries destined for Manipur but which could not reach Imphal due to the Japanese seige were also requisitioned. The 33rd corp also provided vehicle for the transport of food from Kohima to Phek in July August 1944. When the 33 corp left Naga Hills in August 1944 about 40 Jeeps were requisitioned to the government to meet the interim requirements. In addition to the 'guaranteed' daily lift of 10 trucks of food from Dimapur to Kohima, the A.R.M. called in the service of the private fleet of company known as "Assam Transport Operator", which had newly acquired 70 trucks. A number of lorries belonging to private owners were also hired much to the advantage of the local contractors and traders.

During the War period no consumer of goods of any kind could reach the Nagas. There was dearth of tea, sugar and salt. The presence of Army in these areas had brought considerable wealth to the inhabitants and this wealth had raised the standard of living of many people. Steps were taken to supply daily use goods like, cigarettes, matches, tea, sugar etc. for sale until the local traders were able to take over. In the early stages, a lorry fitted as a mobile canteen visited roadside villages in the Naga Hills every week so that local villagers could get their supplies without difficulty. The Nagas were also provided as emergency measure sufficient quantities of vegetable seeds and excellent results were obtained in 1945 spring. Several hundred iron pans were also purchased and sent to the eastern Naga Hills to get their problems relieved.

It was in the midst of such profound socio-economic changes that in June 1946 Zapu Phizo and Angami leader returned to the Naga Hills after his long war time sojourn in Burma to preach his gospel of Naga independence. Although the NNC (Naga National Council) which he had founded initially demanded local autonomy of Naga Hills within the state of Assam, after India's independence, they began to demand the cessation of the place from India.

Notes

1. A. Swanson, *Kohima*, p. 38.
2. *Ibid.*
3. A.B. Bore, A report on the measures of rehabilitation and construction undertaken by the Government of India in the Naga hill and Manipur, p. 62.
4. *Ibid.* p. 79.
5. *Ibid.*, p. 80.
6. T.N. Dupuy, *Asiatic land battles: Allied Victories in China and Burma*, p. 22.
7. W. Churchill, *History of II World War*, Vol. V, p. 432.
8. T.N. Dupuy, *op. cit*, p. 23.
9. A.B. Bore, *op. cit.* p. 3.
10. *Ibid.*, p. 4.
11. *Ibid.*
12. *Ibid.*
13. *Ibid.*
14. *Ibid.*, pp. 5 and 79.
15. *Ibid.*, p. 80.
16. *Ibid.*
17. *Ibid.*
18. *Ibid.*, p. 10.
19. *Ibid.*, p. 17.
20. *Ibid.*, p. 23.

13
British Colonialism and Agrarian Change in Manipur: 1891-1947

Pureshwor Nameirakpam

Introduction

By the end of the nineteenth century, Manipur had an agrarian economy that was naturally shaped by its unique physiographic, climatic condition and isolation from other states in the North Eastern part of India which was reproducing itself without any structural differentiation essentially at the level of self-sufficiency. But the advent of British colonial rule in 1891 subsequently reshuffled the social structure and distorted the state's economy with long term consequences on the growth and development in the state. The process of monetization and marketisation of the economy was started through the commercialization of agriculture and monetary taxation of land under the new land system of British colonial rule. Trade and commerce were expanded and monopolized by the influx of Bengalis and Marwaris at Imphal. The export sector revolved around the rice economy and forest economy (Ch. Priyoranjan Singh, 2005a: 149-159). Institutional changes in management of forest and agricultural land, the administrative and judicial structures, the nurturing of a commercial class of outsiders, modernization of communication and transport structures, all served the expansion of colonial extraction. Imports of new and cheaper consumption goods from outside Manipur brought about de-industrialization and consequent pressure on land for alternative employment in the region.

This chapter brings out the agrarian structure and institutions in the pre-colonial period and how these institutions underwent change, evolution or outright abolition during the British colonialism and how these changes impacted upon the economy and its productive base especially agriculture. Colonialism formed an important stage in the development process of the world, it served as the springboard for global divide of developed and underdeveloped countries in the immediate post-Second World War. European Colonialism had shaped the world in a very immoral and exploitative way and it is still a subject of blame, hatred and controversy. It formed an important perspective for—development from the point of colonizers and underdevelopment from the point of colonies. However, the nature of colonial administration and its ideological underpinning varied over time and across empires.

The main objectives of the study are to identify the agrarian structure and commercialization of Agriculture during the colonial period—New land system and class configurations—Land Revenue and Area-correlates—Productivity, cropping pattern—Agricultural price movement and Real income.

Agriculture was found to be not only the mainstay but also a livelihood of the people in Manipur (Md. Ali. Ashraf, 1988: 242). In this regard, before 1891, the whole area of land in the state belonged to the Raja. Therefore, it was at the will of the Raja (King) either to give or to withhold the land. Some people were allowed to use land permanently without paying tax while others could own only after paying tax. However, after the British occupation the permanent settlement of land was introduced in the state and separate *Pattas*[1] for holding land were issued to individuals. The owners could cultivate their own land by themselves or lease out for rent. But the mode of cultivation in different regions especially in the hills and the valley was different although the people cultivated a variety of crops—both food and commercial. Moreover, the displacement of a number of native people from trade and industry and their joining in agriculture further necessitated to the extension of cultivation to eke out their livelihood. Such indifferent pattern of Agricultural practice was found in the economic activity of the people of the India also. Nearly 80 per cent of the population was depending on agriculture for their livelihood. The progressive realization of the country during the nineteenth century under the initial impact of British supremacy had accentuated the traditional dependence of Indians on agriculture. The British encouraged irrigation facilities for the plantation of commercial crops or of raw materials of textile industries of England in India. Production of food grains increased and became important merchandise both for internal and external market.

Agrarian structure has their roots in history in that the property relations that changed through time shaped the social relations of production. After the Anglo-Manipuri War of 1891, British brought a new economic structure to the state. According to Fei and Ranis model of transition from Agrarianism to open agrarianism (Fei, H. John and Gustav Ranis, 1969: 138), the old closed agrarian economy of the native period was opened up by a new economic agent just after the occupation of Manipur. This factor was instrumental in adding the export sector to the earlier agriculture and service sectors. The export sector rules upon exploitation of cheap labour and natural resources which are productive of specific raw materials, i.e. their agricultural or minerals. Gradually, the non-Manipuri traders became entrepreneurs and monopolized the service sector and the service sector too caters more to the needs of export sector rather less to the needs of the unproductive class or the landed Aristocracy (Ch. Priyoranjan Singh, 2005b: 47). Investments were undertaken on the construction of transportation to connect with the capital Imphal, power, and housing for further export growth. Moreover, there was an influx of consumer goods into the rural areas. The establishments of new service sector brought into the agrarian economy, the commercial class, commercial capital, new production activities and a new consumption horizon. This gradual acceptance of a rational economic behaviour and maximization of profit was the basic purpose of economic life.

This new life was characterized by an insatiable appetite for economic acquisition. However, such conversion was often accompanied by the development of new institutional arrangement replacing the old one. Under the British imperialism, the *Raiyatwari* system[2] was introduced in Manipur. Under this system no intermediary proprietors were recognized and settlement was undertaken with *raiyats* (cultivators) on an individual or collective basis for temporary periods; the *raiyats* were vested with heritable and transferable rights of property in their land and made individually or collectively responsible for revenue payments (P. C. Joshi, 1987: 4).

With the event new land system and introduction of private property in land and taxation in money brought the process of monetization and marketization of the economy and commercialization of agriculture. The valley was divided into four *pannas*[3] for revenue purposes; each division was administered under a *lakpa*.[4] The Imphal *panna* was later added. The *lakpa* gets a commission of 10 per cent of revenue collected and met all expenses from this commission. For political reason Manipuris of influence and standing rather than man of any special capacity for work, were at first appointed to *lakpa's* post.

New Land System and Class Configurations

After the British occupation of Manipur state in 1891, they introduced a new landowning system, which was totally different from the earlier traditional semi-feudal character where private ownership of land did not exist; the new system was based on the concept of western property and proprietary rights. Three types of land systems the *zamindari*[5], *raiyatwari* and *mahalwari*[6] were practiced over the British Indian territory, the *Raiyat* system which had the essence of individual proprietorship were prevalent in the certain areas of Bombay, Sind, Bihar, Assam and Madras. Likewise, the British extended the *Rayatwari* system of land ownership in the native state on experimental basis (J. Shakespeare, 1907 a: 14), then *Pattas* were issued to the individual owners of the valley. The Private ownership of land in turn brought about a change in the system of revenue payments. The earlier revenue system of the kind that specified in the portion of the actual year produce was replaced in the system of fixed cash payment. In 1982, Major Maxwell, the then political agent of Manipur fixed the land revenue to be paid by the people in cash uniformly at the rate of Rs. 5 per *pari*[7] after abolishing *Lallup*[8] duty. And a special house tax of Rs. 2 per house per annum in the valley was levied irrespective of the size of the house or home-stead land or the number of its inmates (M. Lokendra, 1991: 153), and whether the land was cultivated or not and whether the year's harvest was good or bad. In fact such practice made disruption in the traditional village character of the Manipuris and led to change the economic and social relations of the native state.

This new land system granted the rights to every individual to sell his land, purchase land from others and could mortgage over his own land at their sweet will. Hence land became a private property like a commodity in the market (M. Lokendra, 1991:157). The amount of revenue payment in cash was time bound, the old subsistence farmers had to change their objective and were forced to part with some of his produce immediately the harvest for sales. So the peasant required to produce crops for the revenue payments meant for commercial purpose, not just only for their own uses. When the land holders were unable to pay his land revenue to the state due to poor harvest or other natural calamities, he was compelled to mortgage or sell his land. The most contributing factors responsible for the growth of such practices were by the socio-religious function of the Manipuri society like 'saradha'[9] and marriage ceremony which incur huge expenses (M. Lokendra, 1991: 158). Besides, the rich people (money lenders, local merchants, influx Marwari[10] traders, rich urban people, high ranking officials and near relatives of the royal family) got the opportunity of surplus extractions through sales of product sales land or mortgage of land by the peasants. These rich land owners sublet their land to the actual cultivators for cultivation because they did not cultivate by themselves. This practice created a small group of landed aristocrat class and large section of tenants class. Such activities could be witnessed even in the early part of the colonial period. Here, Shakespeare remarked in 1907 that about one-fourth of the land *pattas* issued by the state was held by the rich class of people who sublet out (J. Shakpeare, 1907 a: 14).

During the colonial period land revenue was the main source of income of the state. The revenue assessment for one *pari* of land was Rs. 5 and Rs. 2 for each homestead land. Besides, the Britisher introduced a number of new taxes, *viz.* the hill house tax, the foreigners' tax, the dog tax, the cycle tax, salt tax etc. However, the house tax was removed later on and taxed at the same rate as agricultural land according to area occupied. The rate of revenue in Jiribam region was Rs. 3 and 12 *anna*[11] per *pari* (G.P. Stewart, 1935: 5) and rate of revenue for shop-sites was introduced by the Darbar[12] Resolution No. 10 of August 31st, 1938. Shops can be built at all sites which lie wholly or partly outside *patta* land and within fifty feet of the edge of a road within the precincts of Imphal will be assessed at two *annas* per foot of frontage per month (E.F. Lydall, 1943: 3). The collection of land revenue during the colonial period was comprises dualistic, land revenue for the valley of Manipur and Hill house tax for the hill areas. Valley's actual revenue collection was good, increased with the increase in demand and state government also granted some relaxation for the disabled minority group by remitting their balance arrears revenue and the left balance arrears were to recover in the following year.

The actual revenue collection of 1891-92 was Rs. 62,024 as against the demand of Rs. 1,60,000 and increased to Rs. 6,39,541 in 1946-47 as against the demand of Rs. 11,09,096 in 1946-47. At the early colonial period the demand for revenue was high but its actual collection was very less and leaving behind the balance arrears of Rs. 97,976 in 1891. The percentage collection of actual revenue during the British rule were 38 per cent, 93 per cent, 95 per cent, 69 per cent, 59 per cent and 57 per cent in the year 1891, 1901, 1911, 1921, 1940 and 1946 respectively. Its collection trend shows a sudden increase in the 1st decade of the colonial period in 1901 that rose from 38 per cent to 93 per cent and 95 per cent in 1911, then gradually decreased in the later part up to 57 per cent. The reason for decrease in the payment of revenue it might be of the instant conversion of revenue payment from kind to cash or the natural calamities, diminished exportation of rice. On the one hand, the continuous increase in the actual collection of revenue was due to the imposition of a small fine on defaulting *pattadars* and somewhat high price of rice and the new system of collection that the *lakpas* and their subordinates remain at headquarters, while the *kanungoes*[13] and *amins*[14] whose ordinary work takes them out the villages were employed in hunting up defaulters and sending them into Imphal to pay their revenue. These alterations have had a salutary effect, as they enable a closer supervision to be kept over the work of the collecting staff. After 1911, the balance revenue increased with the increase of remission to the peasant by the government, this might be caused by the worsen of peasantry's economy in the society and unable to pay the total amount fully after the implementation of new land revenue Act or of the improper function of the revenue department. Thus, the extraction policy of revenue adopted in the state by the British subsequently hampered the economy in spite of development. Table 13.1.

illustrate the details of colonial revenue demand, collection, remission and balance of the valley of Manipur.

Table 13.1: Demand, Collection, Remission, Balance of Land Revenue in the valley of Manipur (1891-1946)

Year	*Demand (Rs.)*	*Actual Collection (Rs.)*	*Remission (Rs.)*	*Balance (Rs.)*	%
1891-92	1,60,000	62,024	NA	97,976	38
1901-02	2,71,382	2,53,967	7,469	9,946	93
1911-12	3,33,713	3,20,220	1,729	11,764	95
1921-22	5,74,234	4,01,149	6,718	1,66,135	69
1940-41	8,54,281	5,08,769	74,253	2,71,256	59
1946-47	11,09,096	6,39,541	1,43,441	3,26,112	57

Source: Respective Administration Reports of Manipur state.

As compared to the valley's record some data of the hills revenue were found to be missing or unavailable as per the records given by the subsequent Political Agents of the British in Manipur. In the year 1891-92, the hill house tax was very good, collecting of Rs. 63,566 as against the demand of Rs. 65,728 leaving behind of only Rs. 2,162 as balance arrears. During the colonial rule, the actual collection of the revenue was found to be highly decreased in 1901-02 and later the increased trend of collection was witnessed. It also rose to Rs. 97,683 in the year 1946-47.

Table 13.2 shows the Demand, Collection, Remission, and Balance of Hill House Tax of Manipur.

Table 13.2: Demand, Collection, Remission, Balance of Hill House Tax of Manipur (1891-1946)

Year	*Demand (Rs.)*	*Actual Collection (Rs.)*	*Remission (Rs.)*	*Balance (Rs.)*
1891-92	65,728	63,566	NA	2,162
1901-02	NA	30,325	NA	29,675
1911-12	75,054	69,178	906	4,970
1921-22	83,449	72,678	3,072	7,699
1940-41	NA	94,248	NA	NA
1946-47	NA	97,683	NA	NA

Source: Respective Administration Reports of Manipur state.

Revenue Administration

In the late pre-colonial period the cultivators paid revenue in the form of kind and labour. As no official received salaries in cash, they were remunerated by allowances in paddy. Public buildings, bridges and roads were constructed or repaired by *lallup* or unpaid labour. This system of revenue collections was not useful but there were many advantages connected with it. State labour not being paid for, voluntary labour was cheap, and this enabled people to house themselves well, the *lallup* population possibly 70 per cent of the male adults were strong and industrious and all articles of food were cheap as well. The continuous employment of the people gave no leisure for individual quarrelling or for inciting rebellion against the authorities (H.St.P. Maxwell, 1895: 4). The British reorganized the early revenue administration system by opening a separate revenue department of the state in order to collect revenue or taxes directly or indirectly in cash as far as possible. The hierarchal composition of land revenue department was the Raja - Deputy Commissioner-Sub-Deputy Commissioner- Lakpas or Tahsildar- Amins-Mohurrirs (clerk) - kanungoes-peon (unskilled labour).

During the early colonial period the land revenue was first of all collected by the clerks in the state office, but the system revealed the disinclination of the Manipuri to pay taxes unless personally visited to the house of land holders, this resulted to leave very large arrears. In order to avoid the consequent difficulties of accumulating land revenue arrears when assessed the process of revenue collections for the state. In the year 1894-95, the valley was divided into 4 *pannas* or divisions (Ahalup panna, Naharup panna, Laifam panna and Khabam panna), a *lakpa* or tahsildar (fiscal officer) was appointed for each *panna* to collect land revenue (H.St.P. Maxwell, 1895: 5). In the same manner the house-tax was also collected by the *panna lakpa*. Each *lakpa* kept a writer and a peon for the office, *lakpa* received their salaries directly from the state office but deducted 10 per cent of the collection as their commission for the cost collection. Moreover, the state government skipped of collecting Land Revenue from minority and unabled sections, remitted in favour of the blind and infirm, widows, orphans and women giving birth to twins, and the irrecoverable arrears (Major J. Shakespear, 1905, b: 2). The post of an *amin* was established to check the illicit cultivation and demarcate the boundary of all *pattas* within the season's operations, and it firstly operated in the Laifam panna (H.St.P. Maxwell, 1895: 5). However, the *lakpas* system seems to be more expensive, therefore, the tasks of *lakpas* with settlement business or registration was removed. Then, in the year 1896-97, a post of Sub-Deputy Collector was appointed to supervise the land revenue administration of the state and the government entrusted the entire management of the state land revenue business of the valley to the SDC. For easy assessment of collection the wide size of four *pannas* was reduced by constituting the town of Imphal as a separate *panna* (Government of Manipur, 1898: 4). In the year 1906-07, the settlement of Jiribam region was started.

Disputes of land or cases were frequent because it was difficult to find out the position of any man's land which so far as the *patta* shows. According to the land law, any one can cultivate fresh land just after sanctioning its land *patta* but the people preferred to open up new land and took out *pattas* afterwards. With this recklessness character many persons had added much land to their previous *pattas*. Such irregular procedure causes much confusion and disputes for the boundaries of the land. To prevent the encroachment on village-grazing-lands, lands have been demarcated with earthen mounds and boughs of some quick growing tree (A.W. Davis, 1908: 3).

In 1907, Mr. Cosgrave appointed a *mauzdar*[15] and the year 1908-09, a plane table survey was made of the principal roads and rivers which form the natural boundaries of the various *laikais* or quarters of Imphal and also for the entire British reserve to ensure greater accuracy.

To stop such confusion into which the records had fallen, owing to the absence of anything in the form of a *dagchitha*[16], to which the lands in any given *patta* could be referred and from which it could be ascertained where lands were situated, the measures were taken up by the state, rough survey to the whole valley by rod was done (Government of Manipur, 1898:4). After carefully measuring to few villages, 40 per cent of the land in cultivation were found in *patta* at all, therefore, escapes the taxation (H.St.P. Maxwell, 1895: 5). On the other hand, the state used to transform the existed system by removing or adding a new norm in the administrative process. The reason for rapid changes in the system was only to increase the collection of revenue with little investment. For effective collection of revenue the previous *amins* system was again abolished and transformed into new one by recruiting a temporary staff of 4 *Kanungos* and 40 *amins* on varying pay of Rs. 20 to Rs. 10. A survey school was also established to train the *amins* under the eye of the SDC himself (Government of Manipur, 1898: 4), this resulted improvement in the collection (H.St.P. Maxwell, 1899: 5). As a result the area under cultivation increases partly due to the extension of cultivation and partly to the discovery of concealed cultivation. Areas were newly surveyed and relinquished.

By the new system of permitting the *raiyats* to pay their revenue directly to the headquarters, the Sub-Deputy's inspections were confined to examining the works of *amins* and *kanungos*. On 15th January, 1904, when Lt. Colonel H.St.P. Maxwell saw that of the Rs. 2,18,000 due on that date only Rs. 8,000 had been paid, he was compelled to alter the system and returned on the former method of collecting the revenue. The question arises whether the new system was practicable; Maxwell was feared and believed that would be impracticable so long as human nature remains unchanged.

The DC was the in charge of all land revenue disposes of all rent cases but to reduced the tasks of DC the *lakpas* first enquired the cases and reported to DC and he passes the final order (J. Shakespeare, 1905 b: 3). When tenants fail to pay up their dues on or before the 15th March, their holdings are occasionally put to sale as a last resort, they also confined in the civil jail (J. Shakespeare, 1905 b: 2).

Area-correlates—Productivity

For every agricultural country, rice became the major crop that can be called the crops of monsoon Asia which had been also an important export article in these regions, probably the most exportable in trade deal(Roy. Tirthankar, 2006: 45). In the context of Manipur state, rice was the only food crop that was produced abundantly for being the staple food of the people living in Manipur and majority of the inhabitants survive by means of agriculture. There was competition to own land as far as possible during the colonial rule. The customary mode of cultivation during the British period was highly advanced even though the development of science and technology was very slow. This mode of cultivation was not lack behind from the 20th century cultivation because they wisely practiced the art of *Pung-hul*[17] in the dry or high land where scarcity of water, transplanting was same as of now, *Pamphel*[18] was also practiced in the land where cultivators had to transplant the nurseries in the rocky soil. There were three types of cultivation *viz.* '*Pung hul*' or dry seed cast in the dry ground, *Ling-ba*[19] or transplanting the plants from nurseries and '*Pamphel*' or cast of seeds in the wet field. But the transplantation of the native was same as that practiced in the Eastern Bengal (E.W. Dun, 1981: 61) and the way of soil tilling was a bit different from other parts of Bengal. The soil quality of the valley was excellent due to its own inherent richness of deposition of silt by the river in the rainy season (E.W. Dun, 1981: 60).

In the year 1893-94, the total acres under cultivation according to the revenue office books was 28,845 *paris* of which 1,514 *paris* were held as rent free by the King or have been granted as service lands to various revenue and judicial officers or to the police. The greater part of these service lands and about 25 per cent of the lands held under ordinary *patta* and were cultivated by *raiyats* who pay rent (usually in kind) to the officer holding the land or to the *patta*-holder. This rent was by custom fixed at 12 pots[20] of 50 seers or 15 maunds[21] per *pari* worth rates about Rs. 14 (A. Porteous, 1894: 4). For the rest of the lands assessed to revenue the occupant *raiyat* himself holds the *patta*. 24,887 *pattas* have been issued, for the 27331 *paris* of land not held on service tenure and of these only 2242 had not actually been delivered to the *patta*-holders. The average size of a holding appears from the above figures amount to about 2 ¾ acres. The whole settlement then in force was based on the figures obtained from the records of the village officials, dating from before the revolt of 1891, and no remeasurement has yet been attempted nor do *pattas* contain the boundaries of each holding. They are merely occupancy permits with the village (A. Porteous, 1894: 4). During the colonial period, the agricultural land in the valley which was only 26,500 hectares in 1891 had risen to 75,370 hectares in 1941. The population had grown from 1,35,782 in 1891 to 3,43,694 in 1941. Thus, the man land ratio had risen from 0.195 in 1891 to 0.219 persons in 1941 whereas by the end of the colonial rule, a hectare of land supported only 4.56 persons. Table 13.3 illustrates the quantum of surplus generation of rice. Based on the estimates of the rice demand and production, the agrarian sector in the valley had the surplus potential of 26, 35, 42, and 35 per cent of production in 1891, 1901, 1931, and 1941 respectively. It can be verified from the Brown's Report and Administration Report of 1894-95 that 'At present moment a two-year food surplus is stored in the village'. But the actual rate of production was varied depending on regions where they cultivated the rate of production per *pari* was 40 pots; Least of 75 pots (R. Brown,1874), 43 pots (Government of Manipur,1898), and 40 pots (A.E. Woods, 1902: 1).

Table 13.3: Area, Production and Rice Surplus in Manipur Valley (1891-1941) cited in Ch. Priyoranjan, 2005 b: Unpublished Thesis, 49

Year	*Valley Population*	*Area (Hectare)*	*Demand (Tonnes)*	*Rice Production (Tonnes)*	*Surplus (Tonnes)*	*Per cent Surplus*
1891	1,35,782	26,500	28,107	38,160	10,053	26
1901	1,91,207	42,283	39,580	60,755	21,175	35
1931	2,86,843	71,316	59,376	1,02,695	43,319	42
1941	3,43,694	75,370	71,145	1,08,533	37,388	34

Cropping Pattern

Rice was the staple food of the state Manipur, and peasantry had become a solid aspect of life by the Twentieth century (Oinam Somorendro Meitei: accessed 7 June, 2009) A paddy crop was the most important crops in the state. Cultivation of wet rice of settled agriculture was practiced through irrigation system of dams and canals in the valley. The developed culture of crop husbandry, especially for rice, led to the abundance of rice production and staple food security in the valley region. The crops varied for different season of the year and its productions condition depended on the seasonal monsoon rain, the fate of the harvest whether good or bad was determined by the natural calamities which disturbed the crops specially by heavy rainfall, flood, drought, hail and storms moreover by the widespread attacks of crickets on the nurseries and severe affected consequences of the ravage of water hyacinth. An immense damage of crops was found over the state by floods in 1929, but it made a useful impact of clearing the water hyacinth weeds which very difficult to root out from the cultivating field since there were no pesticide of the weeds. Plantation of paddy crops preferably to proceed in the months of June, July and August of the rainy season. Sali rice was most productive over the valley and Aus rice crops were suitable at the high land rather than any other regions (A. Porteous, 1894: 3). However, just after the rice crops the other important crops were pea, sugarcane, potatoes, chillies, beans, mustard, *matikalai*[22], *mung*, *khesari*, several kinds of pulses etc. were also cultivated in the valley. Cultivation of *matikalai* was favourable in the month of September. In 1893, plantation of wheat, barley, oats and potatoes crops were firstly experimented in the state jail with the imported tubers (A. Porteous, 1894: 3) and found successful in Manipur. The native potatoes did grow but in a miserably inferior sort. Further, in the year 1915, an experimental garden was opened at Kanglatongbi in the northern part of the valley in which plantains, Shillong potatoes, sugarcane, foreign and indigenous *arhar dal* and *buri kapas* were planted.

During the colonial period, both shifting (jhumming) and settled (terrace) crops cultivation were practiced in the hills, the *dhan* crops or rice crops was started in the month of April and May. The other crops cultivated in the hills were potatoes, tobacco, cotton, maize, millet, kachu, job's tear, Indian corn, chillies, *pan*, plantains, plantains leaves, various kinds of fruits and vegetables etc. Hills crops was mostly disturbed or damaged by rats and to a lesser extent by wild pigs and rebellion as well (A.G. McCall, 1928: 11) Shifting cultivation was the ordinary system of cultivation in the hills. Amongst the hills communities Tangkhuls and Mao practiced terrace cultivation. The Kukis of the South-West area and the settlers from Lushai hills also practiced the wet rice cultivation in the valley of Kuga Valley. Generally; the Kukis not take keen interest in wet rice cultivation because they prefer the shifting system from their forefathers (C.S. Mullan, 1922: 10). In 1919, an experiment of wet rice cultivation was made at the South-West area of Kukis, two intelligent Nagas of Mao group who went to France with the Labour crops were sent to the areas to look round the prospect of terrace cultivation or extension of wet rice cultivation. Unfortunately, nowhere in those areas was practicable due to the steepness of the hills and the shortages of water. Then in 1922, two rain gauges were established at Ukhrul and

Tamanglong. The Kukis and the Kacha Nagas of the North-west area did not cultivate rice on an extensive scale because they found the easier way of purchasing the rice with the sales of the forest product such as cane, wax, lac, chillies, cotton and *pan* which they could easily collect and cultivate without much labour (C.G. Crawford, 1923: 11).

Another rain gauge was also established in 1925 at Churchandpur, wet rice crops was tried in the North-west sub-division but people were not persuaded to diverge from their traditional method of cultivation. In the year itself some grains like wheat, barley, oat and fruits were also found to cultivate on the trial basis. Many kinds of fruits trees were planted and the villagers were employed in destroying weeds (water hyacinth) at their respective villages.

Agricultural Price Movement and Real Income

Commercialized in agriculture, monetary taxation of land under the new land system of British colonial rule made expanded the trade and commerce of the economy and gradually monopolized by the influx Bengalis and Marwaris at the Imphal town (N. Lokendra Singh, 1998: 63), the absolute source of exportation from the state revolved around only in agriculture (specially in rice economy) and forest economy. The institutional changes in management of forest and agricultural land resulted the changes in agricultural products and marketed supplies of food grains. Apart from that unpredictable climatic and weather conditions also determined the productivity of rice in the state. When weather patterns are favourable, yield per acre will be high and *vice versa* (Dharma, Kumar, 1982: 880).

Since the rice production was surplus throughout the British rule in the native state, the prices of the paddy crops would be almost in the normal position. In 1892-93, the price of paddy per maund of Rs. 2 and 12 *annas* was increased to Rs. 40–Rs. 50 in 1946-47. From 1898-99 to 1940-41, the price remained constant, i.e. below Rs. 2 per maund. Then, the price of paddy immediately rose to Rs. 25 to Rs. 50 per maund in the next following two years of 1941-42 to 1943-44. The average price for the entire works at about Rs. 3 and 12 *annas*. The reason for steep rising of paddy price might be the excessive exportation of rice towards Kohima for the troops and to Dimapur for coolies employed on railway construction. In 1939, a great agitation called the Nupi Lal (Women's Agitation) occurred to stop the excessive rice exports to the outside state or to safeguard the extraction policy of food grains of the Indian Government for the economy of the state. Such excessive exportation of rice immensely affected the prices of rice in the state and in the local consumption. In this year price of rice rose from Rs. 2 to Rs. 3 per maund. But in the later four years, the prices of Rs. 3 per maund was increased to about thirteen times per maund. During the colonial rule the internal trade and market was managed by the women folk (Yambem Sanamani, 1976: 325-331) apart from the economic activities, the market took an important venue of the social and political interaction. It was the aspect of the Khwairamband Bazar which played a crucial role in the outbreak of the women agitation and it has been observing this agitation till today in the state. The relevant prices of forty-two years are shown as in Table 13.4.

Table 13.4: Price of Paddy per maund in March (1892—1943)

Year	*Price (Rs. anna. paisa)*	*Year*	*Price (Rs. anna. paisa)*	*Year*	*Price (Rs. anna.paisa)*
1892-93	2-12-0	1913-14	1-2-0	1930-31	1-0-0
1893-94	2-4-0	1914-15	1-3-0	1933-34	0-15-2
1894-95	1-4-0	1915-16	1-3-0	1934-35	1-4-0
1897-98	3-8-0	1916-17	1-0-0	1935-36	3-0-0
1898-99	1-6-0	1917-18	0-12-0	1936-37	1-8-0
1899-1900	1-2-0	1918-19	1-4-0	1938-39	1-12-0 to Rs. 2.00
1900-1901	1-4-0	1919-20	1-10-0	1939-40	2-0-0
1902-03	0-10-0	1921-22	1-5-0	1940-41	2-8-0
1904-05	0-9-6	1922-23	0-14-0	1941-42	3-0-0 to Rs. 25 in Aug. 1942
1906-07	1-10-0	1923-24	1-0-0		
1907-08	0-14-0	1924-25	1-5-0		
1908-09	0-14-0	1925-26	2-8-0	1943-44	Rs. 40 to Rs. 50 in June 15th 1943
1909-10	0-11-0	1926-27	1-7-0		
1910-11	0-12-0	1927-28	1-7-0		
1911-12	1-2-0	1928-29	1-2-0		
1912-13	1-5-0	1929-30	1-2-0		

Source: Respective Administration Reports of Manipur state.

The prices of some other crops per maund of the valley were found much higher than the paddy price. During the British period, the least price of *matikalai* was Rs. 3. per maund in 1915-16 and maximum price reached to Rs. 8 per maund in 1920-21 in the month of March. Average price of *matikalai* for the 26 years records from 1904-1930 is about Rs. 5 and 4 *annas*. This average price of *matikalai* is higher than the average price of paddy. This means that the production of *matikalai* was scarce than the paddy. The prices movement of *matikalai* can be seen in Table 13.5. Potatoes also cost only Rs. 1 and 8 *annas* per maund even though its price was again higher than the price of paddy for thirty two years. Table 13.6 shows the price of potato.

Table 13.5: Price of *Matikalai* (Maize) per maund in March (1904-1930)

Year	*Price (Rs. anna. paisa)*	*Year*	*Price (Rs. anna. paisa)*
1904-05	4-0-0	1918-19	6-10-0
1906-07	3-6-0	1919-20	6-7-0
1907-08	5-0-0	1920-21	8-0-0
1908-09	8-0-0	1921-22	5-12-0
1909-10	6-3-0	1922-23	7-4-0
1910-11	4-0-0	1923-24	6-8-0
1911-12	4-0-0	1924-25	6-3-0
1912-13	5-0-0	1925-26	6-11-0
1913-14	4-0-0	1926-27	6-3-0
1914-15	3-5-0	1927-28	5-8-0
1915-16	3-0-0	1928-29	4-5-0
1916-17	5-14-0	1929-30	3-9-0
1917-18	5-0-0	1930-31	3-10-0

Source: Respective Administration Reports of Manipur state.

Table 13.6: Price of Potatoes per maund in March

Year	*Price (Rs. anna.Paisa)*
1901-02	1-8-0 to Rs. 2.00

Source: Administration Reports of Manipur State, 1901-02.

Conclusion

The invasion of British brought some development in the economy, a new economic structure of open agrarian economy instrumental in adding the export sector to the earlier agriculture and service sectors. The new established service sector brought into the agrarian economy, the commercial class, commercial capital, new production activities and a new consumption horizon. Monetized and marketized economy with the commercialized agriculture and monetary taxation was also made during the colonial Manipur. The export exploited cheap labour and natural resources, which are productive of specific raw materials—agricultural or minerals and started giving due importance rather on the needs of the export sector by the service sector. The adopted policy of the British to the state gave a great impact, though surplus in production of agriculture people fought for their food since the Second World War due to scarcity of food in the state. The adverse extraction policy was the only significant result for distorting the self-sufficient society into different classes among the peasants. It developed a class of rich people like money-lenders, local merchants, influx Marwaris traders, rich urban people and high ranking officials and near relatives of the royal family provides the opportunity to gain with the sales of agricultural product, sales of land or mortgage of land by the peasants. Thus, the nature of British colonialism called the exploitative colonialism was given a negative impact to the economy and still carried out its image uptill now.

Notes

1. *Patta*: land holding registration certificate issued by the British authority to the private individuals.
2. *Raiyatwari system*: the system of collecting revenues directly from the cultivators of agricultural land.
3. *Pannas*: means the territorial divisions. In the early period, there was no clear-cut administrative division. The area represented by a Phamdou consisted of specific names of villages under a supervisor, was not based on any geographical or territorial demarcation. Traditionally the kingdom had four *pannas*, believed to have been established during the reign of King Pakhangba. Loiyamba, established six divisions known as *Lup* according to the royal chronicle. *The Loiyamba Shilyen* edited by Kh. Chandrashekhar and translated by N. Sanajaoba refers to six *pannas* adding two more, Hitakphanba and Potshangba. The names of the divisions were different: *Lup* and *Pana*, but the function might be similar. During the zenith of Manipur's power, we have a fully developed *Panna* system.
4. *Lakpa:* chief, official incharge of revenue collection in various institutes as well as subdivisions and specific areas within the land, it was not a hereditary but a post appointed by the king and the

reigning king's male relatives often were the first choice, some posts were automatically allotted to the king's brothers only.

5. *Zamindari system*: A way of collecting taxes from peasants in which the *zamindar* (landlord) would collect all taxes on his lands and then hand over the collected taxes to the British authorities, leaving a portion to himself.
6. *Mahalwari system*: The unit for revenue settlement in the village. The village lands belong jointly to the village community technically called the body of co-shares. The body of co-shares is jointly responsible for the payment of land revenue though individual responsibility is always there.
7. *Pari*: unit of measurement of land used in Manipur; 1 *pari* = 2½ acres; 1 acre = 6.25 bigha in *Wikipaedia*, the free encyclopedia.; *1 hectare* = 2.471 acres.
8. *Lallup*: an old system of tax in terms of labour given to the state. It was organized on the *Panna* basis. The people were allotted a plot of land for which they were not required to pay revenue, instead had to serve the state 3 months in a year, or 10 days in every 40 days. This service of the people was used by the King in various parts of the administration such as guards, construction work and in providing some sort of informal policing; the same person was not continually employed for the purpose nor paid any salary.
9. *Saradha* (*sorat*): death ceremony that is performed after the death of a person. In natural death, the day of *sorat* will be usually fixed by the person before his/ her death or will be fixed according to the will of the family members.
10. Marwaris are the foreigner and called as *Mayangs* by the local people of Manipur.
11. *Anna* the small unit of money, 1 *anna* = 1/16 rupee or 64 paise or 192 pies, during British India.
12. Darbar can be described as a ruler's court, it came into being in the State Manipur in 1907 and the Administration of Manipur, except the British Reserve, was transferred to the Maharaja and to his Darbar, formal and informal meetings were held in this Darbar.
13. *Kanungoes*: A post of supervisor in the revenue and collection department of the British Manipur. The field *Kanungo* should be constantly moving about his circle supervising the work on the spot, except in the month of September when he stays at the Tehsil to check the *Jamabandis* received from the cultivators. He also disposes of the demarcation applications marked to him by the Circle Revenue Officer. The office Kanungo is the Tehsildar Revenue clerk and he is the custodian of all the record received from the *patwari*.
14. *Amins*: land surveyors or a post of Revenue Field Staff under the administrative control of Collector, The land system comprises surveyed and unsurveyed land during the colonial period and land

were surveyed for the efficient land administration and collection of land revenue in the valleys and house tax in the hills by the government.

15. *Mauzadar:* A term referring to a person who takes tax of a mouza (revenue collection unit) during and after the British Raj in the modern-day Bangladesh and India.
16. *Dagchitha*: A kind of register containing information about the plot number of land.
17. *Pung hul*: A method of cultivation which was adopted in dry land. In this method the soil are well tilled, the dry seeds are sown over it and covered with the soil by tilling again once so that the seeds might get germinated quickly with the moisture from the ground. This is commonly operated in the months of May and June.
18. *Ling-ba*: A most popular method of cultivation, suitable to the land surface where inundated is possible or dry whenever required. Here, both the process of soil tilling and soaked of seeds with water are almost same as *pamphel* but the seed used to grow paddy in the nursery and then transplanted them to the fields which have been made ready for the purpose.
19. *Pamphel*: A method of cultivation suitable for the wet land, here the land is tilled to make muddy and well leveled the field then the soaked germinated seeds into an air tied bag with the water are sown in such a manner that each seed might occupy its regular space. This is generally done in June and July.
20. *Pots*: unit of weight usually used to measure food grains. One pot of paddy = 54 kg *vide* R. Brown, Paddy gives 2/3 rice when husked.
21. *Maund*: unit of weight, 1 maund = 37.3 kg.
22. *Matikalai*: a kind of local pulse like maize.

References

A. Porteous, 1894, *Administration Report of the Political Agency, Manipur, 1893-94*: Eastern Bengal and Assam Secretariat Office, Shillong.

A.E. Woods, 1902, *Administration Report of the Political Agency, Manipur, 1901-02*: Assam Secretariat Office, Shillong.

A.G. McCall, 1928, *Administration Reports of Manipur State, 1927-28*: State Printing Press, Imphal.

A.W. Davis, 1908, *Administration Report of the Manipur State, 1907-08*: Eastern Bengal and Assam Secretariat Office, Shillong.

C.G. Crawford, 1923, *Administration Report of Manipur State, 1922-23*: State Printing Press, Imphal.

C.S. Mullan, 1922, *Administration Report of Manipur State, 1921-22*: State Printing Press, Imphal.

Ch. Priyoranjan Singh, 2005 a: *Manipur's Economy: Historical Roots and Structural Evolution.*

Ch. Priyoranjan Singh, 2005 b: Agrarian Production relations of Manipur. *Unpublished Thesis,* Manipur University.

Dharma Kumar, 1982, *The Cambridge Economic History of India. Volume II: c.1757- c.1970,* Orient Longman in association with Cambridge University Press, Hyderabad.

Eastern Quarterly, Vol. 3, Issue III.

E.W. Dun, 1981, *Gazetteer of Manipur,* Vivek Publication Company, New Delhi.

E.F. Lydall, 1943, *Administration Reports of Manipur State, 1938-39*: State Printing Press, Imphal.

Fei H. John and Gustav Ranis, 1969, *Agriculture in the Open Economy in Erri, Thorbecke*:

G.P. Stewart, 1935, *Administration Reports of the Manipur State, 1934-35*: State Printing Press, Imphal.

Government of Manipur, 1898, *Annual Report on the Native States and Frontier Tribes of Assam, 1897-98*: Assam Secretariat Office, Shillong.

H.St.P. Maxwell, Lieutenant Colonel, 1895, *Administration Report of the Political Agency, Manipur, 1894-95*: Assam Secretariat Office, Shillong.

H.St.P. Maxwell, Lieutenant Colonel, 1899, *Administration Report of the Political Agency, Manipur, 1898-99*: Assam Secretariat Office, Shillong.

J. Shakespear, 1907, a: *Manipur under British Management from 1891 to 1907.*

J. Shakespear, Major, 1905, b: *Administration Report of the Political Agency, Manipur, 1904-05*: Assam Secretariat Office, Shillong.

M. Lokendra, 1991, Social change in Manipur: *Unpublished Thesis,* Manipur University.

Md. Ali Ashraf, 1988, Economic History of Manipur. *Unpublished Thesis,* Manipur University.

N. Lokendra Singh, 1998, *The Unquiet Valley.* Mittal Publications, New Delhi.

Oinam Somorendro Meitei, *"Economic History of Manipur (1826-1891)"* www.manipuronline.com/Economy/November2005/econhistory03_1.htm - 48k

P.C. Joshi, 1987, *Institutional Aspects of Agricultural Development,* Allied Publishers, New Delhi.

R. Brown, 1874, *Statistical Account of the Native State of Manipur and the hill territory under its rule,* Office of the Superintendent of Government Printing, Calcutta.

Roy Tirthankar, 2006, *The Economic History of India, 1891-1947.* Oxford University Press, New Delhi.

"The Role of Agriculture in Economic Development." *National Bureau of Economic Research,* New York.

Yambem Sanamani, 1976, "Nupi Lan: Manipur Women's Agitation, 1939", *Economic and Political Weekly,* Special Articles, Vol. XI, 8, 21st February.

14
Colonialism and its Effect on the Culture of North East India

Ningthoujam Munish Singh

Treaty of Yandaboo in 1826 marked the entry of British Colonialism to North East India by capturing the plain areas of Assam. Manipur and Tripura remained its status of a princely state. Most part of the hill areas of North East India were under the Inner Line Regulations with British Suzerainty.

North East India has been a depositor of Culture through ages. There exists several numbers of tribes whose dialects, costumes is completely different from other although way of life, food habits are almost similar. Unique identity of each tribe remains with their own traditional customary rituals and independent administration. Hence, there has been always an unseen wall even today within those tribes and it is not that easy for any foreign culture to intrude beyond these walls. However, there is a thin line of mutual understanding within these tribes which help them coexist. I call this unseen wall Abhimanyu's *Chakravyuh*, as it has got its own mechanism to safeguard its ethnic identity not only by force but through various means of alienation. Hence, a proper channel has to be maintained in order to understand each other's culture. Resistance will always be there for any kind of transformation in each *chakravyuh*. Hence, during the time of British colonization it was not easy even for the big empire to penetrate and transform people of North East India. The *Chakravyuh* exists and strongly resisted to any kind of cultural transformation. Inside this *Chakravyuh* everything that is needed for the subsistence of a society exists with years old wisdom and practices that has been passed on from generation after generations. Each of these tribes celebrate annual harvest festival with merry making indigenous folk dance and music as heathen worship some of which is fortunate enough to continue till today. Respect to the women folks is also one of the main similarities amongst all the tribes. Women were never look down in the society. As T.H. Lewin had said, "Let us not govern these hills for ourselves but administer the country for well-being and happiness of the people dwelling therein."

However, The Charter Act of 1813 permitted missionaries to propagate their religion in British India. The European Modern Education was the major factor that could break the *chakravyuh* to some extent in North Eastern part of India. Christian Missionaries brought modern European education which vastly affected the traditional indigenous North East Indian culture. It was creating a rival society with an effort to erase the indigenous faith and trying hard to breakdown the *chakravyuh*. It was an effort to transform the existing society from its beliefs and way and life to a modern way of life through European education. But the British had spread modern education with vested interest and a motive behind it. From the Macaulay minutes 1835, the intention of the imposing modern education could be well understood. If we go into the details of the minutes a particular point mentioned an abolition of native institutions and promotion of European modern education. This affected the aged old traditional education system of the natives of North East India. In order to achieve their goal, the modern education system started discouraging the traditional practices. The missionaries believed that by imparting their so-called superior modern education, they are on to a civilizing mission. Being ignorant of one's culture causes him to lose part of his identity and pride of his culture instead he is trained for Western culture and ideas. Further modern education discouraged traditional way of life beyond their class room which naturally forced change in traditional pattern of life which leads to cultural deprivation. On the other hand, the motive of Western education was to ensure supply of cheap educated Indians to manage the British administration as expansion of British Empire necessitate more administrators. Hence, modern education was more for the administrative convenience of the British Government and to save money by paying a comparatively less salary for the educated Indian officials. It was an effort to Westernize life of the native people. Missionaries interfered in the social and cultural practices of the tribes of North East India by putting restrictions such as stopping on eating flesh of animals used in sacrifices at heathen festivals or certain form of indigenous dance or music which was part of heathen practices. Hence, the process of Proselytization was followed by changes in the Indigenous culture of the people of North East India. Hence, it gave a big set back to the tribal folk songs, dance, indigenous festivals which were part of the heathen worship as they were barred from these practices. Hence, this created social and cultural conflicts within the same society whereby the well protecting mechanism of the chakravyuh is given a jolt. This affects the tribal people destroying their solidarity enjoying their communal activities.

This transformation for the native of North East India was difficult as they were forced to struggle the new way of life. The belief system of the indigenous people has itself a correlation with their knowledge and attitude to the environment which was no doubt disrupted by the Colonialism. Colonialism and missionaries with their presence in North East India has no doubt benefited from each other. The influencing factors of the Missionaries have brought in cultural assimilation amongst the different tribes of North East India, hence losing their own culture and identity. Detribalizing the various tribes of North East India was at its peak during the colonial period.

15
Social Implications of Colonial Intervention

M. Amarjeet Singh

The economic change and infrastructure development in Assam in the nineteenth century attracted large number of migrants in Assam. Also, in order to serve the colonial interests, new administrative boundaries were drawn and redrawn. In addition, the Bengali was introduced as the language of Courts of Justices and the government schools for a number of years. It was viewed as an act of disregarding the indigenous inhabitants of Assam. Likewise, the assumption that the advent of Hinduism in Manipur affected the relationships between the plain dwellers (the Meiteis) and the hill dwellers (the Nagas and Kukis) is debatable. It is rather due to the colonial policy of separation of the hills and the plains as separate administrative units. Thus, in the name of administrative convenience, policies having far-reaching implications were introduced and tested from time to time. These policies had led to the consolidation of ethnic identity as an inevitable instrument for political mobilisation by different communities.

Colonial Experience

Like elsewhere, the colonial rule consolidated in India's North East through alliances, annexation and even war with the local rulers. Expeditions were carried out in the hill areas to draw maps, assess resources, develop friendly alliances, punish those who defaulted, extract tributes. They used Kukis as buffer between the area under their control and the Nagas (*see*, Misra, 2012). As Ahom rulers experienced declining power in the eighteenth century, Burma and Assam became the rival powers. The former gone on to annex the eastern and southern parts of the region in 1762, and also shown interest consolidating towards Bengal. As a result, the Anglo-Burmese war (1824-26) broke out which led to the signing of the Treaty of Yandaboo in 1826. Under this treaty, Burma surrendered its claims over Assam to the British while the independence of Manipur was recognised which, however, gradually came under the protection of the British.

The advent of colonialism brought significant socio-economic transformations which can be broadly classified as: introduction of education, modern system of administration, infrastructure development, expansion of money economy in remote areas, commercialisation of agriculture especially tea, advent of Christianity, and consolidation of ethnic identity.

Due to the capitalist economic measures introduced by the British, rapid transformation took place in Assam due to tea plantation, coal mining, oil exploration etc. As a result, large number of people, including soldiers and office assistants were brought. In due course of time taking advantage of new opportunities in agriculture and business, large numbers workers and businessmen also came to the region. Rail lines and other infrastructure development were constructed. Thus, Assam became an important destination for migration.

Additionally, in order to serve colonial interests, reorganisation of administrative boundaries took place. Assam was administratively attached to Bengal Presidency for about half a century, during 1826-1873. In 1874, Assam became a separate province along with Cachar, Sylhet and Goalpara districts of Bengal. Boundaries were redrawn again in 1905 in which eastern parts of Bengal and Assam became East Bengal and Assam (with Dhaka as the capital), and Bengal, respectively. It was, however, dissolved in 1911.

Large number of Bengalis comprising both job-seekers and land-seeking farm settlers arrived in Assam (Nag, 2018: 88). Due to their advanced education and long exposure to the colonial administration, they were best suited to play a crucial role in the administration of Assam and beyond. This naturally facilitated in consolidating the use of Bengali language in the spheres of administration and school education. Ultimately, Bengali became the language of Courts of Justices and of the government schools during 1837-1874 (*see,* Report of the Administration of Bengal 1871-72, Part I). It was said to have acted against the Assamese language, and also in 'the interest of tea plantation and trade' (Nag, 2018: 87). Assamese was ultimately recognized in 1874 by retaining Bengali script.

Sensitive language issue and economic marginalisation soon became the twin pillars of political mobilisation of the Assamese-speaking and Bengali-speaking peoples. This mobilisation of ethnicity became the root cause of conflict. In fact, the colonial rule 'halted the centuries-old process of amalgamation and homogenization in Assam' (Nag, 2018: 87). The situation remained so as the Partition of India into India and Pakistan was a painful exercise which affected the lives of more than 14 million people, as Muslims in India fled to Pakistan and Hindus in Pakistan fled to India.

Hills and Valleys

Colonialism inherited a highly destabilising state of affairs in the region. The lower part of the region was under colonialism for a long time, while the hilly areas were consolidated much later. Colonial administration and ethnographers treated today's North East India as a frontier and some of its people as *wild* and *savage.*

Colonial ethnographers collected social and cultural data of the people 'from the position of authority'. They were more interested in studying family, marriage, folklore, rituals and cultural practices of the tribals, not the 'vital' livelihood issues (Misra, 2012: 58). Some held that the colonists adopted the 'policy of fragmenting and splitting Indian people' (Misra, 2012: 63).

The concept of North East was popularised by the colonial rulers. The term 'North East' was initially used by the colonial administrators to connote the geographical areas lying beyond the frontier of Bengal and hence termed North East Frontier. The North East Frontier included Assam along with the adjoining hills and native states of Manipur and Tripura. The tendency to see this region as a frontier area continued in the post-colonial period and this contributed to the construction of a separate identity of the region. Now the region is the only region of the country which has a dedicated central ministry and a regional planning body.

The economic changes and infrastructure developments due to colonialism did not integrate the plains with the hills. The plains were governed by direct rule, while the hills were governed by indirect rule. The hills and plains were never integrated administratively. Efforts were not made to do so also. As a result, separate identities of hills and plains were reinforced as a result of the colonialism. Under the colonial rule, a number of laws governed the administration of hill areas of Assam and Manipur. The Bengal Eastern Frontier Regulations, 1873 prohibited the entry of all British subjects in the area within the inner line without a permit issued by the competent authority. It was enforced in several hill districts (such as Kamrup, Darrang, Nowgong, Sibsagar, Lakhimpur, Garo hills, Khasi and Jaintia hills, Cachar and Chittagong hills). Although such restriction was thought to safeguard the lives of the hill people, its other motives were to safeguard the tea plantation in the plain and the hill peoples into enclaves and restricted trade and communication with other communities along the foothills (*see*, Kikhi, 2018).

Also, the Government of India Act, 1919 declared major parts of Assam as the backward tracts such as Garo hills, Khasi and Jainitia hills (excluding Shillong municipality and cantonment), Mikir hills in Nowgong and Sibsagar districts, North Cachar hills in Cachar district, the Naga hills district, Lushai hills district, Sadia frontier tract, Lakhimpur frontier tract. From 1937 onwards, under the Government of India Act, 1935, these backward tracts were renamed as *excluded* and *partially excluded areas*[1] placing those areas outside the jurisdiction of the provincial administration and bringing them directly under the Governor of Assam.

As a result, the hill tribes were encouraged to distance themselves from the plain dwellers and developed a special kind of identity that had remained crucial for subsequent political developments. The British indirectly ruled over the hills that were left to the management of the traditional authorities who would be easily manipulated. It was a simple paternalistic British rule in the hills unlike the plains.

Moreover, the Christian missionaries were licensed to operate in the hills, who published *Bible* in many dialects. Before they left Assam, a vague promise was given to carve out Crown Colony from Garo Hills to upper Burma by the then Governor of Assam Sir Robert Reid and supported by several local officials. As a result, many of the tribes were encouraged to ask for independence away from India. This was the background in which the Constitution Drafting Committee of free India set up a Sub-Committee (North East Frontier Tribal and Excluded Areas Committee) under Gopinath Bordoloi, then Premier of Assam. The Sub-Committee recommended autonomous districts and regional councils to safeguard the hill tribes of Assam in respect of their land, social customs and usages, language and culture (Barpujari, 1998). These special provisions were listed under the Sixth Schedule to the Constitution of India for the administration of hill tribal areas. While reporting to the Constituent Assembly, Gopinath Bordoloi reminded the members on the ethnic background of Assam Hills:

> "... It is not unknown to you that the rule of the British Government and the activities of the foreign missionaries always went together.... During the war, the then rulers and officers developed in the minds of these tribal people a sense of separation and isolation and gave them assurances that at the end of the war they will be independent states managing their affairs in their own way. They were made to believe that the entire hills would be constituted into a province and put under some irresponsible government. You might possibly have read in the papers that plans were hatched in England in which the ex-Governors of Assam evidently took part, to create a sort of kingdom over there ... "[2]

The Sixth Schedule classified two sets of tribal areas of undivided Assam using the administrative categories that were then in effect: (i) the United Khasi-Jaintia Hills district (excluding Shillong), the Garo Hills, the Lushai (Mizo) Hills, the Mikir Hills (now Karbi Anglong), the Naga Hills and the North Cachar Hills; and (ii) the North Frontier Tracts and the Naga Tribal Area.[3] The autonomy under this provision provides for autonomous district and autonomous regions within those districts with elected councils which enjoy powers to levy taxes, to constitute courts for the administration of justice involving tribals and law-making powers on subjects including land allotment, occupation or use of land, regulation of '*jhum*' or other forms of shifting cultivation, establishment and administration of village and town committees, appointment or succession of chiefs, inheritance of property, marriage and social customs.

Initially, the Sixth Schedule was not intended to protect all the tribal groups of North East India. Only those who were considered to be relatively backward in the former 'excluded' and 'partially excluded' areas were termed 'tribal areas' and these came under the purview of the Sixth Schedule.

Since 1952, district councils were formed in the United Khasi-Jaintia Hills district, the Garo Hills district, the Lushai (Mizo) Hills district, the Mikir Hills district (now Karbi Anglong district), and the North Cachar Hills district. The Nagas were not impressed with such arrangement and rejected it outrightly and went on to insurgency. Incidentally, the most backward tribal area of the region (present Arunachal Pradesh) continued to be under the special dispensation of the governor of the province, who was guided by a tribal adviser in his tribal administrative duties.

Along with the introduction of the Sixth Schedule, the demand for a separate hill state had come in the then Khasi Hills. Meanwhile, such a claim for autonomy further intensified with the growing insistence of the Assamese speakers for maintaining linguistic dominance in the state. On 10 October, 1960, when the Assam Official Language Bill was moved, there was an unprecedented polarization of non-Assamese communities both outside and inside the Assam Legislative Assembly. The move alienated non-Assamese people who had also apprehended the suppression of their language and cultures in Assam. The Bodos and other plains tribes too joined the wagon of protests in course of time and Assam became turbulent in early 1960s.

The Naga Hills district along with Tuensang Hill district had been promoted to statehood in 1963. Thereafter, the Khasi and Jaintia Hills were made a sub-state[4] and then upgraded into a full-fledged state of Meghalaya in 1972. Again, in 1972, the Mizo Hills District and Arunachal were separated from Assam and made Union territories first, and then into a full-fledged state of Mizoram and Arunachal Pradesh respectively in 1987. In this way, the experiment of tribal autonomy became subject to increasing balkanization of Assam.

The special needs of the plains tribes of Assam, such as, the Bodos, the Misings, the Lalung, the Sonowal, the Deori and Tiwas, were the responsibility of the Minority Rights Sub-Committee of the Advisory Committee of the Constituent Assembly. They were essentially cultivators, agriculture continues to be the mainstay of their economy and land is of supreme importance to them. However, there has been constant encroachment on the plain tribal land by non-tribals. Added to this has been the unabated influx of East Bengal [now Bangladesh] immigrants. The erstwhile protective measure of Tribal Belts and Blocks provided in the Chapter X of Assam Land and Revenue Regulation Act, 1886 miserably failed to protect the tribal land. Unabated encroachment on the tribal land, gradual deterioration of the general economic condition of the plains tribals and increase of landless people among the tribals deeply perturbed their minds.

Along with the advent of the colonial rule was the introduction of the permanent land settlement system. Commencement of revenue collection from agricultural land was a burden for the plain tribes. Poor tribals who could not pay land tax sold their land to the relatively advanced immigrants and others. The rulers were interested in enhancing revenue collection and hence wasteland, riverine and forestland were made available to the Muslims peasants from Bengal. The tribes could not compete with the advanced Bengali people. When the British came to Assam, the population was sparse and hence the land was abundant. As the revenue collection was minimal, the settlement of immigrants were actively encouraged for enhancing revenue collection.

Consequent to the departure of the Burmese from Manipur, the British started interfering in royal succession disputes which ultimately led to the Anglo-Manipuri war in 1891. Thereafter, the kingdom became a princely native state, and since 1907, the kingdom further lost its autonomy when the administration of the hill region was entrusted to the British. The colonists consolidated control over Manipur by interfering in settling succession of the throne. The office of the Political Agent, opened since 1835, acted as the agent of the government under Chief Commissioner of Assam became an important agency to exert more control. Although this office was to maintain friendly relationship between Manipur and British and a medium of communication between the two, but in reality it "became more and more powerful because of the internecine quarrel among the princes ... which gave an opportunity to the Political Agent to interfere directly or indirectly in every domestic affairs of the state" (Laldena, 2012: 31).

The king's authority was further reduced when the Darbar (the highest court) was reconstituted in 1907. The reconstituted Darbar comprised the President, the Vice President and six members. The members were jointly appointed by the king and the Political Agent. The Darbar which acted as the highest court had no jurisdiction over the Europeans, British Indian or hill people who were tried in the court of the Political Agent, and the capital punishment had to be confirmed by the Chief Commissioner of Assam (Parratt, 2005: 15). The Vice President (an Indian Civil Service officer under the Government of Assam) was entrusted with the administration of the hill region. The Chiefs of villages were assigned the duties to "collect hill house tax and extract forced labour (*Pothang*)" (Laldena, 2012: 82). The Chiefs assumed two important judicial roles—as interpreter of customary laws and as judges within their respective chiefdom. The Vice President tried all criminal cases concerning the inhabitants of the hill region, but in civil cases, the people had no right to appeal. Therefore, "the only officials with whom the people came into contact were the petty Manipur *Lambus* who were something like peons or messengers" (Laldena, 2012: 82-83).

Under the "Rules for the Management of the State of Manipur, 1916", the "His Highness the Raja will be responsible for the administration of the State." He was assisted by a Darbar headed by an ICS officer (President) selected by the Government of Assam. There were three ordinary members appointed by the King in consultation with the Political Agent to oversee various departments. In addition, there were three additional members who did not hold charge of departments. The administration of the hill region was entrusted to the President of the Darbar. The *Rules for the Management of the State of Manipur*, 1916 stated that the hill tribes are administered by the President assisted by one or more officers on His Highness' behalf in accordance with rules approved by the Government of Assam but His Highness shall be consulted in all matters of importance and the Political Agent, in consultation with the President shall give effect to His Highness' wishes so far as is consistent with the orders of the Government of Assam. If the Political Agent is unable to agree His Highness' proposals, the matter shall, if His Highness so wishes be referred to the Government of Assam.

"The justification for this", according to John Parratt (2005: 15) "was that the Maharajah might exploit the tribal population for its own advantage. While it was true the hill peoples did have a different social, legal and religious system, it was also the case that the Meitei kings had exercised jurisdiction over the hills within their boundaries for long before." One should not entirely see the advent of Hinduism and the subsequent advent of Christianity in Manipur as the root cause of the existing political divide between the hill and plain in the state. The root cause was the restructuring of the administration in which the hill was separated from the plan in administrative matters. The Sanamahi religion (Lainingthou Sanamahi is the most prominent god) was adopted as the state religion of Manipur prior to the advent Vaisnava Hinduism. Charairongba who ascended the throne in 1697 A.D. was the first king to initiate Hinduism in the kingdom (he adopted Sanskrit name Pitambar Singh), but he did not impose Hinduism to his subjects (Nilabir, 2010: 66). After his death, Garibniwaz persuaded the people to abandon Sanamahi religion to embrace Hinduism. In due course of time, the relationship between the Meiteis and hill people gradually turned into a relationship marked by subordination-superordination, and inferiority-superiority (Saha, 2005: 233-234).

Colonialism, Christianity and Ethnicity

Although Christianity came into the region before British colonization of India, the advent and popularity of Christianity in the hill areas of the region have immense impact on the indigenous religion of the tribal people. The traditional beliefs, values and customs underwent tremendous changes as a result of their conversion to Christianity. This happened because the converts abandoned their own religious rites, beliefs and rituals in due course of time. The tribal became more adaptive towards western way of life than that of the Indian way of life. This is due to the spread of Christianity and Western education in the hill areas of the region. "It is striking that the Christian churches spread more comfortably in the hills and plains of the region after the incorporation of these territories into formal empire" (Syiemlieh, 2012: 513).

No doubt the Christian missionaries had played a significant role in transforming the lives of the hill people of the region. They had experienced faster social mobility than ever before. The Church activities have uplifted them. They would not have reached much social advancement had there been no colonialism and missionaries activities. In the name of civilising the 'wild' and 'savage' peoples, the colonists encouraged missionary works (Misra, 2012: 67). Under the patronage of the British, rule, the Christianity flourished in the hill areas of North East India. Soon Christianity became the most favourite religion of the hill people. It was during the colonial period the hill people adapted Christianity. The hill areas were much more exposed to the missionary-led education. It is often claimed that the Christian missionaries were more attracted towards the backward and remotely located communities.

Apart from the religion, an important impact is related to the outlook of the recently converts. At least in Assam and Manipur, they were least interested to learn Assamese or Manipuri. They are thought to have western orientation in their daily lives.

Conclusion

Naturally, the plain areas already had long connection with the erstwhile Bengal and hence had influenced by the Bengali culture. It was not so in the case of the hill areas because of the difficult terrain and the remoteness. If Hinduism already had significant influence in the plains, it was not so in the case of the hills. However, colonialism had added a new religion in the region. As a result several groups have even discarded their old religion, which is really unfortunate. This also creates social tension among these communities. Along with this, the division of hills from the plains for administrative convenience have only enhanced the divide between the hills and the plains. This in turn have aggravated the ethnic identity politics in the region. In fact identity unites people, it also divides people.

Notes

1. Excluded Areas included Naga Hills, Lushai Hills, North Cachar Hills, and North East Frontier (Sadiya, Balipara and Lakhimpur) Tracts; and Partially Excluded Areas covered Garo Hills, Mikir Hills and the Khasi-Jaintia Hills.
2. Constituent Assembly Debates, Vol. IX, p. 1011.
3. The first set of areas today comprises the States of Meghalaya, Mizoram, Nagaland and parts of Assam, and the second set consists mostly of the State of Arunachal Pradesh and a part of the State of

Nagaland. The Sixth Schedule institutions were meant for both sets of areas, but the latter set of territories, which were mostly un-administered during the colonial times, were considered to be not quite ready at that time for such self-governing institutions. The administration of those areas was going to be carried out directly from Delhi—with the Governor of Assam acting as the agent of the President of India.

4. On 24 December, 1969, parliament passed the Assam Reorganisation (Meghalaya) Bill to create "an Autonomous State to be known as Meghalaya within the State of Assam (the executive power of the new unit was vested in the Governor of Assam, aided and advised by the Council of Ministers of Meghalaya, in relation to the autonomous state."

References

Barpujari, H.K. (1998). *India's North-East: Problems, Policies and Prospects since Independence*. Guwahati and Delhi: Spectrum Publication, pp. 6-7.

Kikhi, Kedilezo. (2018). "A Critical Understanding of Sociology of North East India: Geo-political history and migration", in Jyoti Prasad Saikia and Partha Pratim Borah (eds.), *Sociology of North East India: Empirical Reality and Disciplinary Practice*. Guwahati: DVS Publishers, pp. 17-33.

Laldena, (2012). *History of Modern Manipur 1762-1949*, Imphal: Reliable Book Centre.

Misra, P.K. (2012). "J.H. Hutton and Colonial Ethnography of North East India", in T.B. Subba (ed.), *North-East India: A Handbook of Anthropology*. New Delhi: Orient Black Swan.

Nag, Sajal. (2018). "Assamese Nationality Question", in Bhagat Oinam and Dhiren A. Sadokpam (eds.), *North East India: A Reader*. Oxon and New Delhi: Routledge.

Nilabir, S., (2010). "Sanamahi Religion", *Sandhan*, Volume X, No. 2, July-December, 53-90.

Paratt, Saroj Nalini Arambam, (2005). *The Court Chronicles of the Kings of Manipur: Cheitharon Kumpapa*, Vol. 1. Routledge, New York, p. 4.

Saha, R.K., (2005). "Where Civilizations Meet to differ: The Hill-Valley ethnic cleavage in Manipur", in Tanka Bahadur Subba, Sujit Som, 2005. (eds.), *Between Ethnography and Fiction: Verrier Elwin and the Tribal Question in India*, New Delhi: Orient Longman, 227-241.

Syiemlieh, David R. (2012). "Colonial Encounter and Christian Missions in North East India", *Proceedings of the Indian History Congress*, Vol. 73 (2012), pp. 509-527.

SECTION IV
Colonial Legacy and Inter-Community Relationship

16
Colonial Legacy and Inter-Community Relationship

Atul Debbarma

History of Colonialism

The first colonial empires were formed after the great geographic discoveries by those of Spanish and Portuguese. The discovery of America in 1492 by Spanish conquerors colonized the Central America and the South America. The seed of colonization of India was sown after having discovered the sea route to India in 1498 by the Portuguese explorer who consolidated their position on the west coast of India. The British were late comers in the Indian subcontinent. They came just as a trading company, like all other European trading companies who went throughout the world. By the first decade of the seventeenth century, the British were able to get permission from the Emperor of India to establish their trading company East India. After the victory of Battle of Plassey by Robert Clive in 1757, the so-called East India Company did not remained as mere trading company, it transformed to a company of expansionism and aimed for imperialism. The victory over the Nawab of Bengal made the East India Company the master of Bengal and their victory in the Battle of Buxer in 1764 gave them Diwani rights of Bihar, Orissa and Bengal. Gradually they take over charges and control over Burdwan, Midnapore and Chittagong and became the virtual authority of the Presidency of Bengal. The victories in the Battle of Plassey and Buxer bolstered the ambition of the company in higher magnitude. The experience of trading in Bengal gave them idea that without political power they could not do trading and commercial activities unconditionally. The English accordingly endeavoured for aggressive policy of territorial expansion within the border of India and beyond. The acquisition of territorial rights by the Company became a major change in the development of British colonial policy. The British came into contacts with the local Kings and chiefs of the north-eastern India long before the first Anglo-Burmese war and Treaty of Yandaboo in 1826. Following this treaty, the occupation of Assam state by the British became permanent. Subsequently, the British annexed and administered over the Naga Hills, the North East Frontier, the Khasi Hills, Jayantia Hills, Garo Hills and the Lushai Hills. The states of Manipur and Tripura were left as semi-independent states.

Pre-colonial History of Tripura and North East India

The history of the North East of India is as old as history of India. North East India is basically created by the British. In fact before India's independence, the whole of North East India other than Manipur and Tripura was Assam. The historic states of Kamrup, that is the present day Assam, Manipur and Tripura is mentioned in the great Indian epic of *Mahabharata* and other scriptures like *Puranas*. In that Great War of Kurukshetra, the kings of these states participated. Chitrangada, the princess of Manipur was married to Arjuna, one of the Pandavas and their son Babruvahana took part in the war. Hidimba, the princess of Dimapur was married to Bhim, second Pandavas brother and their son Ghatotkach took part in that Great War in favour of Pandavas. Similarly, the Maharaja of Tripura, Trilochan fought in that famous war in favour of Pandavas and attended the Rajsuya Yajna of Yudhisthir where he was gifted with a white colour umbrella and a thrown which is the symbol of Tripura's royal dynasty.

But just after the Independence of India ethno-centric political inspiration lead to the division of greater Assam resulting in the formation of seven North Eastern states, namely Arunachal Pradesh, Assam, Manipur, Meghalaya, Mizoram, Nagaland and Tripura.

The geographical boundaries of different states of North East were not the way they are now. The borders of Tripura kingdom once extended up to the Burma in the east, up to the Meghna river of Bagladesh in the west, Barak river in the north and up to bay of Bengal in the south. There were other states like Cachar, Koch kingdoms in the past which were annexed by the British Company. Similarly, the borders of Manipur, Assam had also expanded and shrank in different times of history. The final borders of different North Eastern states were drawn when the Sikkim state joined with Indian Union on 1975. North East was considered as a single geographical regional entity and nicknamed as 'seven sisters' excluding the state of Sikkim. But during the Vajpayee government Sikkim was included as part of North Eastern states though separated by the northern part of West Bengal and a separate geo-political recognition was given by establishing Ministry of Development of North East Region.

Interest of British in the North East

The British quickly annexed Lower Assam after the first Anglo-Burmese war, because they found that the revenue prospect in this area was very high. If Lower Assam can be permanently occupied that would led to considerable increase of revenues of the company. Subsequently after a gap of a decade they occupied and annexed the Upper Assam also. After the annexation of Assam, the British government turned their attention towards different frontier hills of North East India. They adopted different policy to deal with the frontier tribes on the basis of economic needs of the people without interfering with the internal affairs of the tribes. The frontier hill tribes used to make frequent raids and outrages on the people of plains controlled by British Government. For this reason, the British had to annex the hill tracts of Naga, Garo, Lushai and others alike to maintain law and order and security among the plains subjects. Apart from this, the frontier hill tracts are also strategically very important and act as buffer zone for Bengal and Assam against the aggression of Burmese people. Annexation of Chittagong gave access to port and sea link which would be great advantage to the East India Company.

Colonial Policies

The superiority syndrome that the British had after occupation of most of India's geography can be guessed by Macaulay's speech while in deciding in favour of English education: "believe that the present system tends, not to accelerate the progress of truth, but to delay the natural death of expiring errors. We are a Board for wasting public money, for printing books which are less value than the paper on which they are printed was while it was blank; for giving artificial encouragement to absurd history, absurd metaphysics, absurd physics, absurd theology ... I have no knowledge of either Sanskrit or Arabic ... But I have done what I could to form a correct estimate of their value ... Who could deny that a single shelf of a good European library was worth the whole native literature of India and Arabia ... all the historical information which has been collected from all the books written in the Sanskrit language is less valuable than what may be found in the most paltry abridgements used at preparatory schools in England...It is impossible for us, with our limited means to attempt to educate the body of the people. We must at present do our best to form a class who may be interpreters between us and the millions whom we govern; a class of persons, Indian in blood and colour, but English in taste, in opinions, in morals, and in intellect. To that class we may leave it to refine the vernacular dialects of the country, to enrich those dialects with terms of science borrowed from the Western nomenclature, and to render them by degrees fit vehicles for conveying knowledge to the great mass of the population."

Application of Doctrine of Lapse

The British saw the strategic importance for location and huge economic potentialities in the Kingdom of Cachar. To safeguard the plains of Assam from the invasion of Burmese in the near future Cachar would act as first frontier of British government. While the economic prospects of the kingdom were sufficiently lucrative and could yield high revenue if can be managed in better way and efficiently, the fertile land of Cachar could become the grain house of the surrounding regions. Taking into consideration of all these factors, the East India Company proposed to the king Govindachandra to sign a deed making over the kingdom to the Company which he declined. However, he was killed in a conspiracy soon and the territory of Cachar was annexed by the British applying the Doctrine of lapse policy, as Raja Govindachandra died without leaving an heir. Though there were several claimant for the vacant throne including the eldest queen of the King was denied her rightful demand as the British were the biggest claimant because of its strategic and economic importance.

Non-intervention Policy

The British had annexed all the frontier hills inhabited by different hill tribes, after the annexation of Lower and Upper Assam. But they applied a different policy to deal with the frontier tribes than that of the subjects of plains of Assam. The British did not interfere with the internal affairs of the frontier hills tribes. There was a minimum of interference with the powers and functions of the tribals' headmen of the villages, their organizations and other local authorities. The British were of the views that the complex rules, laws, and procedure applied in the administration of the plain areas were not appropriate for the hills tribes. The policy of simple and just administrations was applied to the hills tribes and it was left to the village chiefs to maintain the law, order and tranquillity in the frontier hills. But this non-intervention policy did not succeed in maintaining the law and order of the plains and the hills frontier. The hills tribes would still continued to make frequent raids and outrages in the plain land of Assam and Bengal, make huge economic and human loss in the area and thereby disturbing the peace and tranquillity. Not only that the hills tribes would invade and plunder the plains of British territory, they would also conduct raids and outrages on rival the villages and would cause substantial loss of human and property. Therefore, the British had to abandon the Non-intervention policy for new approach to deal with the frontier hill tribes.

Forward Policy

The British Government applied 'Carrot and stick' policy and refrained from taking over the direct administration of the hill areas, but it had failed miserably. Subsequently, the British departed from the above policy and they had to apply the so-called 'forward policy' with strong hands, to prevent and counter the frequent raids and outrages conducted by the hill tribes upon the plains. By applying this policy, the British Government brought all the hill areas under their direct control and administration. They also annexed a vast area of hills which were still untamed and wild under the British territory by the offensive approach of 'forward policy'. Consequently, the British Government could bring back the peace and tranquillity in both the plain land area and frontier hill areas. The new policy had brought the confidence and support among the people of the plain and cooperated with the British Government.

Annexation of Chakla Roshanabad

Might is right, the proverb truly proved by the British in the states of Tripura. The districts of Komilla, Brahman Baria and Sylhet which were together known as 'Chakla Roshanabad' were integral part of Tripura kingdom since the ages. These districts are vast cultivable plain land from where the kingdom received revenue of considerable amount. The kings would pay taxes yearly to the British Government for these districts. The British Government annexed this large territory of Tripura with East Pakistan at the times of India's Independence in 1947. The Muslim government of East Pakistan did not protect the life and properties of Hindu Bengali citizens of the erstwhile Chakla Roshanabad rather abetted the Hindu-Muslim communal riots, resulting in large scale migration of Hindu Bengali refugees in Tripura. It has changed the demographic profile of the state, the once majority indigenous Tripuri people was reduced to a minority. The refugees created the pressure on the land, natural resources and job opportunities in the state. There were unequal competitions in every sphere of life both in terms of quantity and quality, in which the Tripuri people lacked behind. There was a sense of being sidelined, deprivation, exploitation and cheating, partly perceived and partly factual among the indigenous Tripuri people. These feelings went on accumulating from generations to the next ultimately exploded into full-flagged fratricidal communal riots between Hindu Bengali and Tripuri people in 1980 which were worse than the infamous Gujarat riot. In the long history of Tripura, there was not a single incidence of communal riot in Tripura, rather it was unheard to the indigenous people. Again incidences of ethnic conflicts between the Tripuri people and Hindu Bengali broke out sporadically in different parts of Tripura during 1998-2001 affecting many lives and property. The Tripuri people are still bearing the brunt of colonial policy and its legacy in their daily life.

Annexation of Lushai Hills

The eastern boundary of Tripura kingdom once extended up to Burma, and the Lushai Hills were part of her territory. But the British Government annexed these hills unilaterally without any considerations or consultation of Tripura kings. The Lushai (now Mizo) and the Riang, who are one of Tripuri tribe were subjects of the Tripura King. The Riang who are mostly Hindus, the original inhabitant of these hills were driven out of their ancestral land in the 1997-98 in communal riots by the majority Christian Mizos. About 40,000 Riang tribes were sheltered as refugees in the North district of Tripura and over 21 years they are living in sub-human conditions in different refugee camps devoid of basic human facilities. Infant mortality rate is very high; more deaths are taking place than the births in the Riang refugee camps of Tripura. There had been repeated attempt to repatriate and settle the refugees by the concerned governments but every time it failed. This is another case of ethnic conflict meted out by the Riang community who became refugees in their own homeland on account of colonial policy.

Divide and Rule Policy

The 'divide and rule policy' of the British administration was most successful policy of colonial government to divide in the lines of race, caste, creed, religion, language, culture, tribes and ethnicity. In the princely state of Manipur, the colonial power divided the states between the people of plains and hills and introduced the Christianity amongst the tribal groups of Nagas and Kukis which had further widened the gap with Meiteis who are a predominantly caste Hindu society. The British used the Kukis to counter and control the stronger and bigger Naga tribes from attacking and raiding the plain British territory. This had created a wide gap and misunderstanding between the Naga and Kuki tribes, which passed from generation to generation and continued till recent times. The demand for greater Nagaland and rumour of inclusion of the Naga dominated areas of Manipur in it, which overlaps with the territorial claims of the Kuki created insecurity and anxiety against the perceived hegemony of Nagas leading to communal riots between the historically created rival tribes—the Nagas and the Kukis. Thus, historical prejudice is keeping hatred and animosity among different ethnic groups alive in Manipur.

Humanizing Policy

The British had an arrogance of supremacy over the conquered territories and subjugated human races. They had a notion that everything they possessed and practices were superior to what the defeated races follow and practice. According to them, the tribes practice the superstitions and worship false gods. They termed tribals' religious rites and rituals as heathen, pagan, animist or by any other name, considered the tribal culture as primitive and substandard. So they need to be given true God and taught right way to worship and follow rites and rituals. The British considered that it was their duty to civilize and teach the 'Uncultured' and 'Uncivilized' tribes.

The Evangelist found the hills of the North East India as a fertile soil for conversion to Christianity and save the souls. The British officials shrewdly utilized the service of the Christian missionaries to proselytize the heathen tribes. Though the aims of 'humanizing mission' of the tribes was apparently to educate and uplift the uneducated and uncivilized but in reality it was to Westernize them so as to keep these tribes away from Sanskritised main land India and it was a colonial's politically motivated policy. Thus, proselytizing the tribes of North East was a part of this strategy to separate the people of hill North East of India both racially, culturally and religiously. The proselytization of the North Eastern people bore the fruits and fulfilled the aims of policy. The converted and missionaries educated tribes exerted the separate identity; ethnicity became more important over the nationalism. Most of the tribes considered that they are racially, culturally, religiously separate and distinct from the plains and main land India. The Evangelist also could convince the false belief that the different tribes of the hills are ethnically, culturally and linguistically different. This idea lead to claim and counter claim their respective cultures are superiors to others which caused frequent attacks and riots among various tribes and clans. The awakened and cultured tribes exerted their exclusive rights over hills they inhabited. The identity politics took deep roots among the tribes of North East India. So the demand of Koki land, Garo land, Khasi land, Jayantia land, Mizoland, Bodoland came out, along with this the demand of self rule and autonomic council like Chakma council, Mara council, Lai council, Dimasa council, Karbi council, and many more. There are different arm rebel and extremist group mushroomed in recent past to achieve their goal of creating ethnically exclusive land or autonomous councils. Often the groups fought each other as most of the times the territories they claim were overlapping and their interests are compromised by the counter claims of the other tribes. The British colonial policy of separating and dividing the people between the plain and hills and among the tribes of the hills was a grand success in the disguise of 'Humanizing the tribes' of the North East India.

Conclusion

The colonial policies had affected every aspect of human life of North Eastern people in particular and all over India in general. The fact that I am speaking now in English is also the effect of colonial education policy. It is easy to destroy but difficult to construct. The colonial policies framed centuries ago did not end after the departure of British Government from Indian soil. The soul of colonialism is still alive and actively haunting in different *avatars* as Breaking India force to smash Indian nation into pieces. In the age of app revolution, there is no need of physical presence at all to engineer the destruction of India, a virtual person is equal to a million real people and is enough to disturb inter-community relationship.

17
Colonial Legacy of Identity and Insurgency in North East India

Rami Niranjan Desai

Introduction

In the Indian collective imagination, North East India has been perceived as a remote and isolated region. It has often been labelled ethnically diverse and distant from the rest of India. Complicating the perception of the North East further is the many conflicts the region has endured for over six decades, fuelled by a number of issues like land distribution, immigration, ethnicity, religion, political autonomy and secession. However, the genesis of majority of these conflicts as well as the alienation of the region from the rest of India lies in the role played by the British Empire. Their involvement in the North East not only seriously eroded the economic and political future of this resource rich region but also created a perception of "otherness" to the rest of the country.

Today, the popular narrative of the North East region being culturally, religiously and ethnically diverse and distant defies the collective knowledge and comprehension of India's past. The narrative overlooks the role of the North Eastern population in India's ancient past as well as recent history. For instance, the Idu Mishimi tribe of Arunachal Pradesh traces their lineage to Rukmini, the wife of Krishna. Till date Idu Rukmini is highly venerated as Inyi Maselo or the Great Mother. The Parshuram Kund in Arunachal Pradesh is also mentioned in the *Kalika Puran* as the lake where Parshuram came to wash his sins away, Hidimba the wife of Bhima and mother of Ghatotkach of the *Mahabharata* were progenitors of the Kachari and Kirat dynasties, many from the Bodo tribe consider themselves descendants of Brahma and the Karbi tribe descendants of Sugriva. The Manipuri princess Chitrangada married Arjuna, the Naga princess Uloopi fell in love with Arjuna and raised his son Babruvahana. Ancient Indian literature and history is replete with such mentions of a robust inter-cultural respect amongst the people and their indigenous ways as well as a common evolved acceptance of diversity. However, this narrative was lost with the advent of the British in North East India. They were driven by their colonising agenda and ambition to control the strategically located region. Not only did they diminish the value of the ancient Indian collective civilization but they also through administrative and religious policies created an identity crisis, religious conflict and a psychological sense of distance from the rest of India.[1]

Against this context, the chapter attempts to analyse the role that was played by the colonialists in the North Eastern interplay of identity, religion and conflict. This chapter on the other hand does not attempt to blanket the various other conflicts in the region. It specifically aims at analysing British administration, policy and religion and the subsequent consequences of their expansionist agenda.

Colonial Expansion in North East India

The British East India Company was one of the several international trading companies that was operating in India in the seventeenth Century. It was in 1609 A.D. that Emperor Jehangir gave permission to the Englishman William Hawkins who was representing the British East India Company, to set up a trading port in Surat, the most important port of western India. However, by 1757 A.D., the British East India Company had managed to minimise the presence of the Dutch, the Portuguese as well as the French Trading Companies in India. They firmly entrenched themselves in the political power play in the country and their victory in the Battle of Plassey in 1757 A.D. won by Robert Clive "lay in the logic of circumstances that the traders should compete for political primacy."[2]

After the Battle of Plassey their colonial agenda came to the forefront and they took advantage of the declining power of the Mughal and Maratha empires in India, to push forth their vision of colonising the entire country. The defeat of the Nawab of Bengal Siraj ud-Daulah in the Battle of Plassey made them the most powerful of the contenders in the region and it was only three years after the Battle of Plassey that they gained their first bastion in the North East. In 1760 A.D. Mir Qasim, the British supported Nawab of Bengal (1760-1763 A.D.) signed a treaty with the British East India Company to give them "the three districts of Midnapore, Burdwan and Chittagong", Chittagong being their foothold in the region.[3]

The East India Company now firmly established in Bengal slowly came into contact with various tribal populations from the North East. The Company had never lost sight of its trade opportunities and had a keen interest in exploring the possibilities with China and Burma (Myanmar). Local rulers also started approaching the Company with requests for assistance and defence against other warring tribes and in the case of the Ahom King Gaurinath Singha against the expansionist invading Burmese as well. Colonel L.W. Shakespear giving an insight on the state of affairs in Assam said, "In the later part of the Ahom rulers, whose power was deteriorating, the country became tilled with the turbulent ruffianism of great bazaars in Bengal, with disbanded soldiery and fighting fanatics, who pilled villages and laid waste fields reducing the country to ruin. British intervention in 1792, when Captain Welsh's expedition to quell the state of civil war and anarchy produced no good effects was followed by incursions of Burmese forces which only increased distressful condition of affairs."[4]

The British took advantage of all the infighting in the region and on "August 12, 1765 the undivided Goalpara district came under British rule after the transfer of the *Deewani* from the Mughal Emperor. Due to tribal influences on the region the police *thanas* of Dhubri, Nageswari, Goalpara and Karaibari were placed under a special administrative unit called "North-Eastern Parts of Rangpur" (note: this Rangpur is in present-day Bangladesh) in January 1822.[5]

The expansion of the Burmese towards India led to the British colonialists gaining an opportunity to colonise and expand towards the east. They had surely noticed the opportunities in the North

East region, tea Cultivation being of primary interest. They had also accounted for the strategic position of the region. Surrounded by China and Burma, the lucrative opportunities of trade and commerce with these countries as well as the vantage point of the Indian frontier encouraged the British to turn their sights to the North East and engage with the Burmese forces.

Immediately after the conclusive victory of the "First Anglo-Burmese War (1824-1826), the British occupied Guwahati and rudimentary administrative arrangements were made by October 1824. The Burmese occupiers retreated from the Ahom capital of Rangpur in January 1825 and nearly the whole of Brahmaputra Valley fell into British hands."[6]

On 24th February, 1826, the Treaty of Yandabo was signed ending a nearly two-year long war between the British and the Burmese.

According to the treaty, the Burmese agreed to[7]:

- Cede to the British Assam, Manipur, Rakhine (Arakan) and the Tenasserim coast, south of the Salween River;
- Cease all interference in Cachar and Jaintia Hills district;
- Pay an indemnity of one million pounds Sterling in 4 instalments;
- Allow an exchange of diplomatic representatives between Ava and Calcutta; and
- Sign a commercial treaty in due course.

Unfortunately, by the end of this disastrous war both sides had suffered. It had been the most expensive war in British Indian history."Fifteen thousand European and Indian soldiers died, together with an unknown (but almost certainly higher) number of Burmese. The campaign cost the British five million pounds sterling (roughly 18.5 billion in 2006 dollars) to 13 million pounds sterling; this expenditure led to a severe economic crisis in British India in 1833."[8]

Nevertheless, the British expansionist agenda continued, the Kachari Kingdom was annexed in 1828, the Khasi King surrendered in 1832 and by 1833 upper Assam became a British protectorate under the erstwhile ruler of the Ahom Kingdom Purandhar Singha, but in 1838 the region was formally annexed into the British empire. This was followed by the annexation of the Maran/Matak territory in the east in 1839, part of the Naga Hills between 1866-89 and the Garos in 1873. Simultaneously, the Lushais (Mizos) were brought under the control by the year 1871-1889. The annexation of Assam was considered complete. The Burmese on the other hand remained under immense pressure paying out the huge indemnity. The British eventually expanded their control to all of Burma as well by 1885.

British Administration and Segregation

The period in the North East after the British subjugation of the region was highly volatile. The policy of exclusion and exploitation in the North East region began almost immediately after the Burmese withdrawal. The British governed from the plains of Assam and made it their seat of power in the North East. Though, they had previously come in contact with various tribal groups, they failed to understand the distinctions, mindset, needs and aspirations of the tribal population. On the other hand, the spirit of the independent people of the North East did not take kindly to British rule and their agenda of not only exploiting their resources but also restricting their free movement in their own land. The territorial authority imposed by the British was alien to the tribals in the region. While a couple of tribal *rajas* were allowed to stay in power in their remote principalities, the ancient egalitarian political administration systems were suppressed and replaced by new administrative frameworks destroying complete social systems that were closely attached to their way of life. The British rulers exploited the vast mineral and natural resources of the region, but they did not pay attention to the economic and social needs of the population alienating them even further. Though, they never lost sight of the value of the untouched resources as well as the importance of a strategically located geographic area in Asia under the direct rule of the British Empire.

It is a fact the seeds of "otherness", separate identity and acrimonious relationships with the government was sown during this period of British mishandling of North Eastern affairs. Due to the negligent attitude towards the tribals by the British there were rampant raids on British trade routes as well as political uprisings against the authorities. The Lushai-Kuki tribes in Assam raided the British posts as early as 1826. The Aka/Khamti resistances, Naga resistances, the Sonaram movements, Kuki rebellion and Jadonang-Gaidinliu uprising also reflected growing resentment against the British administration and repressive policies of colonialism.

However, to prevent these frequent raids and uprisings by the tribes, the Inner Line Regulation (ILR) was established. At the outset, the reason given for this was to protect the tribes from outside interference, however, the ILR was created to protect the British interests from the marauding hill tribals who used to raid the British subjects, loot and kill. Issued under the Bengal Eastern Frontier Regulation in 1873, it was the first act on the part of the British segregating the hill tracts of the North East India from the plains of the valley. The ILR demarcated the limits of the administered areas all along the northern, eastern and south-eastern confines of the Brahmaputra valley. The British had sought to confine the movement of the tribals and limit outside contact to the tribes. To enter the areas beyond the demarcated area for any purpose, a permit would have to be obtained from the Deputy Commissioner. The ILR finally resulted in segregation and alienation of the tribes further causing a massive hindrance in integration with the rest of the nation.

Furthermore, the creation of the Excluded and Partially Excluded areas also added to the alienation of these tribes from the rest of the country. The British policies were narrow-minded. Instead of mitigating with the raiding tribes, the tribes became a point of sociological and anthropological fascination. They did not receive any benefits nor were they beneficiaries of any development. The Indian National Congress at the time was extremely critical of the provision for Exclusion and Partial Exclusion of hill areas. At its annual session held at Faizpur (1936), the Congress declared, "This Congress is of opinion that the creation of the excluded areas is yet another attempt to divide the people of India into different groups with unjustifiable and discriminatory treatment and to obstruct the growth of uniform democratic institution in the country. The separation of these areas is intended for the exploitation of the mineral resources and forest wealth in these areas and keeps the inhabitants of these areas apart from the rest of India for their easier exploitation and suppression. The Congress, therefore, demands the suppression. The Congress, therefore, demands the abolition of excluded and partially excluded areas."[9]

The report of the Pataskar Commission stated that, "the administration in these areas was confined mainly to maintaining the peace and undertaking sociological studies. Its anxiety was marked by the negative idea of preservation and protection, and we believe, little thought was given to possible ways of stimulating progress. The general outlook was, therefore, in many ways static rather than dynamic. The administrative machinery was sketchy...."[10] The report further remarked: "A kind of distinct barrier was maintained between these hills and the plains during the British rule. Non-tribals were not given admittance to these areas without special permission, which was given rather freely to foreign missionaries. Such restriction deepened the isolation of these areas from the rest of the state."[11]

It is evident that there was considerable opposition towards this policy of exclusion. The concern being the irregular distribution of benefits, the future of these excluded areas, concerns on the imbalanced development of the North East region and the sheer isolation of these tribes from the rest of the nation. Not only was this policy discriminatory but there were questions on the role of the missionaries in the region. The colonial agenda was clearly more insidious than previously imagined by many. The seed, thus, for the political development in regional context was sown during this period.

Emergence of a New Religious Identity

During this period of debilitating British policies of exclusion and isolation, the only contact that the Hill tribes had with the outside world was through Christian missionaries. David Scott, the first Commissioner of Assam was of the opinion that "rude tribes were more likely to profit by the teachings of the Gospel." The then Commissioner of Assam, Major Francis Jenkins also held the same opinion that "tribes on the Assam frontier should be brought within the scope of missionary activities as early as possible as the influence of persons skilled in the languages of these tribes, devoting all their time and attention to humanize these rude races could not fail from being useful to us and to them."[12]

However, in 1793, the Baptist Missionary Society of England had already laid the foundation for missionary activity in the North

East but without much success. The British Administration further created the Charter Act of 1813 which stated the importance and necessity of the British administration taking more responsibility for the religious and moral improvement of the people of India. The Act firstly asserted the Crown's sovereignty over British India and secondly, it allowed the free movement of the missionaries to teach English and propagate Christianity.

Since the Charter Act, there was a determined flow of missionaries to the North East region as well as the rest of the nation working hand in hand with the administration. E.W. Clark started his work in 1871 with the Ao Nagas, William Pettigrew attempted to penetrate the Manipuri Vaishnavite Hindu population (but failed so set his sights on the Nagas and the Kukis) and Miles Bronson were some of the earliest missionaries to set foot in the tribal areas in the North East.

The missionary zeal in the region changed the social and cultural fabric. They deconstructed existing ideas of nationality, identity and attitude towards the political process in mainstream India. Both the administration and missionaries functioned parallel to each other. Although the colonial regime initially focused on a policy of non-interference with tribal identities, later on they changed the policy. This was mainly because of the awakening of political uprisings against the British rule in the region against arbitrary tax policies. The Lushai-Kuki tribes in Assam raided the British posts as early as 1826. Hence, after the visit of the Simon Commission in 1929, the colonial rulers initiated missionary activities as a policy to assimilate the tribes into the administration and reduce the growing discontent and marginalization among them.[13]

To make matters worse, the missionaries did not limit their work to religious conversion but to cultural conversion as well. The indigenous tribes had their own animistic methods of worship and spirituality that was closely associated with their culture and lifestyle. The missionaries played the leading role in destroying age old social, cultural, political and spiritual values. Their solutions to many of the problems was from the lens of a Western system and endeavoured to create a standardized homogenous society in sync with the West. However, this religious and cultural pomposity started changing the outlook of the innocent tribals. The missionaries looked upon them as heathens and themselves as civilised, therefore, creating aspirations amongst the tribal populations to imitate the Westerners. This prolonged emotional process and building up of ethnic-minority based identity became more explicit and articulate in the post-independent period and eventually culminated in unrest and terrorism in the region.[14]

For instance, in Nagaland, Christianity played the role of a cementing factor that binds people of diverse ethnic identities of Naga sub-tribes. Most of the leaders of the insurgent movement including Phizo were early converted Baptists and the slogan "Nagalim for Christ" was predominantly used in the region by insurgent groups (Das, 2009). The role played by Rev. Michael Scott, a Christian missionary in supporting the Naga rebels and negotiating with the government of India on behalf of the insurgent groups, is a classic example. Both the leaders of the Mizo movement and the Nagaland movements received immense aid and assistance from the church.[15]A separate identity that is different from the national identity of India was created by the missionaries and the Naga nationalism was perceived largely as a Christian sub-national identity consciousness. This has influenced the other states as well.[16] Even in Manipur, the insurgents received support from the church and were helped in garnering international support as well as platforms to articulate their demands.

The eventual success of the combined efforts of the administration and missionaries is evident in the conversion rates in the region. In 1901, the Christian population in Nagaland was only 0.59 per cent of the total population, in 1947 it had jumped to 46 per cent and by the 1980s at the peak of insurgency the figure reached nearly 87 per cent. More often than not religious conversions are understood to come through a deep spiritual experience propelling one to leave behind ancient beliefs to embrace a new faith. However, it is evident through the gigantic jumps in conversion in the last century as well as documented evidence that the use of force, intimidation and inducement was rampantly used by Christian insurgent groups. Though, it is also important to keep in mind that while there was a rise in insurgency based on a neo-colonial identity there was also a subsequent rise in the distrust and discontent against the British Empire and its missionaries. A powerful factor in the unification of Indian people as a nation was the common bond forged in the course of the freedom struggle. The struggle for independence by North Eastern freedom fighters was highly relevant to the entire unification of the Indian Nation. Rani Gaidinliu, Jadonang, Shoorvir Pasaltha Khuangchera, Hijam Irabot, Moje Riba are amongst the many great freedom fighters that fought against the British Empire for a unified India, especially Rani Gaidinliu and Jadonang who fought vehemently against the pressures of the missionaries on their tribe.

The "Secret Plan"—Crown Colony

Towards the end of the colonial rule, the British rulers were still reluctant to leave this region. The region was rich in resources and strategically located and therefore, they made an alternative plan called the "Crown Colony" to carve out a new independent region comprising the hill regions of the North East and Burma. The idea of amalgamating the "Backward Tracts" of Assam and Burma was initiated in 1928. During the visit of the Simon Commission it had been recommended to separate Burma Province from the British Indian Empire. Two British Officers N.E. Parry and J.H. Hutton were the first to suggest a "North East Frontier Province" consisting of the hill districts of Assam and Burma. This suggestion was based on the premise that the hill tribes were intrinsically different to the people in the plains.[17]

In 1941, then Governor of Assam Robert Reid further proposed combining the hill areas in Assam and Burma and creating a British colony. His plan made clear the intentions of the colonialists. Their policy of exclusion and isolation of these hill tribes nearing fruition. Robert Reid in his proposal pressed upon the importance of India's North East frontier in relation to Tibet, China, Burma and Japan—a country that had invaded Burma and reached the frontiers of the North East. Reid's plan proposed to cover adjoining hilly tracts of India and Burma, the Shan States, and the Chittagong Hills of present Bangladesh, into a separate political entity under the direct control of a Crown Agent. However, this plan was seen as an extension of the British colonialists "Divide and Rule" policy that would eventually lead to unrest. Unfortunately, the British had already laid the seeds for tribal secessionism from the time they entered the region, resulting in the North East bearing the brunt of India's longest running secession movement—the demand for "Greater Nagalim." The Naga insurgency not only took shape during the "exclusion and isolation period" but it also was fired by their new religion—Christianity. The same tribe that the British considered "rude" and "uncivilised" armed with the Bible were asserting their new identity based on the geographical location of the Crown Colony.

Reginald Coupland, Professor at Oxford University in his exhaustive report on the future of India expounded the Crown Colony idea. He also propagated the same limited vision and understanding that many British administrators, anthropologists and sociologists had put forth before—the Mongoloid races of these areas are culturally, ethnically, religiously (missionaries had started seeing success in the region) different from the rest of India. Due to Coupland's report, the Crown Colony plan was also called the Coupland Plan.

Fortunately, the plan could not materialize but the psychological impact on the hill tribes took shape. But as for formalising the plan, it faced immense opposition from leaders in Burma and India. The Indian leadership was vocally against any such plan taking shape. However, the Crown Colony plan was a failure in many aspects, it still played a vital role in creating a sense of exclusion and a separate identity consciousness among the tribes. This ultimately resulted in the emergence of insurgent groups among many tribal communities.[18]

Even though the British reluctantly withdrew from the region, the Church never abandoned the dream to make their own stronghold in the hill region. They instilled a new identity among the tribes based on Christian morality, education, ethnic bonds and projected this new sense of nationalism as something directly opposed to the mainstream Indian nationalism.[19]

The continuation of the missionary work even after Independence changed the religious composition of the region. As a result, in Mizoram and Nagaland, more than 80 per cent of the population is Christian whereas in Manipur, majority of the Kuki and Naga tribes are now Christians.[20] As in the case of Myanmar, Thailand and many South East Asian countries, Christianity in the North East was adopted largely by the tribes rather than non-tribal people. As a result, they developed ethnic as well as religious identity consciousness separate to that of the rest of the nation.

To expand the theory of common Christian brotherhood

among the tribes and to spread the movement for the demand of *Greater Nagalim*, insurgents converted tribes from other states as well. For example; in Arunachal Pradesh a fraudulent theory was promoted by missionaries and insurgents alike, that all of them belong to a common genetic Naga stock and therefore, should support the struggle for a common land for the Nagas. In fact, it was the church that united these tribes. These tribes had no common bonds, they were inter-warring tribes with even separate dialects.

Most of the tribes in Arunachal Pradesh have already converted into Christianity. The tribes including the Adis, Apatanis, Galos, Idu Mishmis, Nyishis and Tagins, now believe that they are part of a long tradition of Nagas and should fight with them to preserve their common identity. The leap in the percentage of converted population is equally extraordinary. The Census records show that in 1971 Christians were 0.79 per cent of the population, in 2011 they were well over 30 per cent and by 2020 a projection of 40 per cent would not be off the mark. The tribes of northern hill districts of Manipur have already converted into Christianity and carry on the false myth of Nagalim, forgetting their actual tribal identity and clan affinity.[21]

The Naga National Council (NNC) and Mizo National Front (MNF), the two oldest political arms of Cristian insurgency in the region even used Biblical imageries in their separatist rhetoric. Slogans like 'Nagaland for Christ' were visible on insurgent camps.[22] In Tripura and Manipur also, Christianity was perceived as a new identity that instilled in them the motive to fight against the Hindu culture of Bengali migrants.

Nevertheless, the failure of the Crown Colony plan limited the damage that otherwise would have resulted in India having to endure another partition. India's North Eastern frontiers would have been lost. A natural defence barrier, the rich history of the region, unique culture and most importantly its age old connections with the rest of the country would have all disappeared. Reid's plan only benefited the British Empire and suited the colonialist defence design in the geo-politics of South East Asia.

Conclusion

After independence Assam became a state in India. Thus, until the 1960s, Arunachal Pradesh, Assam, Meghalaya, Nagaland and Mizoram were all part of one state—Assam. The two other states—Manipur and Tripura—were princely states during British colonial rule, and subsequently became Union Territories.[23] After independence also security and geo-politics played vital role in determining mainland Indian approach to North East. The existence of China as a dangerous threat, proximity with East Pakistan and Burma and the emergence of insurgency forced policy makers to realize the strategic significance of the region, the same strategic significance that the British colonialists had observed a century ago. Moreover, the North East was linked to mainland India only through the strategic corridor of Siliguri in West Bengal.[24] Nevertheless, the rise of separatism in the region due to the seeds sown by the missionaries with the aid of the British administration as well as international media and organisations, led to a reorganization of the entire region.

In 1963, Nagaland was given separate statehood. Then, in April 1970, Meghalaya district was created around Shillong and the capital of Assam was shifted to Guwahati/Dispur. The most significant reorganisation took place on January 21, 1972. With the passing of the North Eastern Areas Reorganisation Act, 1971, by the Union Parliament in New Delhi, Arunachal Pradesh (former NEFA) and Mizoram (former Mizo Hills) were granted Union Territory status while Meghalaya, Manipur and Tripura gained full-fledged statehood. Mizoram and Arunachal Pradesh received separate statehood in 1987.[25] The North Eastern Council (NEC) was created to promote development programmes and coordinate the economic projects in the region. However, in the reorganization process of Assam, ethnicity and neo-colonial identities played a vital role. The Christian hill states of Nagaland, Mizoram and Meghalaya demanded autonomy and the right to represent their separate identity from the Hindu dominated Assam which was later culminated in the formation of separate statehood representing their identities.[26]

The formation of different states and pouring of Central financial assistance did not address the damage the British colonialists caused by their policy of physical, emotional, cultural and religious alienation. The consciousness of a neo-colonial identity created a rift amongst the population resulting in the crumbling of political loyalties and formation of identity and ethnicity based groups.

The British had encouraged ethnic, sub-ethnic and tribal identities on one side and fostered conversion into Christianity on the other during their time in the North East. They not only saw proselytization in the region as an opportunity to 'civilize' and Westernize the tribal way of life but also a way to forge bonds on the basis of religion in an area they had recognized as strategic.

After two hundred years of colonialism, when the British withdrew from India, they left a trail of horror. The partition on India's North Western frontier was ruthlessly demarcated in only fourty days by Cyril Radcliff, who had never stepped foot in India before. This was done regardless of the population that lived there, the strategic implication or the subsequent safety of the common man. One can only imagine if the same callousness was applied to the North Eastern frontier what the implications would have been.

The role of the British administration, their policies of exclusion and isolation and the crucial role of Christianity in building neo-colonial identities was successful to an extent. But the eventual failure of the Crown Colony plan gave the region an opportunity to integrate, just as over six hundred other tribes did in India. However, the legacy of colonialism in the North East will be defined in history by their denial of equality and opportunity to the people of North East India.

Notes

1. *https://www.sanskritimagazine.com/india/north-east-tribals-connection-ancient-india/*
2. K.A. Nilakanta Sastri and Srinivasachari, (1966). *India: A Survey*, Allied Publishers Pvt. Ltd., New Delhi, pp. 47- 48).
3. V.D. Mahajan (reprinted 1993). *Modern Indian History from 1707 to Present Day*, S. Chand and Company Limited, New Delhi p. 32.
4. L.W. Shakespear, (1929). *History of the Assam Rifles—With a new Introduction by Dr. N.N. Acharyya*, Spectrum Publications, Gauhati, p. 3.
5. A.C. Bannerjee, (1992). "Chapter 1: The New Regime, 1826-31." In Barpujari, H.K. (ed.). *The Comprehensive History of Assam: Modern Period*. IV. Guwahati: Publication Board, Assam, pp. 1-43.

6. *Ibid.*
7. *https://en.wikipedia.org/wiki/Treaty_of_Yandabo*
8. Thant Myint-U, *The River of Lost Footsteps—Histories of Burma. Farrar, Straus and Giroux*. p. 113. Anthony Webster (1998). *Gentlemen Capitalists: British Imperialism in South East Asia*, 1770-1890. I.B. Tauris, pp. 142-145.
9. Report of the Commission on the Hill Areas of Assam, 1966, p. 13, para 29.
10. *Ibid.*
11. *Ibid.*
12. M. Horam, *North East India: A Profile*, op. cit., p. 196.
13. Mackenzie, A. (2007). *History of the Relations of the Government with the Hill Tribes in North East Frontiers of Bengal*. New Delhi: OUP.
14. Baruah, S. (2004). *Durable Disorder: Understanding the Politics of Northeast India*. Oxford: Oxford University Press.
15. Bijukumar, V. (2013). "Social Exclusion and Ethnicity in North East India." *The NEHU Journal, 11* (2), 19-35.
16. Bhaumik, S. (2004). "Ethnicity, Ideology and Religion: Separatist Movements in India's North East." In S.P. Limaye, M. Malik, and R. Wirsing (Eds.), *Religious Radicalism and Security in South Asia* (pp. 219-244). New Delhi: Asia-Pacific Centre for Security Studies.
17. *Simon Commission Report on India*, Vol. XIV: Memorandum Submitted by the Government of Assam to the Indian Statutory Commission (London: H.M.S.O., 1930; reprinted ed., Delhi: Swati Publications, 1988). pp. 111-122.
18. *Ibid.*
19. *Ibid.*
20. *Ibid.*
21. Mohapatra, B. (2012). "Ethnic Conflicts, Politics of Regionalism and the Demand for NAGALIM: Perspectives on the Politics of Regional Accomodation and Autonomy." *Indian Journal of Political Science, 23* (2), 311-320.
22. Subba, T.B., Puthenpurakal, J., and Jos, S. (2009). *Christianity and Change in Northeast India*. New Delhi: Concept Publishing Co. Pvt. Ltd.
23. Dutta, M., Flavia, A., and Neera, A. (1996). *The Nation, the State and Indian Identity*. Kolkata: Stree.
24. Ahmed, R., and Biswas, P. (2004). *Political Economy of Underdevelopment of Northeast India*. New Delhi: Akansha Publishing House.
25. Menon, S. (2008). *India's North East Economy: Problems and Prospects*. Hyderabad: ICFAI University Press.
26. Barpujari, H.K. (1998). *North East India: Problems, Policies and Prospects*. New Delhi: Spectrum Publications.

18
Colonial Implication and South Nagalim Movement
Socio-Political Unrest and Trust Deficit in Manipur

Laitonjam Muhindro

Colonial Implication in Manipur

During 1945-46, Manipur witnessed a political turning point when many leaders of different political parties came to know of a British plan to give freedom to the princely kingdoms. Many leaders wanted Manipur to form a democratic country, while some wanted constitutional monarchy. Political parties like Praja Samelini, Praja Mandal, and Manipur State Congress pressed the demand for establishing a legislative assembly. On November 20, 1946, the then king of Manipur, Maharaja Bodhachandra, declared the formation of a constitution-making committee with 21 representative members of the hills and the valley people. Later, Manipur State Durbar was dissolved on July 1, 1947, and Manipur State Council was established on the same day.[1]

Mention may be worth that Naga integration (or South Nagalim) movement which captured public discourse after the June Uprising in 2001 in Manipur has a long genesis. In a manner of speaking, its roots can be traced as far back as 1929, whereby the Simon Commission responded to a memorandum signed by Nihu Angami and 19 other members of Kohima Club (a forum for interaction with British officials that was established in 1881), granted "Excluded Area" tag to some areas of Naga Hill District. In 1945, Kohima Club metamorphosed into the Naga Hill District

Council (NHDC) and, later in 1946, into the Naga National Council under the initiative of Angami Zapu Phizo. These events in Nagaland impressed upon the contiguous tribal areas of Manipur, particularly Mao sub-division of Manipur North District. The gradual influence from the neighbouring state of Nagaland was witnessed among the Mao Nagas. Athiko Daiho[2] was the pioneer of this Naga integration movement in Manipur.

By 1946, there were some voices from the Mao area of Manipur for secession of Naga-inhabited areas from the state, though not from India. A memorandum was submitted to the Governor of Assam by the *khullakpas* (village chiefs) and elders of the Mao Nagas, mentioning that their "people would be humiliated if the British officers make them to step in Manipur state and their administration is put directly under the Manipur State Durbar." They also asserted that except for "occasional inroads of the Manipuris in very limited hill villages, the Manipuri Maharaja had never subjugated the hill villages in pre-British days" and that they "were quite independent." So they requested the Governor "to make their hills a directly British controlled territory as the other neighbouring hill districts with whom they share common customs, traditions, social organizations, etc."[3] In 1947, under the leadership of Phizo, Naga National Council (NNC) had emerged and demanded independent Nagaland for Naga-inhabited areas of Tuensang from Arunachal Pradesh and Mao from Manipur. Phizo might have believed that his demands could strengthen with the involvement of Naga people of Manipur and Arunachal Pradesh. He was later joined by Athiko Daiho.[4]

During the drafting of Manipur Constitution, Daiho strongly argued that the hill tribes should have the right to secede from the state after five years. His proposal was rejected.[5] Another major step towards Naga unification was circulation of a document by Daiho in September 1948 "to a select circle of influential leaders" who dealt with future Naga situation in view of the approaching British departure. He explained his contention from many points of view. Historically, Manipur hills had probably been taken under state administration immediately after 1891, and that though "there might be irregular and occasional inroads of the Manipuri kings' forces in the hills on its way to Dimapur, Silchar or Burma and might possibly have taken spoils from the surrounding villages of the paths", the hills were "not formally conquered and no regular levy or tribute was paid by the Hills to the then king of Manipur."[6] About the then Hill administration he said, "Hills cadre is separate from that of the state proper, Valley. The Hill administration is run by the President of Manipur State Durbar. So, Hills matters do not come under the State Durbar as a whole." From a political point of view, he said that though the hills comprised 7/8th of the total area of the state, its inhabitants will always be a minority in Manipur as their population comprised roughly 2/5th of the whole population. This problem, he insisted, was "created" by accidental political distribution of boundaries at the advent of the British."[7] He further expressed his fear that if the hills of the Manipur forms a part of Manipur state, the inhabitants of the hills would be in a socially inferior position amongst the "more educated and civilized" Hindus.

Therefore, he wanted the "British officers of the Hills who are acquainted with Hill opinions" to decide the hills' future or that a "plebiscite of Hill men be summoned on elected or nominated representative basis of one man in every 1000 people and decide."[8] Thus what he desired was either (i) a federal Hills formed by "Lushai Hill, Somra Tract, Chin Hills, Naga Hills etc.", or (ii) that the hills of Manipur "be formed into a separate district by itself directly under the provincial control", or (iii) that the different parts of the hills may be disintegrated and joined with Naga Hills, North-Cachar Hills, Lushai Hills, Chin Hills and Somra Tract according to convenience.[9] Simultaneously with the demand for secession of Naga-inhabited areas of Manipur, two different and contesting political trends were also noticeable amongst the Nagas. One was represented by the Naga chiefs and their allies who had not changed their traditional values and outlook. The other trend was represented by the educated Christian Nagas who had distanced themselves from their root/past and were quite conscious of the then changing situation all-around.

The educated Christian Nagas decided not to join the Interim Council of Manipur. This stand followed the removal of the clause "'Right to Freedom of Action' after five years" from the final draft of the Manipur State Constitution Act, 1947. The said provision was seen by these Christian Nagas as "right to secession" from Manipur as well as from India.[10] When this clause was ultimately removed, they began toying with the idea of secession of Naga areas of Manipur from the state as well as from India. On

August 14, 1947, some Nagas in Kohima had declared independence for the Nagas of Manipur hills and Cachar, and that they were "negotiating to join Pakistan Dominion on suitable terms."[11] A meeting of Manipur Hills Special Conference, held at Imphal on August 14, 1947, demanded that since India is going to be free, all parts of it and the people thereof must be allowed to run the government. But, it did not mention secession either from Manipur or India.[12] Meanwhile, the NNC at Kohima tried to interfere in the Naga problem in Manipur. Having closely observed the situation in Manipur, the President of NNC wrote to the Maharaja of Manipur: "The political upheaval of the hill people in your state has attracted the keenest interest and close attention of the Naga National Council. Surely the National Council attaches very great importance to the fact that, though no fault of ours, that "upheaval" has directly touched the root of our National Council. As hill men we have interest in them; as neighbour, we are equally interested in your people and your state. Naturally, as a freedom fighting organization the NNC observes, with great sympathy, all the freedom fighting forces.[13] Hailing the development as "a natural corollary of national consciousness" and their right to secession as a "reasonable demand", the President of NNC expressed his belief that Maharaja would lose no time in granting the demand thereby paving the way of goodwill between the hills and the valley and also the state and the NNC as a whole."[14] Maharaja asked the Chief Minister to take urgent action, but the Chief Minister replied that "the Council has not been recognized by the state and is not of the state. No action need be taken."[15] This indifference of the authority made Daiho retrace his stand of secession from India. In a resolution of Naga National League (NNL) under his presidentship, Daiho stated that the organization shall primarily speak on behalf of the Nagas of Manipur but pledged itself to stand together with other hill tribes in the state as well as outside it in order to demand self-determination of the hill peoples in general without in any way injuring the general interests of Assam or India.[16] The main idea of the League was unity of all the Naga tribes as well as the non-Naga tribes of the state and work out their future according to the inclination, wishes and aspirations of the respective tribes. It also aimed to "bring together under one district administration the different scattered, allied tribes who happened to be in different districts of Assam but contiguous in area."[17] The term "self-determination" mentioned in the resolution was defined as "consolidation of tribes of the same stock under the district administrations in order to facilitate working of the future of that tribe who happen to be scattered living under different districts but contiguous in area."[18]

Another memorandum was also submitted to Sardar Patel, the then Deputy Prime Minister of India, on January 24, 1948 by A. Daiho and N. Modoli of NNL along with some Mao Naga chiefs and headmen. The memorandum opined that the conservation "of their culture, tradition, customary right, usages and political practices" would not be possible if the Naga people and their contiguous geography were placed under different influences and policies."[19] They insisted that "on the basis of linguistic provinces and consolidation of the same stock of people", the Nagas of different areas but contiguous in geography should be consolidated under one administrative unit and that nothing short of this demand would be acceptable to the Nagas of Manipur. As no positive response was received from the Government of India (GoI) and Government of Manipur, a "Provisional Government" was set up in order to start various agitations. As the first strategy, a no-house-tax campaign was started. In the following month, Daiho declared himself as leader of the Mao Nagas and did not pay tax to the state government. Instead, tax was collected by him for the Provisional Government.[20] His followers indulged in subversive activities by way of violating state rules. They forcibly broke through the Mao Gate and allowed lorries full of potato to cross the state gate without paying duties, even seized members of the state police and tortured them.[21]

On March 9, 1948, Daiho submitted a memorandum to the Government of India arguing that his movement was "not at all communal, but broadly based on linguistic provinces of India", and they wanted to secure their "due rights and liberties within free India as a freedom loving people." Further, NNL Secretary K. Sashipri sent a letter to the Secretary, Ministry of State, New Delhi, expressing that A. Daiho may enter into an agreement with the Government of India on behalf of the Mao and other allied Nagas of Manipur in connection with their right to self-determination. Daiho was arrested but released on August 26, 1948 by Chief Minister of Manipur M.K. Priyobarta. Later when Daiho refused to appear before the Hill Bench of Manipur Court, the state authority rushed to arrest Daiho. War cries were heard on the arrival of the police with the crowd gesticulating and shouting anti-state slogans. An attempt to peacefully arrest Daiho failed as the mob did not allow the authority to pass through the barricades they had built. Assam Rifles took to force with *lathi* charge. After about 50 minutes, mob became very tense, and as soon as the police confirmed that some unlicensed arms were to be used by the followers of Daiho from the nearby jungle, Assam Rifles opened fire resulting in two deaths and two wounded. Later, Daiho along with Medoli and Loili were arrested from the area. They were later kept in Calcutta jail.[22] Their arrest had greatly demoralized the followers. Meanwhile, an event of historical significance was building up. Manipur was merged into India in 1949, thus diverting the first movement for the Naga integration or secession of Naga inhabited areas from Manipur for the time being.

Trust Deficit and Diabolic Phenomena in Manipur

In Manipur, multifaceted conflicts situations have been appearing since long back and more deteriorating with the coming up of ethnic based AOGs that have different objectives to strengthen their rights so to say third generation rights for particular community in one or either form of movement. During the last few decades, Manipur has been wrecked by armed conflict that has left thousands killed and rendered thousands of others homeless. In the 1990s alone, various ethnic clashes took place—Meitei-Pangal, Kuki-Naga and Kuki-Paite, apart from the five-decade-long insurgency and counter-insurgency operations.[23] With this view the state of conflict in Manipur may be described as (i) Conflict between state and non-state actors; (ii) Inter-Ethnic Armed Conflict; and (iii) Intra-AOGs conflict etc. Each of these has interrelated as it can be considered as the source of the chains of conflicts.

Human rights in Manipur seem to be handled by state and non-state actors. It is known to all that Manipur was merged with Indian Union, w.e.f. 15 October, 1949.[24] "Since the day when Manipur was annexed in the most undemocratic way, the people of the state who are of Mongoloid stock, speaking a language of Tibeto-Burman family and having a separate culture and history of its own, have been struggling to regain the lost sovereignty."[25]

The then pioneer leader Hijam Irabot established the first ever armed revolutionary organization of Manipur, Manipur Red Guard (MRG). However, he breathed his last on 26 September, 1951 at Tangbo, Myanmar, before his Red Guard could attract popular attention (Tarapot, 2005: 175). Another underground group called Manipur Revolutionary Nationalist Party (MRNP) was also surfaced in 1953. It demanded the restoration of independent status of Manipur. The MRNP also went into oblivion soon following mass arrests of the Party leaders and tightening of security measures across the state (*Ibid*). By 1960s insurgent movements have been in new dimension with the coming of United National Liberation Front (UNLF) and others demanding sovereignty.[26] With a view to suppress any secessionist movement, various inhumane Acts including Armed Forces Special Power Act, 1958 (AFSPA) has been executing by India since 1980 till today.[27] Significantly, political executives and chief of the armed forces and elite groups have often observed that only the 'political dialogue should resolve the issue of armed conflict'. On the other, no sincere effort is being made by the authority which is evidenced by the ongoing peace talks of NSCN (National Socialist Council of Nagaland)[28] that started 15 years back in 1997. Besides, it seems to regenerate ethnic conflict in the north-east India.[29] Mention may be made that during 1992-96 there was Naga-Kuki conflict, ethnic cleansing (Singh 2006: 65) in many parts of hill areas in Manipur where many lives were lost.[30] Indeed it is precondition for Naga integration as well as ethnic dominance and ground preparation to undergo political dialogue in between NSCN-IM (National Socialist Council of Nagaland-Isak and Muivah) and Government of India.

Peace Initiative and Polarisation of Conflict

With a view to settle or manage existing conflict, Government of India has been initiating peace process (political dialogue/ suspension of Operation) with different Armed Opposition Groups (AOG) in India's North East. As a result of this political dialogue conflict between hill and valley in particular to Meitei and Naga was seemingly deteriorated and further resulted conflict between those who stand for territorial integrity and those who demand for Greater Nagalim. Subsequently, June uprising was broke out in 2001 when the Government of India extend ceasefire agreement (without territorial limit) including Manipur against the aspirations of the people of Manipur (Mani, 2001). Since this neo-conflict, in addition to various intractable/diabolic age-old issues of hill and valley, confidence building in between the hill and valley was suddenly deteriorated. With three major ethnic groups in Manipur, its insurgency is also primarily divided into insurgent groups of Meitei, Naga and Kuki. While the Meitei insurgents' prime objective is to free their pre-British territorial boundary from "Indian occupation", the Naga insurgents of Manipur support the demand of sovereign 'Nagalim' (Greater Nagaland) comprising Nagaland along with the Naga majority areas of Manipur, Assam, Arunachal Pradesh and Burma (Myanmar). The Kukis on the other hand support the demand of separate Kukiland for which Kukis of Burma are also fighting (*Ibid.*). Today, Manipur is one of the worst insurgency affected states in the North East India.[31]

So far the strategic plan of the Government of India may be in the right direction what they had thought earlier. That the strongest and oldest insurgent group NSCN (NSCN-IM and NSCN-K) is in the fold of political dialogue/ceasefire talk since August 1997 and November 1998[32] and carry forward various conflicting issues with a hope to resolve within the framework of the Constitution of India. It may be noted that many Armed Opposition Groups (AOG)/ insurgent outfits are being operated in North East India. Most of them had started with a vision of sovereign state. As such NSCN-IM's demand for sovereignty was shifted to Greater Nagalim to unite all the Naga inhabited areas of North East region and even including some neighbouring parts of Myanmar. In this context, though the union government has the power to change state boundaries, neighbouring states have condemned and warned the India Government to protect territorial integrity of their respective states. Since political dialogue started in between NSCN-IM and GoI from 1997, socio-political and ethnic conflict added to be worsening on the enduring conflict of Manipur.

Socio-Political Unrest and Territorial Integrity

The threat to territorial integrity of Manipur started around 1946 with the upsurge of ethnic secessionism. Mao Nagas started an agitation to integrate Mao areas with Nagaland. In Manipur, there were two agitations after 1947. One was Hmar Movement for the merger with Lushai Hills as inspired by the Mizo Union of the Lushai Hill District. The other was that of Naga People's League which stood for the independence of Nagas in Mao area of northern Manipur. But other Nagas and Kukis of Manipur did not participate in these movements. The Nagas of Manipur did not participate in the plebiscite of 1951 which was regarded as the bedrock of Naga independence movement. Their non-participation in the plebiscite was regarded as a unique feature of the politics of the Nagas of Manipur.[33]

The demand for integration of Naga-inhabited areas of Manipur was influenced by Phizo, the pioneer of Naga revolutionary group Federal Government of Nagaland (FGN), who demanded independent Nagaland. Peace talks were started on the issue after a ceasefire agreement was clinched between the FGN and Government of India in 1964. The next peace attempt in 1975 (Shillong Accord) between the FGN and the Government of India was thwarted by Th. Muivah and Isak Swu. The latter two along with Khaplang formed another revolutionary group, National Socialist Council of Nagalim (NSCN) in 1980 with Issac Swu as President, Khaplang as Vice-President and Th. Muivah as General Secretary, marking a new phase in the Naga independence movement. The year 1988 saw NSCN breaking up into two factions: NSCN-IM led by Isak Swu and Th. Muivah, and NSCN-K by Khaplang.

With the emergence of NSCN-IM, the demand for independent Nagalim, or integration of Naga-inhabited areas of Manipur into a new state, or to form a "Southern Nagaland" comprising the districts of Senapati, Ukhrul, Chandel and Tamenglong of Manipur got a new impetus. NSCN-IM made public its vision of a "Greater Nagaland" comprising 1,20,000 sq. km. by expanding the present 16,579 sq. km. of Nagaland. The expanded area includes four districts of Manipur (mentioned above), five districts of Assam (parts of Sibsagar, Golahgat, Jorhat, Karbi Anglong, North Cachar Hill districts) and two districts of Arunachal Pradesh (Tirap and Changlong), with a section of Myanmar territory.[34] While NSCN-K has remained focused on sovereignty for the Nagas, NSCN-IM seems to have scaled down their goal from sovereignty to "Greater Nagalim" and/or federal relations with India. Many Naga elite groups and some civil society organisations have condemned NSCN-IM's flexible demands as sacrifice of the movement and devaluing those whose lives were sacrificed in course of the long struggle for a sovereign Nagaland. The gulf between different factions seems to be increasing day-by-day. Without a peaceful settlement between the two major factions, larger peace settlement seems a distant dream. In several phases of the peace talk, the Government of India has seemingly, so far, taken cognizance of the general feeling of the people in Assam and Manipur, particularly on the issue of reshaping the existing state boundaries and shelved the demand for "Greater Nagalim" for the time being, at least.

South Nagalim and State Politics in Manipur

Though the movement for integration of Naga-inhabited areas started in 1946 in Mao area of Manipur, this became an important political issue in the state politics of the late 1960s. One of the most prominent political leaders amongst those who gained political mileage out of the issue, Rishang Keishing[35] carried forward the movement with overt and covert agendas. Though the root of the Naga movement was germinated by Daiho at Mao, it was nurtured by Keishing with the formation of the Naga Integration Council at the far end of the 1960s. With this politics in tow, Keishing could create a record of sorts by winning state assembly elections (from Phungyar assembly constituency) consecutively from 1972 to 2000.

The Naga Integration Council, formed with the aim of promoting integration of Naga-inhabited areas, was later converted into United Naga Integration Council in 1972. Not long after, the UNIC merged with the Congress Party taking assurance from the Congress to support the integration movement. Since then, Keishing has carried forward the Naga agenda as a political weapon to build up his political career. Incidentally, he was the longest serving Chief Minister of Manipur (1983-1997) until he was removed in 1997.

The political dialogue between the Government of India and NSCN-IM has crossed a decade, but it has not progressed much. Largely, this was due to the delaying tactics of the Government of India. Both the parties do not seem to be sincere in their approach, though both make claims of progress and sincerity. The Government of India has been making dual commitment both to the people of Manipur and Assam, as well as to the Naga "national" leaders. It seems that political leaders at the Centre, unable to find any amicable solution, are so far engaging in delaying tactics. On the other side, NSCN-IM merrily continues all their routine activities like taking illegal taxes from the vehicles, demanding huge amounts from the capitalist and business community and other forms of violent extortion except engaging the Indian armed forces militarily. The Government of India finds it convenient to look away from all these goings-on instead of enforcing its writ for maintaining law and order. In the meanwhile, the pot of factional feud and hostility among Naga militant groups is kept boiling. In the circumstances, mutual recognition and reconciliation amongst the NSCN-IM, NSCN-K, and NNC become all the more daunting.

In Manipur, though, several Naga civil society organizations loyal to NSCN-IM have started implementing new strategies of organizing democratic movements since 2000. The United Naga Council (UNC) and allied organizations staged a number of unity rally in the hill districts of Manipur and Nagaland. *Bandhs*, strikes, blockades, and non-cooperation movements[36] of various kinds mark the main components of the new movement that is seemingly aimed at affecting public order and hopefully, earning leverage for a peace settlement with NSCN-IM. Gradually, as a new strategy, NSCN-IM is seemingly entering into state politics, directly or indirectly, by reversing its pre-ceasefire stand of boycotting and banning elections in the hill districts. The State Assembly election of 2002 saw the NSCN-IM backing specific candidates. This was done to strengthen the peace process and also to achieve some political points for negotiation. Then, again, the organization initiated the consolidation of Naga politicians supporting "integration" through the UNC. On the eve of the 2002 election, the Naga candidates had taken an "undertaking" to contribute to the Naga consolidation and integration movement. Thus, the Naga problem has become a major political issue for the entire state. The same policy was continued in the next State Assembly election of 2007, with the UNC instructing the Naga candidate aspirants not to be candidate of a national party, condemning particularly the ruling Congress high command's attitude and its delaying tactics.

Political Dialogue and Diplomatic Dancing

Both the counterpart (GoI and NSCN-IM) have no sincere in the dialogue though both claimed progress and sincerity.[37] The ground rules of ceasefire are often violated and the monitoring committees set up to implement the ground rules have remained callous in their approach. The government has been engaged in talks with the NSCN (IM) for the last sixteen years and managing conflicting issues somehow but there is still no concrete acceptable resolution. The so-called 'violence' is controlled but the outfit has continued all its activities with impunity. From organised extortion to narcotic smuggling to arms running this outfit feeds and raises other smaller groups to expand their area of control. Therefore 'talks' ensure certain legitimacy to the underground activities of these groups across the spectrum.[38] Samir Kumar observed that "the primary objective of peace dialogue is to bring warring groups in the negotiating table, set forth potentially agreeable ceasefire terms and conditions and offer alternative ways of settling conflicts that beset the region."[39] In regard to success of peace process Kishalay observed[40] that those some AOG started with a vision for sovereign state are seemingly deferred to the local issue and ethnic cleansing and rather emphasising federal relations.[41] Significantly, NSCN-IM deferring their demands from sovereignty to federal autonomy and even alternative arrangement within Naga inhabited areas in India's North East. Indian Government has had some success in achieving stability in the region, using tactics from negotiations to military operations to root out militants.[42] In such pandemonium situation the dynamics of peace process and subsequent effect in different ethnic groups in India's north-east is wider day-by-day. On the other hand Suspension of Operation with some minor AOGs in Manipur is indeed success and failure of one and the other. Initiative of the government is somewhat success but its ramification is rather developed a conflict within different ethnic based AOGs. Thus, the ongoing peace process has been advancing with no significance achievement in terms of mutual agreement or acceptable but coercive nature of Government of India is a plenty and widening ethnic divide while trying to manage conflict on the way what the Central Government want *'wait and watch'* which is success of the one side and loser of the other, it is indeed a *diplomatic dancing*.

Successful Democratic Initiation

Obviously, elections in the hill and remote areas are witnessing abnormal election where many electorates could not enjoy the right to franchise. Moreover some civil organizations who are loyal to insurgent groups have been acting like a political party and imposed does and do not to the electorates and intending candidates. The problem of factionalism also casts its shadow over the operation of electoral processes as one Naga underground outfit does to promote its interests by involving in elections, so also other outfits.[43] Besides, political elites have nexus with insurgents and using them for mutual benefit. Perhaps the conflict situation may compel to do so. Politics in the North East are not based on democratic norms as understood in the Western-model democratic system observed by Ved Marwah, former Governor of Manipur.[44] During elections political leaders seek support of the AOGs in the form of muscle power. The entire political system in the region has grown around these unscrupulous politicians.[45] In the hill districts, under the imposition of parallel diktats, intimidations, forces from different underground factions, the voters remain helpless for free exercise of their voting right. The imposition is often exercised through frontal Naga NGOs, Naga political parties etc. It has its beginning after 1997 which was the year in which current ceasefire agreement was inked between Government of India and NSCN (I-M).[46]

It may be noted that general strike / ban on the polling day in Manipur were also very common which totally violates electoral rights but all the concerns seem to consider it as a result of conflict. NSCN-IM boycotted the Seventh Manipur State Assembly Election and 12th (1997) and 13th Lok Sabha Election (1999).[47] The NSCN-IM's call for boycott was stringently observed by some of the over-ground Naga organizations under the banner, "We want solution not election."[48] In the Seventh Assembly Election of 2000, the number of Kuki MLA's had outnumbered the elected Naga MLAs.[49] *The people of Ukhrul had no other option but to abide by the diktat of the NSCN (IM). But this time, the people of Ukhrul have not only participated in the Assembly elections defying the boycott call by the NSCN (IM), but also ensured the defeat of a person, who had reportedly close links with the underground group.* The United Naga Council (UNC) in the State made clear that they would like to be part of a Greater

Nagaland as demanded by the NSCN-IM; for the Meiteis and other ethnic groups, this became a question of defending their territory. This divide has its impact on the political set up in the State, including a realignment in the political parties, the electioneering process and, possibly, on the outcome of the polls.[50] In the Eighth Assembly Elections, 2002 and the 14th Lok Sabha Elections 2004, NSCN-IM decided the fate of the Naga mainstream politics, right from the selection of the candidate to their election.[51] The line of divisions between the various communities in Manipur can no longer be treated as a fall out underground politics with the submission of a Memorandum by Naga MPs and MLAs of the state to the Prime Minister openly supporting the NSCN (IM)'s concept of Nagalim on 27 May, 2005.[52]

Ethnic Organizations for Peace and South Nagalim

On the eve of elections, many Naga NGOs and frontal organisations of Naga Armed Opposition Groups have been trying to make more unite and close cooperation by organizing traditional functions and even campaigned door to door in the entire hill areas to convince and support sponsored Naga candidates on the backdrop of Naga integration. Some Naga politicians and social organizations claimed that the word "Manipur Integrity" is against their aspiration of Naga Unification though some sections of Naga community do not have much interest on the integration demand. Taking the opportunity on this diabolic situation most of the politicians in hill and valley have often been made a great deal on ethnic or communal politics. NSCN-IM, on 13 July, 2005, and ANSAM asked all the Naga MLAs and Ministers in Manipur to resign, declaring that Naga identity and dignity can not be safeguarded under the present arrangement of Manipur state under any circumstances. Only for their political gain politicians often insisted many innocent electorates to condemn the ruling government charging betray or neglect them in any field on communal line. Even former Chief Minister, MP Rishang Keishing himself claimed "Meitei Betrayed."[53]

In the 9th Manipur State Assembly Election 2007, a faction of the Naga rebel group, while considering it as an opportunity of strengthening the ongoing peace process for securing the aspirations of the 'Naga people for a united Naga Homeland' involved in a big way. The UNC, its constituent Tribe Councils/ Hohos and the Naga civil societies have decided to define the objectives with which the Naga people must approach the same for securing representatives through whom the voice of the Naga people can be articulated loud, clear and consistently.[54] The UNC appeals to the Nagas of Manipur to choose/elect only those candidates who have no party affiliation whatsoever, who enjoys the confidence of their respective constituencies who are God fearing and who subscribes to the following four objectives to work unitedly with his/her other fellow Naga representatives elected in the same manner:

- to fulfil the inherent and democratic aspiration of the Naga people for unification of all homeland;
- to mobilize the peoples' fullest support of the ongoing Indo-Naga political dialogue for an honourable solution;
- to provide leadership to society in nation building; and
- to promote the common interest of all ethnic communities in the state.

The UNC appeals to the Naga people of Manipur through their respective tribal council/Hohos, churches; intelligentsia; professionals; women, youth and student's organisations to rally behind the goal to mutually strengthen for the unification of the Nagas (*Ibid.*).

"The Nagas of Manipur have to go beyond the immediate compulsions of personal gains; family, clan, village, and tribal interests and political opportunism. We must ensure the return of responsible candidates with clear visions who will represent the Nagas aspirations and carry forward our struggle for peace, justice, and freedom. It is an uphill task but we must do it because we know what awaits us if we do not", it further says *[UNC]*.

The NSCN-IM has also joined the fray by attacking the candidates of various political parties.[55] The UNC has fielded 11 independent candidates in 2007 Manipur State Assembly Elections in the four-Naga dominated districts of Manipur under the United Naga Democratic Front (UNDF) with the twin objectives of intensifying their agitation for the integration of Naga-inhabited areas under one administrative unit and mobilising support for talks between the GoI and NSCN (IM).[56]

The UNC took a resolution (3 August, 2006) wherein Naga candidates had been instructed against contesting the 9th Manipur State Assembly Elections under any national political parties and intimated to all the sitting Naga MLAs.[57] In the UNC sponsored meeting of the all the intending Naga candidates for the Manipur State Assembly Election 2007, 60 Naga intending candidates signed the Eight Point Declaration. [58]

I wilfully support the ongoing Indo-Naga Peace talks for a negotiated and honourable solution. On being elected I will steadfastly defend the interest of the Naga people for the integration/Unification of the Naga Areas; That I will resign from the Manipur Legislative Assembly if called upon to do so by the Naga people represented by the UNC; ... I declare that I will accept without any reservation whatsoever, the candidature of the particular person who is determined by the Naga people represented by the UNC to be the consensus candidate; ...I shall not defect/split/merge to any political party without the approval of the Naga people represented by the UNC. Failing to fulfil the above Commitments and Declaration, I and my witness shall be made liable to any measures adopted by the Naga people.

In another meeting of the UNC held on 28 December, 2006 at Senapati resolved to totally ban and restrict the political party affiliation of whatsoever and holding of political parties' conventions and campaigns in the Naga areas.[59] The UNC had afterwards served ultimatum on 24 January, 2007 to all those candidates who had not been nominated by the UNC to withdraw their candidates.[60]

Conclusion

Opposition parties' attack of ruling party is a common phenomenon in democratic politics; but the mode of consolidation of the opposition in recent times carries certain significance in the state politics of Manipur. The Naga integration movement continues to play a major catalyst in this respect leaving no stone unturned in its efforts germinate and consolidate oppositional democratic politics along ethnic lines and furthering hill-valley divide in Manipur. In the foreseeable future, too, there will be no dearth of leaders and organizations to keep the pot of Naga integration politics boiling. The price for this obsessive agenda of the NSCN-IM will be pushing two equally important agenda of the Naga struggle—one, ending of hostility among the three factions (NSCN-IM, NSCN-K and NNC), and, two, a more comprehensive and sincere engagement with/by the Government of India—on the back-burner. This, of course, is easier said than done. Future of Naga politics in the state of Manipur, and the region as a whole, lies in the dynamics of this engagement.

Notes

1. Irom Khamba Singh, "Manipurgi Houkhraba Leingaklon (since 1891)" in *Voice of People's Democracy*; vol. 1, 53rd Anniversary Souvenir; Imphal: PDF, 2002, p. 55.
2. Daiho was a Mao Naga leader (member of Manipur Constitution Drafting Committee and later Minister of Finance during Territorial Council 1963 and also elected as MLA from Karong AC in 1972, 1st Assembly election after statehood.
3. A memorandum was submitted by the Khullakpas, Gouburas and elders of the Mao Nagas to the Governor of Assam, apparently, when he visited Mao on January 2, 1946.
4. A. Ibobi, "Manipurgi Ngamkheida Pirakpa Cheitheng V-1", Poknapham, November 2, 2005.
5. Gangmumei Kamei, "Ethnicity and Politics in Manipur", in *Selected Writings on Issue of Identity*, Imphal: Imphal Free Press 8th year of publication, 2003, p. 36.
6. A. Daiho, "My views on the tendency of future Hills administration of Manipur or Demand of the Hills", *General People*, September 5, 1946.
7. *Ibid.*
8. *Ibid.*
9. *Ibid.*
10. Proceedings of a meeting of hill men held on August 13, 1947, at Imphal under the chairmanship of R. Suisa, quoted in S. Mangi, A Study on Selected Socio-Political Problems in Manipur (1947–1980), unpublished Ph.D. thesis, Department of Political Science, Manipur University, p. 344.
11. Telegram from President of Naga state, Kohima to the Maharaja of Manipur on August 14, 1947, in S. Mangi, *A Study on Selected Socio-Political Problems in Manipur (1947–1980)*, p. 345.
12. *Ibid.*, p. 346.
13. *Ibid.*
14. *Ibid.*

15. *Ibid.*
16. Memorandum dated January 20, 1946 signed by N. Modoli and A. Daihom, President of NNL, *Ibid.*, p. 347.
17. *Ibid.*
18. *Ibid.*
19. *Ibid.*, p. 349.
20. *Shillong Times*, September 3, 1948.
21. S. Mangi, A Study on Selected Socio-Political Problems in Manipur (1947–1980), p. 349 unpublished Ph.D. Thesis, Department of Political Science, Manipur University.
22. *Ibid.*, p. 350.
23. Anjulika Samom, "Prostitution: Sex trade thrives in conflict-ridden Manipur", *India Together*, 12 June, 2007.
24. The leaders of the then Dominion of India, who had all along maintained that the people of the princely state should decide the future of the state, failed to take into confidence the opinion of the people's representatives in the then existing national house of Manipur. Instead, the 'Merger Agreement' was forced upon the king in Shillong...
25. Dhanabir, L., Resolution of Armed-conflict in Manipur: An Alternative Perspective, Manipur Research Forum, Manipur and Delhi, retrieved from http:/www.manipurresearchforum.org/resolution_armed_conflict.htm, accessed on 22 January, 2010.
26. The emergence of insurgency in Manipur is formally traced to the emergence of the United National Liberation Front (UNLF) on 24 November, 1964. The alleged 'forced' merger of Manipur and the delay in the conferring of full-fledged statehood to it was greatly resented by the people of Manipur. Since then several other outfits, like the People's Liberation Army (PLA), founded on 25 September, 1978, People's Revolutionary Party of Kangleipak (PREPAK) set up on 9 October, 1977 and the Kangleipak Communist Party (KCP) that came into being in April, 1980 have emerged in the valley areas consisting of four districts of the State. All these insurgent groups have been demanding a separate independent Manipur. Centre for Development and Peace Studies, "Overview: Insurgency and Peace Efforts in Manipur" (Online) available at: http://cdpsindia.org/manipur_insurgency.asp, accessed on 30 March, 2010.
27. Rakesh, P. Meitei, "AFSPA, 1958 And The Jeevan Reddy Review Committee" retrieved from http://www.e-pao.net/epSubPage Extractor.asp?src=news_s ection.opinions.Opinion_ on_Killing_of_ Manorama.AFSPA_1958_and_The_Jeevan_Reddy_Committee, accessed on 22 April, 2010.
28. The hill areas of the State, comprising five districts, have been affected by different brands of militancy. From Nagaland, violence by the Naga groups has also spilled over into Manipur, a substantial

part of which is claimed by the Issac-Muivah faction of National Socialist Council of Nagaland (NSCN-IM) as part of Nagalim, the proposed unified territory of the Nagas as claimed by the Naga rebels. Several clashes between the NSCN-IM and the Khaplang faction of National Socialist Council of Nagaland (NSCN-K) have been reported from the hill districts of the State. STAP, retrieved from http://www.satp.org/satporgtp/countries/india/states/manipur/terrorist_outfits/kna.htm, accessed on 22 December, 2010.

29. The Nagas of Manipur were supporting the movement of National Socialist Council of Nagaland (NSCN) demanding a sovereign 'Nagalim' (Greater Nagaland) including the Naga inhabited territory of Assam, Manipur, Arunachal Pradesh and Burma. The Kukis, who live side by side with the Nagas, however, never supported the latter instead often clashed with them and formed underground group to fight for their separate sovereign identity. Moreover, Meitei community strongly reacted that they stand for territorial integrity of state that has more than 2000 history.
30. The Kuki-Naga clashes which started around the middle of 1992 continued till the middle of the 1990s. Though it was popularly described as the Kuki-Naga clashes, it was mainly between the Nagas and the Thadou speaking Kukis of the state. Nonetheless, many other tribes of the Kuki-Chin-Mizo group were also affected during the clashes. Once started, the clashes spread like wild fire and within no time the entire state was in the grip of unprecedented ethnic violence. It affected all the five hill districts of the state. Of these five, Chandel was the most troubled and affected district. Manipur Cultural Integration Conference (MCIC) and Ethnic Community in Manipur (A Report of the MCIC visiting team), 1996, p. 2.
31. A report of the State Home Department in May 2005.
32. Indeed NSCN started peace talk during reign of Indira Gandhi's period of Prime Minister 1967, and also referring as Shillong Accord.
33. Gangumei Kamei, "Ethnicity and Politics in Manipur", p. 37.
34. R.K. Mani, "A Reflection on the Indo-NSCN-IM Cease-fire Extension", in R.K. Mani (ed.), *For Our Tomorrow: Perspectives on Naga Ceasefire in Manipur*, SILYA, 2001, p. 27.
35. Rishang Keishing, a Tangkhul Naga, is known as the longest serving Chief Minister of Manipur.
36. Those forms of protests manifest in specific forms, such as including non-payment of hill house tax, longest blockade against June uprising holiday, textbook issue, school affiliation issue, banning Meitei script and entertainment elements in the hill areas, replacing signboards of district headquarters in "South Nagaland" etc.
37. Muhindro, L. (2008) "Political Dialogue of NSCN-IM and Government of India: an Introspection", *South East Asia Politics*, New Delhi, Vol. 7, Issue 6, pp. 21-24.

38. Kishalay Bhattacharjee, (2011) 'Peace Talks' in Assam's Post Election Scenario, IDSA comment, 16 May, retrieved from http://www.idsa.in/idsacomments/PeaceTalksinAssamsPostElectionScenario_kbhattacharjee_160511, accessed on 10 February, 2012.
39. Samir Kumar Das, (2007) "Conflict and Peace in India's North East: The role of Civil Society, East-West Centre", Washington, *Policy Studies* 42, Washington, DC.
40. Kishalay Bhattacharjee, (2011).
41. Besides NSCN-IM Secretary Th. Muivah and Chairman Isak-Swu diverted/reversed their demands of sovereignty to the Greater Nagalim within the Indian Union by disintegrating territory of other neighbouring states in north eastern including large area of Manipur and even some parts of Myanmar, make immense influence to the Naga political leaders and Naga social organizations though some Naga leaders condemned NSCN-IM decisions after devoted many lives on the long way.
42. Bibhu Prasad Routray, Manipur Assembly Elections: Divergence of Ethnic Interests, Institute for Conflict Management, retrieved from http://www ipcs.org/article/military/manipur-assembly-elections-divergence-of-ethnic-interests-703.html, accessed on 23 October, 2010.
43. Benjamin, G., 2013, "Impairing Free and Fair Election: The Emerging Trend Observed Among the Naga Tribes of Manipur", in L. Muhnindro and G.T. Haokip, (ed.), *Emerging Electoral Trends and Violation of Human Rights: A Paradigm of Exacerbating India's Democracy*, New Delhi, Mittal Publication.
44. Ved Marwah, Former Governor, Manipur and Jharkhand delivered a lecture on Ethno-Political situation in India's Northeat, at Centre for Strategic Analysis, Tamil Nadu, 19 May, 2010.
45. The growing nexus between the undergrounds and the over ground political leaders and the civil servants is directly related to the lure for easy money. As the people do not trust the state police to protect them, the different ethnic groups have organized their own armed militias. They need funds to maintain these armed, which they secure by extortion and pilferage of government funds practiced on large scale. Ved Marwah, Former Governor, Manipur and Jharkhand delivered a lecture on Ethno-Political situation in India's Northeat, at Centre for Strategic Analysis, Tamil Nadu, 19 May 2010.
46. Benjamin, G., 2013,
47. The Naga Members of Legislative Assembly (MLA)s sent emissaries to negotiate with the NSCN-IM when the later issued a directive to all Naga MLAs in Manipur to resign their seat by December 31, 1994 in protest against the Central and State Government's alleged assistance to the Kukis in their conflict with the Nagas. This shows the NSCN-IM had a considerable hold on Naga MLAs.
48. The issued NSCN (IM)'s note of appreciation jointly signed by both

Isak Chisi Swu and Th. Muivah, dated 10 February, 1998 expressed appreciation and thanks to UNC and others for "their outstanding decision to disallow the imposition of Indian election in Nagalim. It says, "*The Collective Leadership acknowledges here its profound gratitude to the Naga people for their outstanding decision to disallow the imposition of Indian elections in Nagalim. We would particularly like to thank the Naga Hobo Summit, United Naga Council, Naga Peoples' Movements for Human Rights, Naga Students' Federation, Naga Mothers' Association, Naga Village Chief's Federation Concerned Citizen Forum, Naga GB' Federations, political parties and the Church leaders for their decisiveness in asserting the national rights of the Naga people. Your momentous endeavour is unprecedented since the time of 1951 Plebiscite under your bold pilotage the Naga people have come forward all the more, taking the firm political stand at a crucial moment such as this one.... History is more securely in our hands now. It is indeed your timely efforts and unsparing sacrifices that have proved beyond doubt the unconquerable power of the people in different dimension. Now no one on earth can deny this fact. Thanks be to God, now no force under the sun can hold the Naga people back. We are committed to the national cause heart and soul.*"

49. *Media miss Manipur polls, editorial, Oriental Times, NEN, 2(37-38) 7 Mar.-21Mar. 2000* retrieved from http://www.nenanews.com/OT%20Mar%207-%20Mar%2021,%2000/editorialC.htm, accessed on 22 April 2002.
50. Bibhu Prasad Routray, Manipur Assembly Elections: Divergence of Ethnic Interests, Institute for Conflict Management, retrieved from http://www.ipcs.org/article/military/manipur-assembly-elections-divergence-of-ethnic-interests-703.html, accessed on 23 October, 2010.
51. Aheibam Koireng Singh, Some Reflections on Land Questions and Ethnic Crisis in Manipur, paper presented in National Seminar on *Land Problem and Ethnic Crisis in North East India*, sponsored by Maulana Abul Kalam Azad Institute for Asian Studies (MAKAIAS), Kolkata, orgd. by Dept. of History, Manipur University, 27-28 July, 2005.
52. *North East Sun*, Delhi, 15 July 2005.
53. *North East Sun*, weekly magazine, Guwahati, (7)15: 2005.
54. Koireng Singh, A. (2011) In the Whirlpool of Delhi Bandits' Skulduggery and Insurgency: Manipur Electoral Politics, paper presented on two-day UGC sponsored National Seminar on Emerging Electoral Trends and Violation of Human Rights: A Paradigm of Exacerbating India's Democracy, held on 25 and 26 November 2011, at S. Kula Women's College, Nambol, Manipur
55. According to the former Chief Minister, Reishang Keishing, two candidates from the party contesting the Chandel and Tengnoupal seats have already been forced to withdraw their nominations by the NSCN-IM.

56. The common front floated by the United Naga Council (UNC) has been christened as the United Naga Democratic Front (UNDF) with Kho John as its convenor. In its manifesto, it pledges to mobilize the people for fullest support to the on-going Indo-Naga political dialogue for an honourable solution; to provide leadership to society in nation building; to fulfill the inherent and democratic aspirations of the Naga people for the unification of all the Naga Homeland; to promote common interest of all the ethnic communities in the state. *The Sangai Express*, English local daily vernacular, 7 February 2007.
57. *The Sangai Express*, a local English Daily vernacular, 3 November, 2006. With it a verbal spat erupted between the Congress MLA, R.K. Theko and UNC when a newspaper cited the former saying that the NSCN-IM is attempting to wipe out the Congress organisation from the Naga areas through the UNC. It can be recollected that R.K. Theko was the President of UNC at a time when it issued Quit Notice to the Kukis in 1992. Spat of resignation by Naga MLAs took place ahead of the 9th Manipur Assembly Election in which five sitting legislatures namely Samuel Jendai, Henry Paotei, Danny Shaiza, B.D. Behring and Wungnaoshang Keishing resigned from the Manipur State Assembly in support of the ongoing GoI-NSCN-IM peace process and 'to fulfil the inherent and democratic aspirations of Naga people' for "unification of all Naga Homeland." [*North East Sun*, Delhi, 16-31 January, 2007].
58. *The Sangai Express*, English local daily vernacular, 12 January, 2007.
59. *Ibid.*
60. *Ibid.*, 2 February, 2007.

19

State Policies Towards the Tribal

A Rethinking on the Indian Experience

W. Nabakumar Singh and *Th. Bimola*

I

The term 'tribe', though used indiscriminately both by anthropologists and laymen alike, is a concept burdened with academic vagueness, for it is a term referring to two realities, two fields of facts that are different, yet linked (Godelier, 1977:70). Almost everyone uses it to distinguish a type of society from others on one hand and to designate a stage of evolution in human society on the other. Both the uses of the term, however, are full of disagreements; the former owing to the vagueness of criteria employed to define and isolate different types of society while the latter because of the failure, among anthropologists, to arrive at a decision regarding the existence of a necessary stage in the evolution of humanity. This theoretical crisis that centres around the concept is only half of the trouble; the ideological uses of the concept and its related form 'tribalism' meets with violent attacks from academicians and politicians alike, for they see in the contradictions attributed to the term not so much a relic of pre-colonial structures but as a legacy of the colonial period and the new relations involved in neo-colonial domination. Ideologically it always carries a biased meaning of primitivism and traditionalism. Truly speaking, almost all the so-called tribal groups, though not severed totally from their past, have lost many of their traditional characters; this has necessitated us to view them, both from the theoretical and practical perspectives, as new entities.

In view of the theoretical crisis attributed to the concept, and also in view of the ideological biasness based on the cultural arrogance of the majority/reference group who use the term, it is high time for both the State and the academics to search a new terminology, at least free from biasness, appropriate for these so called 'tribals'. It may be pointed out here that segmentary/lineage society is the new terminology employed by some anthropologists in place of the tribal society.

II

Academically speaking tribe is a concept inherited from L.W. Morgan (1877), but amputated theoretically a century later by functionalists and then again revitalized by neo evolutionists like Sahlin (1961) and Service (1962). It calls for a brief academic exercise on the thinking of various scholars who have for a brief academic exercise on the thinking of various scholars who have studied the so called tribal people theoretically as well as ethnographically so that a glimpse of the characteristic features of tribal societies may be highlighted.

"A tribe is a collection of clans. Each tribe is individualized by a name, by a separate dialect, by a supreme government and by the possession of some territory which it occupies and defends as its very own" (Morgan, 1877). The possession of a common religious faith and cult and the strict observance of the group endogamy are the two further attributes of tribal organization. John J. Honigman in his article on 'tribe' for the Dictionary of Social Sciences (1964), retaining the characteristics as far as Morgan's descriptive idea of a type of society is concerned but rejecting his idea about the stages of evolution, has cited the following characteristics as the defining criteria for a tribe: (i) Common territory, (ii) a tradition of common descent, (iii) a common language, (iv) a common culture, and (v) a common name. He has not mentioned the political characteristics of a tribe as there is a disagreement among anthropologists as to the nature of political organization of the people concerned. He thus abstains from adding political criterion to other already established criteria used to define a tribe. He concludes: "Any primitive society, therefore, (or at least all which have no clear cut forms of class relations or state power) can be characterized as a tribal society."

Sahlin (1961) and Service (1962), both neo-evolutionist, have proposed a scheme of social evolution in four stages; the band, the tribe, the chiefdom and finally the state. They have constructed a possible representation of these processes selecting the functioning traits of some present-day societies. Sahlin (1968) in his *Tribesmen* has revised his four-stage evolution to three-staged evolution taking out *chiefdom* from his original scheme. According to Sahlin, the first characteristic common to all tribal societies is the fact that all elementary social units are multifamilial groups which collectively exploit an area of a common resource and form a residential unit the whole year round or major part of it. He names these elementary units as primary segments. The second common element possessed by all tribal societies is the multifunctional character of kinship relations organizing those primary segments. He shows that kinship relations function simultaneously with economic relations, political relations, ideological relations etc. In short, it may be said that they have the property of being functionally generalized. Sahlin concludes that 'familial more of production' is the basic mode of production common to all different economic systems of tribal societies.

It is evident from the discussion that the expression "tribal societies" has been used to designate those societies, not necessarily primitive societies that have two visible, functioning features in common; the existence of elementary social unit—primary segments possessing the form of multifamilial local groups, the multifunctionality of kinship relations that shape those familial groups. It is an agreed fact that tribal societies are classless societies. It does not necessarily mean that tribal societies are devoid of inequality. They are ranked societies in the sense there are inequalities on the basis of age and sex, and moreover the distribution of power and privilege over the different structural segments of the society is found to be uneven. For instance, the lineages/clans that are the constituent structural segments of tribal societies are ranked according to their proximity to the real/assumed founding ancestor or ancestress. In brief, tribal societies are not stratified societies but ranked societies, for there is no conflict of interest among the structural segments.

III

India is a developing country committed to the goal of democratic socialism in spite of its mosaic socio-cultural setting. As clearly written in our Constitution, the so-called tribal societies of our country participate in the socio-economic life of the nation with certain constitutional safeguards. Since Independence, the developmental programmes taken up by the State for the socio-economic upliftment of the tribal people have been acting as the exogenous force of bringing about institutional and structural change in tribal societies. The present discussion focuses on such a change what we call theoretically 'directed change' because it frequently leads to the unforeseen, unpredicted goal, sometimes socially disastrous, rather than the targeted goal. This is what is actually happening in the contemporary tribal societies of India in general and of Manipur, the home state of thirty three recognized Scheduled Tribes, in particular.

A discussion on the directed change experienced by the present day tribal people can be fruitfully made within the theoretical frames of reference of economism and culturalism (Dube: 1993:86). These two theoretical approaches of development have adapted different images of humankind and society, different sets of cultural orientations and different visions of the future of mankind. The former, following the utilitarian principle of avoidance of pain and maximization of pleasure, has emphasized the enhancement of production through the use and adoption of the new inventions and innovations of the constantly advancing science and technology. It encourages greedy exploitation of the limited natural resources and organization of the society along the functional roles and specialization. It assumes that once the growth process gained momentum, an invisible hand would take care of the distributional dimension. The Indian experience has shown a contradictory result. Today distribution economics is found to be equally important as production economics because there will be no development in its true spirit unless there is distributive justice.

Culuralism, to the contrary, has recognized the specificities of situations and contexts of development. It emphasizes the centrality of culture and the possible positive role of tradition. Different societies, it has argued, should be free to articulate themselves through their historically, derived designs of living, that is, their culture. It holds that no changes should be imposed from without. Its philosophy centres around the cultural pluralism rather than economic determinism. Some developmental programmes meet with disapproval because the people whom they are intended for perceive disadvantages in them. This is the explanation provided by the scholars who have advocated culturalism for the failure of a number of developmental programmes of the tribal people.

IV

It is not an exaggeration to say that many tribal societies have undergone tremendous changes in respect of their social-cultural lives; but the tragic part of the story lies in the cultural disarticulation of the people concerned with the newly emerging social situations. No doubt, many tribal societies have been benefited from the developmental packages given to them by the State. It is also a reality that even after six decades of Independence many tribes are in the underdog position whereas some tribals, who have cornered large share of the benefits of development, have been benefited more than they deserve because of the lack of the distributive justice, and a new, socio-economically advanced category of tribals, which some scholars term "Tribal Elites" have come into existence consequent upon the widening gap between the economically affluent and poor tribals. There is no hesitation to say that it is the consequence of the wrong policy of the administrative machinery of the State which has more faith in the doctrine of economism. Such a social reality has some other attendant social phenomena, such as self-alienation of the tribal people because of their strong feeling of erosion in their cultural capita. It has also generally given birth to a number of disastrous social movements like militarism, ethnicity etc., that can be explained in the light of the lack of the commitment of the State in the doctrine of culturalism. It may be concluded that the previously homogenous ranking tribal societies are found to be transforming into the economically heterogeneous, class societies owing to current strategies of development. Finally, the structure of many tribal societies is now cracking under several strains. The area to which the present discussion has given emphasis is only a part of the problems that are being faced by the contemporary tribal societies in the process of their development.

References

Dube, S.C. (1996). *Understanding Change, Anthropological and Sociological Perspectives*, New Delhi: Vikash Publishing House Pvt. Ltd.

Godelier, Maurice (1977). *Perspectives in Marxist Anthropology*, Cambridge: Cambridge University Press.

Honigman, John. J. (1964). *Dictionary of Social Sciences*, UNESCO.

Morgan, L.W. (1877). *Ancient Society*, New York: World Publishing Co.

Sahlin, Marshal (1961). "The Segmentary Lineage: An Organization of "Predatory Expansion", *American Anthropologist*. 63:322-343.

Sahlin Marshal (1968). *Tribesmen*, Prentice Hall, Inc. Englewood Cliffs.

Service, E.R. (1962). *Primitive Social Organisation*, New York: Random House.

SECTION V
National Integration

20
Defending Integrity by Strengthening National Voices

Kuldeep Chand Agnihotri

Three movements find special mention in the contemporary history of Jammu and Kashmir (J&K). First is the movement launched by the Muslim Conference in 1931 in which Hindus were killed for the first time after the defeat inflicted on foreign Afghan state by Maharaja Ranjit Singh. Kashmir was liberated from, the foreign rule of Afghans by Ranjit Singh in 1818. So, after a gap of 113 years, Hindus were again made a target in Kashmir. What primarily led to it was called a given by a Pathan Abdul Qadeer Khan to the Muslims of Hazratbal to uproot the rule of the Hindu king. But this time, it was not any love for Afghanistan but allegiance to the British that led this Pathan to instigate Muslims against the king of Kashmir. Those who supported Abdul Qadeer were not Pathans or Gujjars but Sheikh Abdullah-led Kashmiri-knowing Sunni Muslims whose ancestors had embraced Islam after abdicating their traditional religion and heritage. This movement claimed the lives of 21 people on whose graves obeisance is still paid by some people even today on July 13. Since 1950, the state government has given declared this day as a government holiday. But this movement had given rise to hushed tones and murmurs of foreign conspirators in the Kashmir Valley for the first time after the end of the state's enslavement under Afghans.

The second movement in the Kashmir Valley was started by the National Conference led by Sheikh Abdullah. The main and only demand of this movement was for and annulment of the treaty of 1946. The strategy of this movement was deeply detrimental to the whole of India. God forbid if this movement had succeeded, the whole of J&K would have become part of Pakistan. The annulment of the 1846 Amritsar Treaty would have lost its status of a princely state to become a part of British India since it had become a part of Indian states only because of this treaty. The government of London could have segregated British India under its occupation but it had no right to divide any of Indian states. If this state had become a part of British India, the London government would have made it a part of Pakistan in June 1946 on the basis of being a Muslim majority state. The British imperialist mindset was somewhere at work behind this movement. It was baffling that Pandit Jawaharlal Nehru had lent his support to this anti-India movement launched by National Conference of Sheikh Abdullah, whereas the declared policy of Congress was not to interfere in the internal affairs of princely states within India.

The Muslim Conference that had launched the movement in 1931 had taken on the grab of National Conference by 1946. This transformation had made logically convenient for the Hindu communists of the valley to be a part of National Conference as they had been supporting the Two-Nation Theory and had accepted the Muslims to be a part of the proletariat under their class struggle concept. It goes to the credit of the than ruler of Kashmir Maharaja Hari Singh that he kept on fighting against this anti-Indian agitation and notwithstanding the pressure from the British government and the clout of Nehru, he was instrumental in court proceedings against Sheikh Abdullah that resulted in his chastisement. This is a separate matter that he had to pay a heavy price for it's after the departure of the British and taking over of Nehru as Prime Minister of India.

The problem being faced by J&K today are primarily born out of these agitations. Indian National Congress had accepted the theory of holding a plebiscite in princely state, according to which after the departure of the English from British India, people of the state will be allowed to exercise their right to seek democracy or monarchy. Several states had seen agitations against monarchy. But after Nehru extended his support to the agitation waged against the annulment of Amritsar Treaty, Lord Mountbatten had given a clever interpretation in the case of the state of Jammu and Kashmir. He had advocated the idea of ascertaining the opinion of the people with regard to becoming a part of India or Pakistan. Pandit Nehru not only accepted this interpretation but also started harping on the unseemly idea of ascertaining people's opinion on the issues in the United Nations.

The first division of India had been presided over by the British government and now Nehru and Sheikh Abdullah joined hands to orchestrate the second division of the country. Lord Mountbatten had firmly positioned himself akin to the proverbial clever monkey in this affair. The agitations of 1931 and 1946 and the new interpretation of ascertaining the will of the people created an atmosphere of fear, misgivings and mistrust in the whole of Jammu and Kashmir. Pakistan had already mounted an attack on the state. Pandit Nehru and Lord Mountbatten were not so much interested in flushing out the aggressor as fanning the debate that it remains to be decided whether the state would go to Pakistan or India.

Mahatma Gandhi had departed for his heavenly abode. Sardar Patel too had died in 1950. Otherwise, he could have prevented Nehru from going ahead on this course of dismembering India. Sheikh Abdullah too had found the time to take an opportunistic stance that the state will form its own constitution in the matter of defence, communication and external affairs. It would have nothing to do with the federal constitution. The state would also have a separate flag, which he used to term as the national flag. The state will be headed by a Prime Minister, not a Chief Minister. Sheikh Abdullah first brainwashed Nehru in the believing that it was at his behest that the Muslim of the state had embraced India instead of co-religious Pakistan. When Nehru had started believing in this baseless assumption, Sheikh too started extraction his pound of flesh. Nehru kept on paying price after price.

Due to wrong policies pursued by the duo of Nehru and Sheikh, Gilgit, Baltistan, some parts of Jammu and Kashmir, Punjabi-knowing Muzzafarabad had gone under the occupation of Pakistan. Instead of wresting them back from Pakistan, Nehru started shedding cowardly tears in the Security Council. Subsequently, there were mounting apprehensions in the minds of people living in Jammu and Ladakh, Hindu Sikhs of Kashmir Valley, Gujjars and Shias that this deadly pair might force them to embrace Pakistan. It gave way to popular saying in Jammu—Aap to dube brahman, jajman bhi dobe (These Brahmins, on a losing course, will be detrimental to the cause of their clients)—people too. It is pertinent to point out that Nehru and Sheikh Abdullah both were Kashmiri Pandits. Nehru's ancestors had left Kashmir and those of Sheikh had embraced Islam long back. People wondered how to counter divisive activities of Nehru-Sheikh. Nehru Sheikh had their own organisation in the Kashmir Valley National Conference, but the people of Jammu-Ladakh and Gujjars had no such organisation.

In this context, the onus of saving the country from a second partition had fallen on the Rashtriya Swayamsevak Sangh. Prof Madhok, a professor of history at Srinagar's DAV College, had been instrumental in the expansion of Sangh in the valley. Pt. Premnath Dogra, who was the state Sangha Sarchalak, had played a crucial role in establishment and consolidation of the Sangh in Jammu. Jagdish Abrol and Kedarnath Sahni were the Sangh Pracharaks there. In the hour of crisis, the RSS mobilized the people and formed Praja Parishad.

Praja Parishad conducted a historical movement from 1949 to 1952 in which 15 people sacrificed their lives, while exposing the whole conspiracy. Its demand transform into a resounding slogan on the lips of children "Down with two flag, two laws and two heads in one nation!" Sheikh Abdullah tried to buy over the man behind the nationalistic movement, Pandit Premnath Dogra, through the lure of power. Sheikh had proposed that Premnath Dogra be content wielding power in Jammu and not interfere with his hegemony in Kashmir. Premnath Dogra spurned his offer. His answer was: "I am fighting, not for attaining power for myself, but for defending the integrity and identity of the nation." At the behest of Nehru, Sheikh Abdullah implicated Premnath Dogra in false cases ranging from rape to murder and got him imprisoned. But bowing to the collective might of the people's will, he had to set him free. People have to pay custom duty for taking goods in Jammu and Kashmir and obtain a passport-like permit for entry in the state. Praja Parishad vehemently opposed it. In those days, the Governor of Jammu and Kashmir was designated as Sadare-Riyasat at par with the President. The workers of Praja Parishad used to shout slogans by placing the photo of the then President Rajendra Prasad over there chest—"Down with two heads in one nation."

The police under Sheikh Abdullah used to *lathi*-charge and even fire at those shouting slogans. The *satyagrahis* of Praja Parishad used to struggle for unfurling the national flag at government offices and the police of Nehru- Sheikh used to deploy all its force for removing them. While Praja Parishad was braving bullets to defeat the destructive strategy of Nehru-Sheikh in Jammu and Kashmir, Dr. Syama Prasad Mookherjee established Bharatiya Jana Sangh, with the help of RSS. Gradually, the whole country was reverberated with the resonant cries of this national movement and *satyagrah*. Bharatiya Jana Sangh decided to support this movement of Praja Parishad with the help of other parties. Jana Sangh disseminated the knowledge about the agitation by celebrating Jammu and Kashmir Day throughout the country. The *satyagrahis* from across the country started entering Jammu and Kashmir without passport-permit. The police used to arrest and subject them to inhuman torture in jails. Premnath Dogra tried many time to meet Nehru in Delhi along with the delegation of Praja Parishad to brief him about the stance of the people of Jammu and Kashmir. But Nehru, who used to swear by his democratic credentials, did not grant him audience. He was not prepared to meet anyone other than Sheikh Abdullah to know about the situation in Jammu and Kashmir. On the other hand, the government of Sheikh Abdullah in Jammu was not prepared to deal with *satyagrahis* other than in the language of bullets. As many as 15 *satyagrahis* fell to the police bullets, while they were unfurling *tiranga* at government office and saying '*Bharat mata ki jai.*' In Delhi, Nehru was unrelenting and hell-bent on crushing this people's movement at any cost. And in Jammu, Sheikh was sending out threats that he would not let the Constitution of India run in Jammu and Kashmir; and anyone attempting to hoist the national flag would pay a price for it.

Dr S.P. Mookerjee decided to meet Sheikh in Srinagar on this issue. But the whole country was abuzz with the talk that Nehru would not allowed Mookerjee to go to Jammu as he wanted to go there without permission. But god knows what deal was struck between Nehru and Sheikh that the Congress government allowed him to proceed for the state, but Dr. Mookerjee was arrested the moment he entered Jammu and Kashmir. If the Congress government of Punjab had arrested him, he would have come under the jurisdiction of the Supreme Court of India. But, it was not the case as he was arrested in Jammu and Kashmir, which was not under the jurisdiction of the Apex Court, as per the agreement between Abdullah and Nehru. A few months after his arrest, Dr. Mookerjee died in mysterious circumstance in jail. The curtains came down on the Praja Parishad movement. Only after this, Nehru grew suspicious that Sheikh wanted to set Kashmir free with the help of America. Sadly, Dr. Mookerjee had to lay down his life to drive home this truth to Nehru.

21
Dismantle Colonial Relics

J. Nandakumar

Introduction

The *Bhagavad Gita*, acclaimed as a most comprehensive summary of the Perennial Philosophy ever revealed, teaches us, "It is better to do your own duty (*swadharma*), however, imperfectly than to assume the duties of another person (*paradharma*), however successfully. Prefer to die, doing your own duty: the duty of another will bring you into great spiritual danger." Following the similar lines, the colonisation was, in fact, a process of syphoning out whatever was inherent or congenital to our culture, delinking us from our cultural past and civilisational ethos (our *Swadharma*). Fulfilling its two-fold evil mission, it has filled the void space with alien contents and principles (*Paradharma*) which ultimately left us at a crossroads at the onset of Independence with no certain path ahead. We have been left with no choice but to move ahead with the seeds of Western values which were spawned by the so called Colonial Masters and nourished by neo-colonial masters with leftist-liberal outfits.

The very term colonialism is not just all about the British, but it typifies the entire gamut of foreign ideas and ideals which are slapped on us. In post-Independent India, the succession has been handed over to the so called eminent historians and academicians. They used the same instruments and apparatus as their colonial masters, that were craftily devised to "divide and rule" the nation. Colonisation, if we put in simple terms, can be of two types: one, the colonisation in the real sense, and the other is an invisible colonisation which happens or continues without our cognizance.

The latter is graver as it inflicts more damages on the national genius and unity. For the same reason, it becomes pertinent to review, if any earnest efforts have been made to decolonise Indian minds and also to ponder over the steps to be taken towards this direction. There is an interesting biological phenomenon seen a species of insect that metaphorically explains the malicious *modus operandi* of colonisation. There are families of colourful wasps, such as the Braconidae and Ichneumonidae that lay their eggs on or inside living creatures like caterpillars, aphids and spiders. Simultaneously, the wasps inject a toxin into their victims that paralyse them but do not kill. When the eggs hatch, the larvae feed on the living prey, consuming the non-vital parts like fat and digestive organs first, keeping the vital organs like the heart and the central nervous system for the very last, in order to prolong the time for which their food remains fresh. (Preface: Global Parasites—500 years of western Culture by Winin Pereira and Jeremy Seabrook, taken from Encyclopaedia of Indian Natural History OUP, 1986, p. 588).

In a way, "the colonisation is also building an independent India, is the socialist pattern of society which is infinitely more abstract and superficial, more mechanical and charged with unsolved problems of class conflict than the foundational ideas of the past." While decolonisation was given high priority in other countries which achieved independence along with India, it was sabotaged in India. Ironically, the pursuit of reinventing the national self-consciousness and linking the young generation to the lost roots of our culture has been impeded by us ourselves.

The responsibility of this great crime falls on the eminent people, who enjoyed a sway over the newly-born Indian republic, and who can be put in three categories. All of them, voluntarily or involuntarily, identify themselves as the vocal advocates of 'colonial values'. One, those who were not at all aware about the importance of *Swadharma*. Naturally, they won't follow it. Instead of fostering it, they will try to weaken it to its core. And they treat the very essence of our cultural existence, *Swadharma*, as a major hurdle which impedes the progression of our nation. Two, who believed they were aware of it, but were reluctant to adopt it as they feared it was not capable or not strong enough to tackle the problems, the present India was facing. Since their bondage with colonial past is stronger and deeper, they would search the remedy for India's present predicament in their foreign counterparts like various communist and capitalist countries (erstwhile USSR or USA). Hence, the post-Independence policies of Nehru were more an extension of India's colonial past devoid of self-respect and self-reliance that ended up in adopting the Soviet model, again an alien development paradigm, which has been happening the same way. Sedated by the glittery Western ideas and ideals, we often fail to realise the pain of the eggs being injected into our minds as the larvae eat up the vital organs of national life which eventually leads us to death.

As far as efforts towards national reconstruction and decolonisation are concerned, the policies of our first Prime Minister, who himself sought pride in calling himself an English man, were rather aimed at 'recolonising' than at 'decolonising'. M.A. Venkata Rao (to whom Shri Guruji dedicated the entire volume) rightly observed in his introduction to Bunch of Thoughts, "The Nehru mind is made mostly abroad and in spite of later proved to be unfit for Indian conditions. While both are native, albeit destructive in nature, the third group is the actual enemies, the perpetrators of 'Breaking India' warfare. As stated above, colonisation is not enslaving a new but also it continues to enslave, more like a nuclear chain reaction, until it is weeded out from the root. As the colonisation was a toxification as far as the national body is concerned, the decolonisation should serve the purpose of detoxification which has to be carried out very systematically and carefully. Those who are seriously contemplating on the condition of present India cannot overlook or tolerate Discovery of India, Shri Nehru never succeeded in catching the spirit of Indian culture at its best. Thus, the blueprint of the new society, he is using as a Prime Minister and leader of national reconstruction for the gross damage inflicted on our national genius by this aforementioned 'invisible colonisation'. As Bhagwan Krishna explicitly said in *Gita*, if we want to live as we are, then necessarily this menace of the foreign body has to be warded off.

As famous journalist Mark Tully rightly said, the predominance of English in India is harmful to intellectual life and to democracy, many academic India-watchers only laugh at the "nativist' position. The ruling elite have thrown full weight behind attempts of the linguistic decolonisation. It was in a way an attempt to preserve the privileged position of English and to prevent the linguistic decolonisation of India. As a result, according to a statistics, the share of total non-English medium candidates who passed Civil Service Preliminary examination was hardly 13 per cent!

Take education, especially Social Sciences and Humanities, for example. We are not yet ready to teach at least our own history of Science in Bharat. The Aryan invasion hypothesis is still a non-disputable fact for History as well as Social Science syllabus in our universities. Hence we are teaching our students that Kautilya is an Indian Machiavelli, Samudra Gupta is an Indian Napoleon, Kalidasa an Indian Shakespeare, who are, in fact, no way peers in any standard, neither historically not chronologically.

Right from Kindergarten level, English has been imposed as a medium of communication as well as learning. History books written by Savarkar, R.C. Majumdar etc. are yet to be recognised as authentic and fact-based by our so called eminent academicians. In media academics there are no Bharatiya theories of Communication. In art and literature no commendable contribution at par with their so called international standard. Can there be any other nonsensical teaching method than enlightening students of Indian Philosophy through Plato and Socrates? What else we can assume other than that we are in a state of toxification effect of colonised mental makeup where an Indian political science student is denied learning Hindu Polity. What is the intention of the eminent educationists, what are they fearing? Is our Indian "*Gana Rajya*" system unworthy to be learned about?

After Effects of Colonisation

The after effects of colonisation are very much evident and alive in our present society that often comes to the fore in various ways. It can be in the form of anti-national slogans raised at the university campus or a pro-secessionist voice raised in the Parliament house or on the streets. Sadly, it has affected all walks of the nation. It did not even spare the agriculture which is a way of life of rural India. The Western approach has been imported into the agriculture sector where the native agricultural techniques and seeds are being replaced with those of the Western in origin. It is needless to comment on the industrial sector and technology as they were completely devoid of anything that can be called Indian.

Despite the reformative steps taken from time to time, our bureaucracy, judiciary, administrative apparatus etc. are nothing but the relics of our colonial past.

The prevailing social order stands testimony to the crime of colonialism which has tampered with the pre-existent social framework and has sowed the seeds of division by infusing the class hierarchy which is essentially a Western construct. As a result, new castes are taking birth everyday. All the evil effects of colonisation can be summarised into six 'I's, such as Inferiority, Ignorance, Inertia, Incompetency, Ill-Will and Irreverence. One of the effects of initiatives of the likes of Rabindranath Tagore (like Vishwa Bharati, Deccan Education Society etc.), the efforts of revolutionary nationalists like Sri Aurobindo, Bal Gangadhar Tilak and others contributed enormously to the pursuit of decolonisation and nationalisation. The sincere attempts of all such nationalists amounted to invigorating the nationalism and the feeling of *Swadharma* in Indian minds. But a comprehensive and conscious effort in this regard came into being in 1925, in the form of Rashtriya Swayamsevak Sangh envisaged by Keshav Baliram Hedgewar.

Despite a Herculean effort is needed to usher in decolonisation in the education field, which was the first and foremost victim of colonisation where it inflicted a gross devastation. The devastation has been of mammoth proportion. So a conscious and consistent effort is needed to Indianise centuries of immersion in a colonial psychology is an inferiority complex and an attitude of self-reproach. Many of us are ignorant about the greatness of our rich heritage because we were not taught about that. As prominent lawyer Nani Palkivala once remarked, a bit harshly, "India is like a donkey carrying a sack of gold. The donkey does not know what it is carrying but it is content to go along with its load on its back."

Another dangerous epidemic which had crept into our very entity is bewildering inertia. Even if we are aware we are under siege, we are not ready to act. The incompetence, rampant in all sectors, is an outcome of delinking ourselves from a social structure based on family-oriented our academic environment, and it can happen only through discussions and debates. More importantly, without our own languages, how can a nation progress. Sanskrit and other Indian languages should get a deserving space in the academic parlance. The re-emergence of Sanskrit and the wide acceptance of *Yoga*, etc, suggest that the young minds are now more inclined to *Bharatiyata* than their immediate predecessors.

They are the shining examples of an India which is being decolonised. The surge of nationalist organisations, both socio-cultural and political, across the nation also signifies that we are on the industries. When the ill-will is manifested as the prevailing shameful servitude mentality, the irreverence towards all that is Indian is a characteristic feature of the intellectuals and academicians in post-Independent India that misled an entire generation. Anything Hindu is being ridiculed as communal, obscurantist, retrograde and what not. This propaganda in the academic circle is being consistently done by the Leftist intellectuals. In a way, they are taking forward the colonisation agenda of the West. A post-modern form of Marxism which denies the very notion of objective knowledge, which assumes that knowledge is conditioned by one's social belonging, and which insists that "all research in the social sciences has a political agenda."

The spiritual movements led by Sri Ramakrishna and Swami Vivekananda, the cultural renaissance sprung from Bengal and spread out to the rest of the nation, the right path. For an instance, BMS (Bharatiya Mazdoor Sangh) has become the largest trade union. Unlike other labour movements rooted in Western thought system, BMS, a movement upholding Indian thought system believes the labour field is a family while the Communist idea of trade unionism treats it as a battle field.

The progenies of colonisation and prisoners of colonial mindset are still up in arm against the decolonising efforts by various nationalist movements. But the enlightened young India with an earth-shattering zeal to break the shackles of centuries-old slavery is taking lead for the cause and striving ahead for the cause. The unusual urge of Indian minds to connect with our cultural roots is a really welcome sign which hopefully delivers a real *Swaraj* even after seven decades of political Independence.

22
Role of Rashtriya Swayamsevak Sangh in Freedom Movement

Rakesh Sinha

Ideological predisposition has been a predominant factor in evaluating the role of various groups and individuals in the freedom struggle. Marxist and subaltern historians, who are ideologically poles apart from the Rashtriya Swayam Sevak Sangh (RSS), have bracketed it with the Hindu Mahasabha and other Hindu organisations formed at various stages of the anti-imperialist struggle, questioning its independent identity, presumably to deride its clout in post-Independent India.

The reality is different. Nagpur, where the RSS was first organised in 1925, was prone to Hindu-Muslim riots. When a riot broke out in 1927, the RSS acted as deterrent to the outbreak instead of playing an offensive role and unleashing anti-Muslim propaganda which was expected by a section of local Hindu leaders and apprehended by the Muslims. This removed the suspicion from the Muslim mind against the RSS whose presence in the Central Provinces (CP) thereupon evoked no protest from the Muslim population.

It was none other than a Muslim member of the CP Council who refuted the allegation that the RSS was a communal organisation. During the debate on the RSS in the Council in March 1934, M.S. Rahman said, "no sane Muslim would take any exception to any Hindu organisation provided its object is not aggressive and militant, but simply the betterment of the Hindu community as a whole." He asked the Government whether "any

Muslim organisation had sent a representation to the Government calling upon the Government to ban the RSS?"

The leader of the House, Raghavendra Rao said that there had not been any representation by any Muslim organisation against the RSS. Moreover, in pre-Independent India barring a few stray incidents confined to Hyderabad, Lahore and Rawalpindi, there had not been single incident of violence between the RSS volunteers and the Muslims till 1945.

The lukewarm response of the RSS to the Hindu Mahasabha's political agenda led the latter to form its own volunteer organisations—the Hindu Militia and the Ram Sena. The RSS was increasingly seen by many Hindu organizers including Savarkar and Moonje as too ineffectual to counter Muslim aggressiveness. Thus, a large number of volunteer organisations, for instance the Mahavir Dal and Agni Dal in UP and Punjab, Hindu Rashtra Dal in Poona, Hindu Rashtra Sena in Bhopal, Mukteshwar Dal and Rashtriya Swayamsevak Mandal in the CP, Shakti Dal in Jabalpur and Hindu Rashtriya Sena in Giridih in Bihar, were formed to fight "Muslim domination."

The RSS came into existence in between the two great anti-colonial movements—the non-cooperation movement and the civil disobedience movement. While the Muslim question was dominant on the political agenda of the Hindu Mahasabha, the only ideology that the RSS recognised was anti-colonialism. Despite the commonalities of views on many issues with the Mahasabha, the RSS preferred the Congress as the prime platform for the anti-colonial struggle. The RSS leaders had a long association with the Congress. K.B. Hedgewar, the founder Sarsanghchalak, joined the Congress in 1919, the year he was assigned the responsibility to collect funds for the Hindi journal to be published by the Provincial Congress.

On the question of cooperation with Gandhi, he differed with the followers of Tilak who were working under the auspices of the Rashtriya Mandal and formed a separate organisation, the Nagpur National Union. The Union under his leadership prepared detailed programmes for non-cooperation and sent it to the special Calcutta session of the Congress in 1920. When the non-cooperation movement was launched in 1921, Gandhi faced resistance from prominent followers of Tilak like B.G. Khaparde and Moonje and others. However, the young troika of Nagpur—

Hedgewar, M.R. Cholkar and Saimulla Khan—captured the leadership of the movement. It was under them that the movement got a wider social base as the lower caste weaving communities—Koshtis and Momins—participated on a large scale.

Hedgewar formed the non-cooperation board to train volunteers to spread the message of non-cooperation in the CP. He was arrested for making "seditious" speeches and sent to jail. During his trial, he questioned the *locus standi* of a foreigner to try an Indian patriot and asked, "Is there any law by which people of one country have the right to rule over the country of others?"

After the formation of the RSS, Hedgewar evolved the convention by which RSS cadres could join hands with the Congress and sometimes with the Mahasabha against the British in their "individual capacity." The anti-Simon Commission movement in the CP was led virtually by RSS leaders. By 1928, the RSS had 18 *Shakhas* mostly confined to Nagpur and Wardha. The CP Congress (Marathi) was headed by Harekrishna Joshi who was General Secretary of the provincial committee and was also Sanghchalak of the Wardha unit of the RSS.

However, the fight between the Moonje and Abhyankar factions led the All India Congress Committee to intervene and it was at this juncture that both Hedgewar and Joshi withdrew from the Congress. The withdrawal was from factional politics of the Congress, not from its programmes as the RSS cadres and leaders participated in all subsequent movements of the Congress.

The Congress in its Lahore session passed a resolution for "complete Independence." The RSS extended uninhibited support to the Congress. It issued a circular to all 37 *Shakhas* which stated, *"the Indian National Congress too has adopted our goal of Independence... through the speeches it should be explained what is the meaning of Independence and why should we work with this end in view. And rallies should conclude with complimenting the Congress for accepting the goal of Independence."*

The civil disobedience movement was launched in the CP in the form of the forest *satyagraha* in which the RSS participated on a massive scale. One of the RSS leaders, Martanda Jog, designated as *Senapati* (commander-in-chief), was made captain of the volunteers' group. He violated the law by reading proscribed literature at a public meeting in Nagpur. Hedgewar gave up the responsibility of Sarsanghchalak to participate in the movement and so did the other central office-bearers. *Maharashtra*, a popular Marathi daily of Nagpur, reported that when Hedgewar proceeded to inaugurate the *satyagraha* he was accompanied by thousands of people including seven to eight hundred women. He and other RSS workers were arrested.

The anti-imperialist character of the RSS and its unconditional support to the Congress movement appalled the British administration which made the first serious attempt to suppress it soon after the civil disobedience movement died out. At the end of 1932, the CP government issued a circular prohibiting government employees and their wards from participating in or associating with the RSS on the plea that it was "political and communal organization."

In December 1933 its scope was extended to the employees and teachers of local bodies. The Government wanted to give it a communal colour since the Local Self-Government Minister was a Muslim. However, the Sangh did not make it a communal issue and targeted the colonial rule. During the budget session in March 1934, a member of the Council, V.D. Kolte, put up a **cut motion** against the government's circular. This led to a four-hour discussion during which all the speakers belonging to Brahmin, non-Brahmin and Muslim communities appreciated the work and ideology of the RSS.

A Home Department report in 1940 said, "the organisation is intensely anti-British and its tone is increasingly becoming militant." The CID report revealed that RSS volunteers were "introduced into various departments of Government such as the army, navy, postal, telegraph, railway and administrative services in order that they there may be no difficulty in capturing administrative departments when the time comes."

The RSS chief M.S. Golwalkar, who succeeded Hedgewar after his death in 1940, suggested indoctrination of government employees and his speech in the Poona Officers Training Camp (OTC) of the RSS on May 3, 1942 was reported by the CID saying that, "the Sangh resolved to stand on its own legs, not minding any opposition. It was not possible to get *swaraj* by begging it from foreigners and this could only be achieved by strength." The history of the RSS, spanning more than two decades before India's Independence, is one of active participation in the anti-colonial struggle and unconditional cooperation not only with the Congress but also with any other group committed to the liberation of the motherland.

Index